Genealogical Records in TEXAS

Genealogical Records in
T · E · X · A · S

By
Imogene Kinard Kennedy
&
J. Leon Kennedy

Baltimore
GENEALOGICAL PUBLISHING CO., INC.
1987

929.1

5-88 Publ 2200

Published by Genealogical Publishing Co., Inc.
Baltimore, Maryland
Library of Congress Catalogue Card Number 86-83384
International Standard Book Number 0-8063-1185-1
Made in the United States of America

TABLE OF CONTENTS

MAPS

Municipalities of Texas

Original colonies of Texas

Land districts of Texas

Formation and organization of counties

FOREWORD

by

Dr.   David B. Gracy II
Governor Bill Daniel Professor in Archival Enterprise
University of Texas at Austin

    Genealogy is History. The genealogist who disregards
this simple fact will, as surely as one generation follows
another, miss valuable information about the person's
ancestors. Yet numbers of genealogical searchers do ignore
the fact. During my nine years as Director of the Texas
State Archives, I saw uncounted genealogists come to the
Archives eager to pursue genealogical research who had not
the least idea of the outline of Texas history and thus not
the least idea what records might exist, what they
documented, and where to look for them.

    The records that genealogists seek in archival
repositories (especially records produced in the offices of
government) were not created to be genealogical records.
They resulted instead from some business of government or
work of individuals. All of these records first
facilitated, then only in time evolved into historical
documentation of, some activity. Muster rolls, for example,
were created to document recruits in the military and gather
enough data about them to distinguish one recruit from
another. To use these records effectively, the genealogist
must know when wars were fought and by whom. Reference
archivists in the Texas State Archives regularly are asked
what records the institution holds on soldiers of the
Mexican War. The Archives, of course, has no service
records. That war was fought over, but not by, Texas.
Lacking a working knowledge of history, researchers limit
the places they can think of to look for records and waste
precious time and energy looking in the wrong places for the
records they do think of.

    Even the best grasp of the history of an ancestor's
times, however, does not guarantee to reveal the history--
and therefore the likely location--of all potentially
pertinent records. It is an axiom that not all records and
sources lie in the obvious places of the state archives,
county offices, or the larger genealogical libraries. Part
of the challenge and pleasure of studying history--and, by
the same token,genealogy--is following unfamiliar paths of
less-known, but no less rich, records.

Imogene and Leon Kennedy here present the sort of
information that a genealogist needs at the beginning of a

search for ancestors in Texas: historical data bearing on the creation and location of records of use in genealogical research. Because they have done so, because they have invested untold hours in gathering names, addresses, telephone numbers, and a variety of other data, users of this book will not have to repeat the work. Researchers should rejoice. Reference archivists will rejoice also. The better informed is the researcher coming to the archives (any archives), the easier and more rewarding is the work of helping that researcher. The better informed is the researcher, the better quality can be the genealogy the person produces.

It is not often that one book has the potential to help so many, so much.

PREFACE

The State of Texas, largest of the 48 connected United States, has a history unique in this nation. The many records that are important to anyone doing research in this state are the result of the activities of various governments over a period of almost 200 years.

From the earliest recorded grants by the Spanish, through the Mexican land grants by both the Empire of Mexico and the Republic of Mexico, to the grants, deeds, and patents by the Republic and State of Texas, the titles to the lands of Texas have remained intact and have passed down by will or deed from that time to the present.

All of these deeds and records have names and information about our ancestors, and they are all still available to us if we know where and how to find them. In the pages of this book we attempt to give you the location of these records and explain where to begin your research based on the information you have available.

There have been many changes in our county boundaries, and even county names, since we became a state. This book will take you back to the beginning. Through text and maps it shows the origin of each county and the location of the records for each portion of that county before it was organized into its present boundaries.

The Spanish and Mexican land grants are, of course, written in Spanish. While it would be necessary to have these documents translated in order to understand them, we have included some names and terms with the translation used at the time they were written rather than that used today.

On the acknowledgements page we express our appreciation to those to whom we turned in order to find the basic information in this book. But we cannot acknowledge by name those men and women who work or volunteer their services in libraries and courthouses throughout Texas who have been so helpful and kind in assisting in the location of records. We do, at this time, express thanks for their help and for the public service they are performing.

We hope this book will help in your research in Texas.

ACKNOWLEDGEMENTS

A book of information, such as this, is only as good and as reliable as the sources of that information. In making the effort to assemble the data for this book, nothing was accepted as fact without personal investigation, and it was through the help, encouragement, and kindness of several people whose assistance we appreciate, that this book was compiled.

Dr. David B. Gracy II, former State Archivist and now The Governor Bill Daniel Professor in Archival Enterprise, Graduate School of Library and Information Science, University of Texas, at Austin.

Dr. Dorman H. Winfrey, Director, Texas State Library and his staff.

Chris LaPlante, State Archivist, Texas State Archives, and his staff.

Dr. Michael Q. Hooks, Director of Archives, Archives and Records Division, Texas General Land Office and his staff.

Mrs. Loretta E. (Tommy) Burns, Professional Genealogist, for advice and research.

Mrs. Barbara H. Franz, Genealogy Librarian, 2nd Assistant Montgomery County Library, for advice and research.

Imogene Kinard Kennedy
Genealogy Librarian
Montgomery County Library
Conroe, Texas

And

J. Leon Kennedy
Genealogist
Conroe, Texas

CHAPTER 1

EARLY MUNICIPALITIES OF TEXAS

The earliest political subdivisions in Texas were created under the rule of the Spanish and the Mexicans. Twenty nine municipalities whose jurisdiction lay entirely or partially in Texas, were created between 1731 and 1836. These municipalities and the dates they were created are listed on the next page.

On the following pages you will find Texas maps showing the approximate boundaries of the municipalities during three periods of history. The first map shows the municipalities created before 1831; the second map covers the period from 1832 through 1834; and the third map covers the remaining period until the end of Mexican rule in 1836.

In many cases the original boundary descriptions have been lost so we have reconstructed boundaries using the material available to us. In some cases we were able to document municipalities on both sides of a third municipality; thus making it easy to locate the boundaries of the central jurisdiction. In other cases the descriptions were so vague and so loosely described as to make exact boundaries impossible to determine. In these cases, the boundaries are approximate as based upon information we have located.

The municipalities listed here, with the exception of the six municipalities along the Rio Grande, were the predecessors of present day Texas counties. Early land records that originate within the jurisdiction of these municipalities, therefore, may be of considerable value in genealogical research, when they are available. Records were lost or destroyed in the Texas counties as listed in later chapters.

Municipalities Created Under Spain and Mexico

MUNICIPALITY	CREATED
Bexar	1731
Reynosa	1780
Laredo	1784
Guerrero	1785
Mier	1785
Camargo	1785
Matamoros	1792
Refugio	1825
Austin	3-07-1827
Goliad	1827 or 1829
Nacogdoches	1-31-1831
Liberty	1831
Brazoria	5-01-1832
Gonzales	1832
Victoria	1832
Matagorda	3-06-1834
San Augustine	3-06-1834
Bastrop (Mina)	4-24-1834
San Patricio	4-24-1834
Milam (Viesca)	1834
Washington	10-16-1835
Shelby (Tenehaw)	11-11-1835
Red River	11-11-1835
Jasper (Bevil)	1835
Jackson	12-03-1835
Jefferson	12-05-1835
Sabine	12-15-1835
Harris (Harrisburg)	12-30-1835
Colorado	1-08-1836

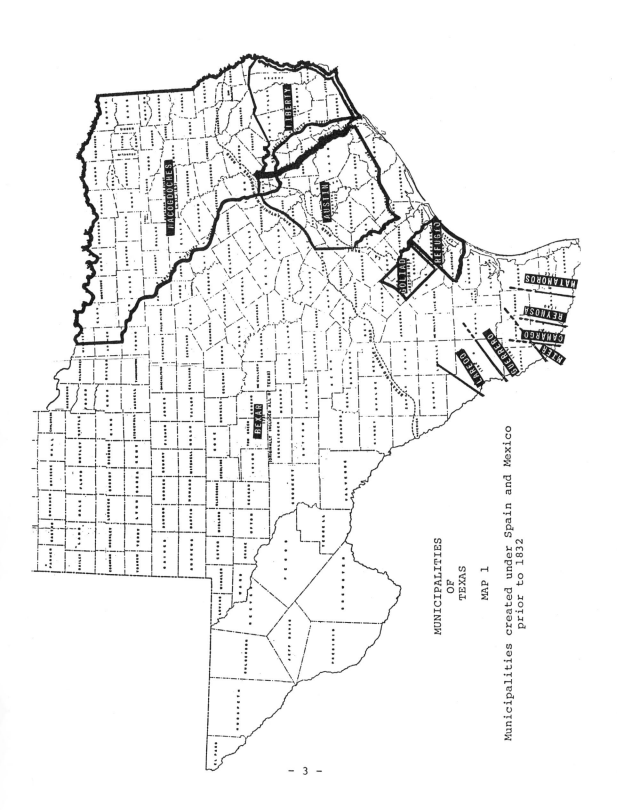

MUNICIPALITIES
OF
TEXAS

MAP 1

Municipalities created under Spain and Mexico
prior to 1832

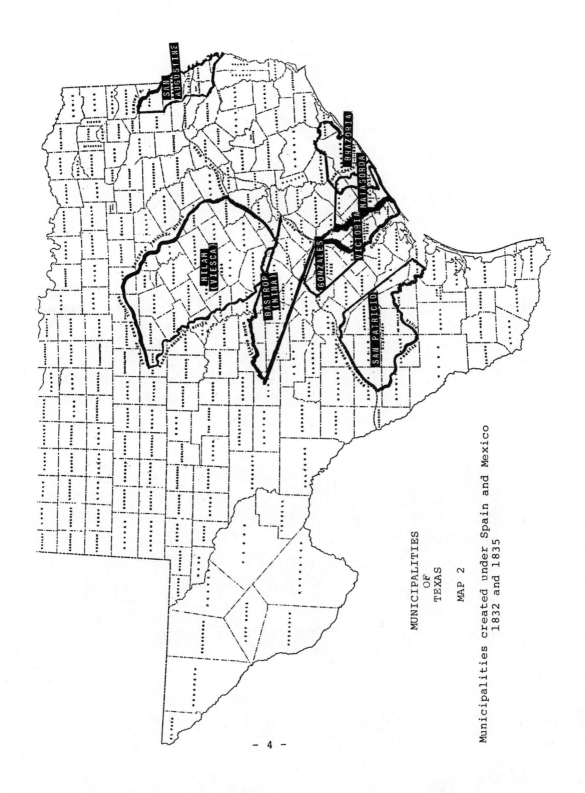

MUNICIPALITIES
OF
TEXAS

MAP 2

Municipalities created under Spain and Mexico
1832 and 1835

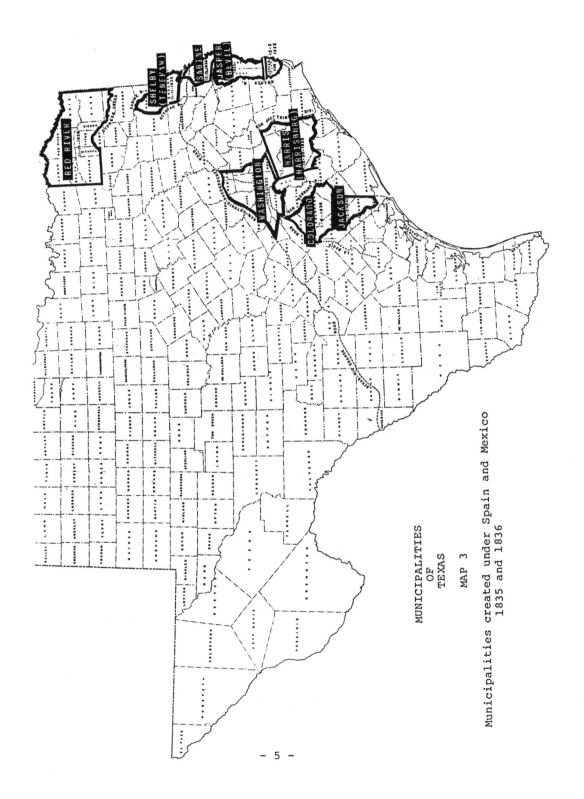

MUNICIPALITIES
OF
TEXAS

MAP 3

Municipalities created under Spain and Mexico
1835 and 1836

- 5 -

CHAPTER 2

MEXICAN LAWS CONCERNING COLONIZATION

The primary purpose of the colonization laws and decrees of Mexico was to secure the possession of the sparsely settled areas of the country by encouraging immigration into them. These laws and decrees became the fundamental authority under which lands in the States of Coahuila and Texas, and Tamaulipas, were surveyed and granted. Because of the political problems and changes that occurred so frequently in Mexico and Texas, a few dates, events, and laws are very important.

September 27, 1821
Augustin Iturbide assumed command of Mexican forces in revolt against Spain.

May 18, 1822
Iturbide was proclaimed Emperor.

January 4, 1823
First colonization law of Mexico promulgated by the Junta that was appointed by Iturbide. Stephen F. Austin was largely responsible for this law.

March 19, 1823
Iturbide abdicated the throne.

April 14, 1823
After a revolution in Mexico, the Provisional Government, in response to Austin's plea, ratified the action taken January 4,1823, by the Iturbide government, relative to colonization.

August, 1823
The Constitutient Congress of the Provisional Government of Mexico assembled and proclaimed the Republican Constitution hereafter known as the Constitution of 1824.

May 7, 1824
Coahuila and Texas were united into one state.

August 15, 1824
The first Congress of the new state of Coahuila and Texas assembled at Saltillo.

March 24, 1825
The first colonization law of Coahuila and Texas was enacted.

April 6, 1830
Colonization law enacted prohibiting further foreign colonization. Parts of the law later repealed.

Transcribed from

THE GENERAL COLONIZATION LAW OF MEXICO.

January 4, 1823

(1 Gammel 27-30)

"AUGUSTIN, by divine providence, and by the congress of the nation, first constitutional emperer of Mexico, and grand master of the imperial order of Guadalupe; To all who shall see these presents: Know ye, That the junta nacional instituyente of the Mexican empire, has decreed, and we sanction the following:

"The Junta Nacional Instituyente of the Mexican empire, being convinced by the urgent recommendations of the government of the necessity and importance of giving to the empire a general law of colonization, have thought proper to decree as follows:

"ART. 1. The government of the Mexican nation will protect the liberty, property, and civil rights of all foreigners who profess the Roman Catholic apostolic religion, the established religion of the empire.

"ART. 2. To facilitate their establishment, the executive will distribute lands to them, under the conditions and terms herein expressed.

"ART. 3. The empresarios, by whom is understood those who introduced at least two hundred families, shall previously contract with the executive, and inform it which branch of industry they propose to follow, the property or resources they intend to introduce for that purpose, and any other particulars they may deem necessary, in order that, with this necessary information, the executive may designate the province to which they must direct themselves, the lands which they can occupy with right of property, and the other circumstances which may be considered necessary.

"ART. 4. Families who emigrate, not included in a contract, shall immediately present themselves to the ayuntamiento of the place where they wish to settle, in order that this body, in conformity with the instructions of the executive, may designate the lands corresponding to them, agreeably to the industry which they may establish.

"ART. 5. The measurement of land shall be the following; establishing the VARA at three geometrical feet; a straight line of five thousand VARAS shall be a league; a square, each of whose side shall be one league, shall be called a sitio; and this shall be the unity of counting one, two, or more sitios; five sitios shall compose one hacienda.

"ART. 6. In the distribution made by government of lands to the colonists, for the formation of villages, towns, cities, and provinces, a distinction shall be made between grazing land, destined for the raising of stock, and lands suitable for farming or planting, on account of the facility of irrigation.

"ART. 7. One labor shall be composed of one million square varas, that is to say, one thousand varas on each side, which measurement shall be the unity for counting one, two, or more labors. These labors can be divided into halves and quarters, but not less.

"ART. 8. To the colonists, whose occupation is farming, there can not be given less than one labor, and those whose occupation is stock raising, there cannot be given less than one sitio.

"ART. 9. The government of itself, or by means of the authorities authorized for that purpose, can augment said portions of land as may be deemed proper, agreeably to the conditions and circumstances of the colonists.

"ART.10. Establishments made under the former government which are now pending, shall be regulated by this law in all matters that may occur, but those that are finished shall remain in that state.

"ART.13. Care shall be taken in the formation of said new town, that, so far as the situation on the ground will permit, the streets shall be laid off straight, running north and south, east and west.

"ART.18. Natives of the country shall have a preference in the distribution of land; and particularly the military of the army, of the three guarantees, in conformity with the decree of the 27th of March, 1821; and also those who served in the first epoch of the insurrection.

"ART.19. To each empresario who introduces and establishes families in any of the provinces designated for colonization, there shall be granted at the rate of three haciendas and two labors, for each two hundred families so introduced by him, but he will lose the right of property over said lands, should he not have populated and cultivated them in twelve years from the date of the concession. The premium can not exceed nine haciendas and six labors, whatever may be the number of families he introduces.

"ART.20. At the end of twenty years the proprietors of the lands, acquired in virtue of the foregoing article, must alienate two-thirds part of said lands, either by sale, donation, or in any other manner he pleases. The law authorizes him to hold in full property and dominion, one third part.

"ART.21. The two foregoing articles are to be understood as governing the contracts made within six months, as after that time, counting from the day of the promulgation of this law, the executive can diminish the premium as it may deem proper, giving an account thereof to congress, with such information as may be deemed necessary.

"ART. 22. The date for the concession of lands constitutes an inviolable law, for the right of property and legal ownership; should anyone through error, or by subsequent concession, occupy land belonging to another, he shall have no right to it, further than a preference in case of sale, at the current price.

"ART.23. If after two years from the date of the concession, the colonist should not have cultivated his land, the right of property shall be considered as renounced; in which case, the respective ayuntamiento can grant it to another.

"ART.29. Every individual shall be free to leave the empire, and can alienate the lands over which he may have acquired the right of property, agreeably to the tenor of this law, and he can likewise take away from the country all his property, by paying the duties established by law.

"This law shall be presented to his Imperial Majesty for his sanction, publication and fulfillment.

Mexico, 3d January, 1823
3d of the independence of the empire.

Juan Francisco, Bishop of Durango, President.
Antonio de Mier, Member and Secretary.
Juan Batista de Arispe, Member and Secretary.

- 9 -

"Therefore, we order all tribunals, judges, chiefs, governors, and all other authorities, as well civil as military and eccelesiastical, whatever class or dignity they may be, to comply with this decree, and cause it to be complied with in all its parts; and you will cause it to be printed, published, and circulated.

Given in Mexico, 4th January, 1823.

Signed by the Emperor.
To Don Jose Manuel de Herrera, Minister of Interior and Exterior Relations."

FROM
GENERAL COLONIZATION LAW OF MEXICO

August 18, 1824

(1 Gammel 38-40)

"The Supreme Executive Power, provisionally appointed by the general sovereign Constituent Congress --To all who will see and understand these presents: Know ye -- that the said Congress has decreed as follows:

"ART. 1. The Mexican nation offers to foreigners, who come to establish themselves within its territory, security for their persons and property, provided they subject themselves to the laws of the country.

"ART. 2. This law comprehends those lands of the nation, not the property of individuals, corporations, or towns, which can be colonized.

"ART. 3. For this purpose, the legislatures of all the states will, as soon as possible, form colonization laws, or regulations for their respective states, conforming themselves in all things to the constitutional act, general constitution, and the regulations established in this law.

"ART. 4. There can not be colonized any lands, comprehended within twenty leagues of the limits of any foreign nation, nor within ten leagues of the coasts, without the previous approbation of the general supreme executive power.

"ART. 5. If for the defence and security of the nation, the federal government should deem it necessary to use any portion of these lands, for the construction of warehouses, arsenals, or other public edifices, they can do so with the approbation of the general congress, or in its recess, of the council of government."

"ART. 6. Until after four years from the publication of this law, there shall not be imposed any tax whatever on the entrance of foreigners, who come to establish themselves for the first time in the nation.

"ART. 7. Until after the year 1840, the general congress shall not prohibit the entrance of any foreigner, as a colonist, unless imperious circumstances should require it, with respect to the individuals of a particular nation.

"ART. 8. The government, without prejudicing the objects of this law, shall take such precautionary measures as it may deem expedient, for the security of the confederation, as respects the foreigners who come to colonize.

"ART. 9. A preference shall be given in the distribution of lands, to Mexican citizens, and no other distinction shall be made in regard to them except that which is founded on individual merit, or services rendered the country, or under equal circumstances, a residence in the place where the lands to be distributed are situated.

"ART.10. The military who in virtue of the offer made on the 27th March, 1821, have a right to lands, shall be attended to by the states, in conformity with the diplomas which are issued to that effect, by the supreme executive power.

"ART.11. If in virtue of the decree alluded to in the last article, and taking into view the probabilities of life, the supreme executive power should deem it expedient to alienate any portion of land in favor of any officer, whether civil or military of the federation, it can do so from the vacant lands of the territories.

"ART.12. It shall not be permitted to unite in the same hands with the right of property, more than one league square of land suitable for irrigation, four square leagues in superficies of arable land without the facilities of irrigation, and six square leagues in superficies of grazing land.

"ART.13. The new colonists shall not transfer their property in mortmain (MANUS MUERTOS).

"ART.14. The law guarantees the contracts which the empresarios make with the families which they bring at their own expense, provided they are not contrary to the laws.

"ART.15. No person who by virtue of this law, acquires a title to lands, shall hold them if he is domiciliated out of the limits of the republic.

"ART.16. The government in conformity with the provisions established in this law, will proceed to colonize the territories of the republic.

Mexico, 18th August, 1824.
Cayetano Ibarra, President.

Pedro de Ahumada, Member and Secretary.
Manuel de Villay Cocio, Member and Secretary.

Therefore, we command it to be printed, circulated, and obeyed."

Nicholas Bravo	)	Members of the
Vicente Guerrero	)	Supreme Executive
Miguel Dominguez	)	Power.

FROM
COLONIZATION LAW OF THE STATE OF COAHUILA AND TEXAS

March 24, 1825

(1 Gammel 40-46)

"The Governor provisionally appointed by the Sovereign Congress of this state; to all who shall see these presents: Know that the said Congress have decreed as follows:

"Decree No. 16. The constituent congress of the free, independent and sovereign state of Coahuila and Texas desiring, by every possible means, to augment the population of its territory, promote the cultivation of its fertile lands, the raising and multiplication of stock, and the progress of the arts and commerce; and being governed by the constitutional act, the federal constitution, and the basis established by the national decree of the general congress, No. 72, have thought proper to decree the following LAW OF COLONIZATION:

"ART. 1. All foreigners who, in virtue of the general laws of the 18th August, 1824, which guarantees the security of their persons and property in the territory of the Mexican nation, wish to remove to any of the settlements of the state of Coahuila and Texas, are at liberty to do so; and the said state invites and calls them.

"ART. 4. From the day in which any foreigner has been enrolled as an inhabitant, in conformity with the foregoing article, he is at liberty to designate any vacant land, and the respective political authority will grant it to him in the same manner as to a native of the country, in conformity with the existing laws of the nation, under the condition that the proceedings shall be passed to the government for its approbation.

"ART. 7. The government shall take care that within the twenty leagues bordering on the limits of the United States of the North, and ten leagues in a straight line from the coast of the Gulf of Mexico, within the limits of this state, there shall be no other settlements, except such as merit the approbation of the supreme government of the Union, for which object, all petitions on the subject, whether made by Mexicans or foreigners, shall be passed to the superior government, accompanied by a corresponding report.

"ART. 8. The projects for new settlements, in which one or more persons offer to bring at their own expense one hundred or more families, shall be presented to the government, and if found conformable with this law, they will be admitted; and the government will immediately designate to the contractors, the land where they are to establish themselves, and the term of six years, within which they must present the number of families they contracted for, under the penalty of losing the rights and privileges offered in their favor, in proportion to the number of families which they fail to introduce, and the contract totally annulled if they do not bring at least one hundred families.

"ART.11. A square of land, which on each side has one league or five thousand varas, or what is the same thing, a superficies of twenty five million varas, shall be called a sitio, and this shall be the unity for counting one, two, or more sitios, and also the unity for counting one, two, or more labors, shall be one million square varas, or one thousand varas on each side, which shall compose a labor. The vara for this measurement shall be three geometrical feet.

"ART.12. Taking the above unity as a basis, and observing the distinction which must be made between grazing land, or that which is proper for raising of stock, and farming land, with or without the facility of irrigation; this law grants to the contractor or contractors, for the establishment of a

new settlement, for each hundred families which he may
introduce and establish in the state, five sitios of grazing
land, and five labors at least, the one half of which shall
be without the facility of irrigation, but they can only
receive this premium for eight hundred families, although a
greater number should be introduced, and no fraction whatever
less than one hundred, shall entitle them to any premium, not
even proportionally.

"ART.13. Should any contractor or contractors in virtue of
the number of families which he may have introduced, acquire
in conformity with the last article, more than eleven square
leagues of land, it shall nevertheless be granted, but
subject to the condition of alienating the excess, within
twelve years, and if it is not done, the respective political
authority shall do it, by selling it at public sale,
delivering the proceeds to the owners, after deducting the
costs of sale.

"ART.14. To each family comprehended in a contract, whose
sole occupation is cultivation of land, one labor shall be
given; should he also be a stock raiser, grazing land shall
be added to complete a sitio; and should his only occupation
be raising of stock, he shall only receive a superfice of
grazing land, equal to twenty four million square BARS.

"ART.15. Unmarried men shall receive the same quantity when
they enter the matrimonial state, and foreigners who marry
Mexicans, shall receive one-fourth more; those who are
entirely single, or who do not form a part of some family
whether foreigners or native, shall content themselves with
the fourth part of the above mentioned quantity, which is all
that can be given them until they marry.

"ART.16. Families or unmarried men who, entirely of their
own accord, have emigrated and may wish to unite themselves
to any new towns, can at all times do so, and the same
quantity of land shall be assigned them which is mentioned in
the last two articles, but if they do so in the first six
years from the establishment of the settlement, one labor
more shall be given to families, and single men in place of
the quarter designated in the 15th article, shall have the
third part.

"ART.17. It appertains to the government to augment the
quantity indicated in the 14, 15, and 16th articles, in
proportion to the family, industry and activity of the colonists, agreeably to the information given on these subjects
the ayuntamientos and commissioners; the said government
always observing the provision of the 12th article, of the
decree of the general congress of the subject.

"ART.20. In order that there may be no vacancies between tracts, of which, great care shall be taken in the distribution of lands; it shall be laid off in squares, or other forms although irregular, if the local situation requires it; and in said distribution, as well as the assignation of lands for new towns, previous notice shall be given to the adjoining proprietors, if any, in order to prevent dissensions and law suits.

"ART.21. If by error in the accession, any land shall be granted belonging to another, on proof being made of that fact, an equal quantity shall be granted elsewhere, to the person who may have thus obtained it through error, and he shall be indemnified by the owner of such land, for any improvements he may have made; the just value of which improvements shall be ascertained by the appraisers.

"ART.22. The new settlers as an acknowledgment, shall pay to the state, for each sitio of pasture land, thirty dollars; two dollars and a half for each one that can be irrigated, and so on proportionally according to the quantity and quality of the land distributed; but the said payments need not be made until six years after the settlement, and by thirds; the first within four years, the second within five years, and the last within six years, under the penalty of losing the land for a failure in any of said payments; there are excepted from this payment, the contractors and military spoken of in the 10th article; the former with respect to lands given them as a premium, and the later for those they obtained in conformity with their diplomas.

"ART.24. The government will sell to Mexicans, and to them only, such lands as they may wish to purchase, taking care that there shall not be accumulated in the same hands more than eleven sitios; and under the condition that the purchaser must cultivate what he acquires by this title within six years from its acquisition, under the penalty of losing them, the price of each sitio, subject to the foregoing condition, shall be one hundred dollars if it be pasture land; one hundred and fifty dollars if it be farming land without facility of irrigation; and two hundred dollars if it can be irrigated.

"ART.25. Until six years after the publication of this law, the legislature of this state cannot alter it as regards the acknowledgment and price to be paid for land, or as regards the quantity and quality to be distributed to the new settlers or sold to Mexicans.

"ART.26. The new settlers, who within six years from the date of possession, have not cultivated or occupied the lands granted them, according to its quality, shall be considered to have renounced them, and the respective political authority shall immediately proceed to take possession of them and recall the titles.

"ART.27. The contractors and military, heretofore spoken of, and those who by purchase have acquired lands, can alienate them at any time, but the successor is obliged to cultivate them in the same time that the original proprietor was bound to do; the other settlers can alienate theirs when they have totally cultivated them and not before.

"ART.30. The new settler who, wishing to establish himself in a foreign country, resolves to leave the territory of the state, can do so freely with all his property; but after leaving the state, he shall not any longer hold his land, and if he had not previously sold it, or the sale should not be in conformity with the 27th article, it shall become entirely vacant.

"ART.34. Towns shall be founded on the sites deemed most suitable by the government or the person commissioned for this effect, and for each one, there shall be designed four square leagues whose area may be in regular or irregular form, agreeably to the situation.

"ART.37. So far as practicable, the towns shall be composed of natives and foreigners, and in their delineations great care should be taken to lay off the streets straight, giving them a direction from north to south, and from east to west, when the site will permit it.

"ART.38. For the better location of the said new towns, their regular formation and exact partition of their lands and lots, the government on account of having admitted any project, and agreed with the contractor or contractors who may have presented it, shall commission a person of intelligence and confidence, giving him such particular instructions as may be deemed necessary and expedient; and authorizing him under his own responsibility, to appoint one or more surveyors to lay off the town scientifically, and do whatever else may be required.

"ART.39. The governor, in conformity with the last fee bill ARANCEL, of notary publics of the ancient audience of Mexico, shall designate the fees of the commissioner, who, in conjunction with the colonists, shall fix the surveyor's fees; but both shall be paid by the colonists, and in the manner which all parties among themselves may agree upon.

"ART.40. As soon as at least forty families are united in one place, they shall proceed to the formal establishment of the new towns and all of them shall take an oath to support the general and state constitutions; which oath shall be administered by the commissioner, they shall then, in his presence, proceed for the first time to the election of their municipal authority.

"ART.41. A new town, whose inhabitants shall not be less than two hundred, shall elect an ayuntamiento, provided there is not another one established within eight leagues, in which case, it shall be added to it. The number of individuals which are to compose the ayuntamiento shall be regulated by the existing laws.

"ART.48. This law shall be published in all the villages of the state, and that it may arrive at the notice of all others throughout the Mexican confederation, it shall be communicated to their respective legislatures, by the secretary of this state; and the governor will take particular care to send a certified copy of it, in compliance with the 161st article of the federal constitution, to the two houses of congress and the supreme executive power of the nation, with a request to the latter to give it the general circulation through foreign states by means of your ambassadors.

"The governor pro tem of the state will cause it to be published and circulated.

Saltillo, 24th March, 1825.
Signed: Rafael Ramos Y Valdez, President
               Juan Vicente Campos, Member and Secretary
               Jose Joaquin Arce Rosales, Member and Secretary

"Therefore, I command all authorities, as well as military and ecclesiastical, to obey, and cause to be obeyed, the present decree in all its parts.

                              Rafael Gonzales, Governor.

FROM COLONIZATION LAW OF THE STATE OF TAMAULIPAS
December 15, 1826

(1 Gammel   454-459)

COLONIZATION LAW
of
THE STATE OF TAMAULIPAS

December 15, 1826

"The Congress of the State of Tamaulipas enacts the following as a General Law.

"ART. 1. Foreigners who wish to colonize vacant lands in the state shall be admitted, and their persons and property protected, provided they submit to the laws of the republic, and those of the State.

"ART. 2. For a foreigner to obtain adjudication of lands he must become domiciliated in some town in the state with a capital of his own to afford him a decent support, or with a trade or useful industrious pursuit which he follows; or he must establish a new town with one hundred families at least. Should he establish himself on the northern frontier of the state, fifty families shall be sufficient for that purpose.

"ART. 3. In either case, they shall make their petitions in writing to the governor of the state, who shall resolve thereon with the concurrence of his council, and audience of the fiscal of the court of justice of the state, making them the concessions of lands that shall be hereinafter determined

"ART. 7. From the very date whereon a foreigner is thus registered, he acquires domiciliation, and may as such an inhabitant, designate (denunciar) the vacant land he thinks best, presenting himself to that effect by writing to the respective Alcalde, who shall decree what is proper for examining, measuring, and marking out the land designated, after citing the adjoining proprietors, should there be any.

"ART. 8. The instructive despatch being terminated, and no opponent of right resulting, the Alcade shall pass it to the executive of the state, by whom the title of adjudication and ownership shall be issued to the person interested, ordering that the Alcalde of the town of his residence put him immediately in possession of the land granted. All these proceedings shall be conducted officially, and the executive shall proceed with the audience of the fiscal of the supreme court of justice of the state.

"ART. 9. Opposition of right of ownership that is commenced shall go through the steps of an ordinary civil trial between the designator and the opponent, the former aided by an agent of the state, whom with the citation of the fiscal, the executive shall appoint. Should the opposition be for the right of option to the ownership, the executive shall examine and decide.

"ART.10. The executive shall take care to repeople by this means, the depopulated, and very particularly that the designations and judicial proceedings that have to be conducted on account of the same, be not paralyzed.

"ART.11. In the same manner he shall take care that no town projected by foreigners be situated within ten leagues upon the coast of the Gulf of Mexico within the limits of the state, without previously obtaining the consent and approbation of the supreme executive of the union. Beyond said line he shall also take care that, so far as the sites permit, the new towns be established in contact with the present ones, and with the conditions he stipulates with the empresarios.

"ART.12. Contracts ratified by empresarios with the executive are guaranteed by this law so far as they are in conformity to the provisions thereof.

"ART.14. A square of land measuring a league upon each side, or what is the same thing, a superficies of twenty five million square varas shall be called a sitio, and this shall be the unit for enumerating one, two or more sitios, in the same manner as the unit for counting one, two or more labores shall be a superficies of a million square varas, or a thousand varas on each side, which shall compose a labor.The varas for these dimensions shall consist of three geometrical feet.

"ART.15. The unit taken as a standard, and observing the distinction to be made on the distribution of lands, between grazing lands, or those suitable for raising stock; and irrigable and temporal tillage land, this law grants to the contractor or contractors of new towns, for every hundred families they introduce and establish in the state, of five sitios of grazing land and five labores, of which one-half at least shall be temporal land; but they shall receive only in the ratio of eight hundred families, although they shall introduce more, and no fraction not completing a hundred shall entitle them to a premium, not even proportionally. Should the northern frontier be settled, fifty families shall suffice for enjoying the benefit of this article.

"ART.16. To each family of those comprised in this contract, whose occupation is that of cultivating the soil, one labor shall be granted; should the family raise stock, grazing shall be added to complete a superficies of twenty four million varas.

"ART.17. Foreigners shall have the same assignment after marrying, and foreigners marrying natives of the country shall have one-fourth more, and those who are entirely alone, or who do not form a part of any family whether foreigners or natives, contenting themselves with one-fourth of said assignment, the sole portion that can be granted them, which shall be completed to them when their assignment is made.

"ART.18. Families and unmarried men, who have emigrated separately and at their own expense, should wish to annex themselves to any of the new settlements, may do so at any time, and their assignment of land shall be respectfully the same as mentioned in the two foregoing articles; but should they accomplish it within the first two years from the establishment of the settlements, one labor more shall be granted to families; and unmarried men, instead of one-fourth as pointed out in article 17, shall have one-third. Men unmarried, and with a family, shall be considered in the light of families.

"ART.19. For the project of new towns, which one or more foreigners offer to settle with families of from one hundred upwards, or from fifty, should they have to settle on the northern frontier, the vacant and deserted lands of the state, proposition shall be made to congress by the executive, in order with his report to accord the contracts.

"ART.20. Adjudication and possession to new foreign settlers shall be subject to the following rules:

First. All deserted lands to which at the expiration of fifty days from the designation thereof for settling, the supposed owners do not appear to prove their right, shall be considered open for colonization.

Second. That, which, having been adjudicated by this law, should be abandoned for five years, and no successor appearing within said term claiming a right to the same.

Third. That, which having been disputed in adverse trial with regard to the ownership thereof, are found to be voluntarily abandoned by the parties for three years; or where the parties have withdrawn from the trial, without the formation of a determinate judgement deciding the right of either, provided, that the time specified by law for the trial to be considered as abandoned, shall expire.

Fourth. The boundaries that are established shall be clearly and distinctly pointed out, expressing the bearings, and specific landmarks, under the responsibility of the judge of survey.

Fifth. The standing waters the lands contain shall likewise be designated and adjudicated with the lands.

Sixth. Until twelve years, reckoned from the date of the publication of this law, they cannot be alienated or transferred to the ownership of anyone not born in the republic, or who resides out of the state.

"ART.22. All adjudication and possession of lands designated for settling shall be made with previous citation of the adjoining proprietors. As little detriment as practicable shall be occasioned to those who do not appear, of themselves or by attorney, and their complaints shall not be heard.

"ART.23. The new settlers shall pay to the state as an acknowledgment, thirty dollars for each sitio of grazing land, uncultivated, or woodland, that is adjudicated to them; and for those having the benefit of running water an estimate shall be made by two competent persons, chosen by the executive and the settler, setting out from the established rule.

"ART.25. The executive shall convoke those born in the republic for the occupation of vacant lands, who shall be preferred to foreigners in the order of the older date of the designations, and, in case of equality, the natives or inhabitants of the place to which the land designated belongs, shall have the first place, those of places within the state the second, and those of the other states of this republic the third, and adjudication may be made up to the amount of one hundred and twenty-five million square varas.

"ART.26. Designators of lands, which, in time of the ancient government did not perfect their adjudication, shall present themselves to the respective authority to continue its course according to the state thereof, effecting the same within the term of forty days from the date of the publication of this law, and on the contrary, said lands shall be considered open to designation as vacant."

"ART.27. Designations that have passed to the congress of the state shall be returned to the executive, who shall cause them to be carried through the steps provided by this law.

"ART.28. Proprietors of extensive deserted and uncultivated lands shall likewise settle them with foreigners or Mexicans within the term of five years with the conditions that may suit them, and on the contrary, opposition to designations made in conformity to this law, shall not be taken into consideration.

"ART.30. All land of which the proprietor makes no use for himself shall be considered deserted and uncultivated land.

"ART.34. Lots abandoned in depopulated towns, wherein they wish to fix their residence, shall be adjudicated to them gratis by the Alcaldes of said towns.

"ART.36. The executive shall appoint two approval surveyors, and in default thereof, two individuals of known education to concur in the operations forwarded by this law, which he shall cause to be published in a manner sufficient for it to arrive to the notice of nations that interest themselves in colonizing.

THE LAW OF APRIL 6, 1830

Papers Concerning Robertson's Colony in Texas
Volume III, page 494-498
By Malcolm D. McLean

Volume 53, page 146-147, Spanish Archives
General Land Office, Austin Texas

"ART.9. The entrance of foreigners under any pretext whatever, at the frontier of the North is prohibited if they are not provided with a passport, issued by the agent of the Republic at the place from where they came.

"ART.10. No change shall be made respecting the Colonies already established, neither in respect to the slaves which may exist in them, but the General Government or the particular one of each State, will heed, under the most rigid responsibility the compliance of the Colonization laws and that no more slaves are introduced.

"ART.11. In the use of the faculty reserved for the General Congress in the 7th article of the law of 18th August 1824, it is prohibited to colonize the foreigners on the frontier border in those States and Territories of the federation, which adjoin their Nation. Consequently the contracts which have not had their compliance and which may be in opposition to this law, shall be suspended.

Therefore I order that it be printed, published, and circulated and that due compliance be given to it."
                              Anastasio Bustamente
                              A D Lucas Alaman

From
Decree No. 190.

STATE OF COAHUILA AND TEXAS

April 18, 1832

(1 Gammel 299-303)

"The Congress of the State of Coahuila and Texas has thought proper to decree as follows:

"ART. 1. To any Mexican, who on the publication of this law, shall resolve to settle any of the vacant lands thereof, the state hereby tenders its protection and aid.

"ART. 2. Any Mexican or Mexicans who offer to effect at their own expense, the removal of ninety families at least, shall present themselves to the executive, with whom they shall ratify their contracts according to this law, and shall fulfill the said contracts within the term of four years. Those who do not settle the aforementioned number of families shall forfeit the rights and privileges granted them by this law."

"ART. 3.   As soon as thirty families are collected, the formal establishment of the new town shall be commenced on the site most appropriate in the judgment of the executive, or person commissioned by him for the purpose; and four square leagues shall be assigned for each new town, whose area may be of a regular or irregular figure, as the local situation shall require.

"ART. 4.   Should any of the sites designed for founding a new town consist of land already appropriated, and the establishment be of evident general utility, it may be taken notwithstanding, observing the provision made by the constitution in restriction fourth, Article 113.

"ART. 8.   To each of the families comprised in the contract mentioned in Article 2, one day for watering, and one labor shall be granted, or two labors should the land be temporal, (land cultivated during ordinary rains) and a lot sixty yards square, whereon said family shall erect a dwelling within two years, otherwise they shall forfeit the privilege. Should the family have neat stock, horse kind, or small stock, exceeding one hundred head of the two former kinds, or six hundred of the latter, the same shall be entitled to one sitio of grazing land.

"ART. 9.   A square of land measuring one league, consisting of five thousand varas on each side, or what is the same thing, a superficies of twentyfive million square varas shall be called a sitio, and this shall be the unit for enumerating one, two or more sitios, in the same manner as one million square varas, or one thousand varas on each side, which shall constitute a labor, shall be the unit for reckoning one, two or more labors.   The varas for this measure shall consist of three geometrical feet.

"ART.10.   This law shall grant to empresarios, for every ninety families they settle in the new town, four sitios of grazing land, and three watering days for the aqueducts or canals that can be applied to the cultivation of the land pertaining to their empresa: but they shall receive premium only in the ratio of ninety families , although they should introduce more, and they shall be entitled to no prize land for a fraction not amounting to ninety.

"ART.11.   Neither the commissioner or any other authority shall grant another lot to the same person until he shall have built upon the first.

"ART.12.   Any empresario who, in consideration of the families he settles, shall acquire agreeable to Article 10, more than eleven sitios, shall alienate the excess within nine years, and should he not, the respective political authority shall sell the same at public auction, and deliver the proceeds to the owners thereof, after deducting the costs of sale.

"ART.13.   The government may sell to Mexicans the lands they solicit, taking care that more than eleven leagues are not united in the same hands, and on the positive condition that, by the fourth year from the acquisition thereof, purchaser shall have introduced upon said land at least thirty head of large, or two hundred of small stock for each sitio. The purchaser shall deliver one-fourth of the value of the land granted, to the state treasury or to where the executive designates, at the time of the sale; and the remaining three-fourths shall be paid, the first on the second, the second on the third and the last payment on the fourth year, under penalty of forfeiting the right acquired in the part wherein this provision is not fulfilled.

"ART.14.   Within the ten littoral leagues upon the coast of the Gulf of Mexico, the price of each sitio shall be two hundred dollars for grazing and three hundred for tillage land, not irrigable.   In the rest of the department of Bexar, the price thereof shall be one hundred dollars for the former and one hundred and fifty for the latter kind of land; and that, of the other vacant lands of the state, fifteen dollars a sitio for the former, and twenty for the latter.

"ART.15.   Lands, whose local situation admits of canals, and not designated for towns, may be sold by the executive, to Mexicans only, at three hundred dollars each sitio in the department of Bexar, and at two hundred in the others of the state; to be paid as Article 13 provides, and under the same penalty imposed therein; on the express condition that by the fourth year from the acquisition thereof, the purchaser shall have cultivated one-eighth of the land, and the same shall be observed with respect to the tillage land not irrigable as mentioned in the proceeding article.

"ART.16.   No change shall be made with respect to the contract which the executive has ratified, or the concessions stipulated to purchasers or settlers by virtue of Decree No. 16, of the 24th of March, 1825; but the executive shall take care that, within eighteen months from the publication of this law, the purchasers enter in possession of the land which he has granted them.   Those who shall hereafter ratify new contracts, or acquire new concessions by purchase, shall be required, the former to have introduced one-sixth of the families contracted within eighteen months from the ratification of the contract, and the latter to enter in possession of the land acquired, within the same term; under penalty of forfeiture for the non-fulfillment thereof."

"ART.19. No new settler, Mexican or foreigner, shall under any title or pretense, sell or alienate the land or water that falls to his share, until after six years from the time of taking possession.

"ART.20. Mexicans or foreigners who undertake to colonize with foreign families, whose introduction is not prohibited by the general law of the 6th of April, 1830, shall be entitled to the privileges granted by Article 6 of the present law.

"ART.25. The executive shall take care that, within twenty border leagues fronting upon the United States line, and ten littoral leagues upon the coast of the Gulf of Mexico, no settlements are made that are not composed of two-thirds Mexicans, previously obtaining by request, the approval of the national executive, to whom he shall forward all petitions made on the subject, accompanied by his report, whether the empresarios are Mexicans or foreigners.

"ART.28. That no vacancies be left between the tracts, which shall be carefully avoided in the distribution of lands, they shall be distributed in square or other forms, although irregular should the locality so require, and to prevent litigation and dispute, in making the distribution aforesaid, as well as in the designation of the sites, whereon new towns are to be founded, the adjoining proprietors, should there be any, shall be previously notified.

"ART.29. The survey of vacant lands that shall be made upon the borders of any river, running rivulet or creek, or lake, shall not exceed one-fourth of the depth of the land granted, should the land permit.

"ART.30. Should any appropriated land be taken possession of through error in the concession, on proof thereof, an equal quantity of land entirely vacant shall be granted to the person who obtained the same, and moreover, he shall be idemnified by the owner of the land aforesaid, agreeable to a just estimate made by competent judges, and according to law, for the expense he has incurred in the improvements that appear thereon.

"ART.33. New settlers, who shall resolve to leave the state to establish themselves in a foreign country, shall be at liberty to do so with all their property, but after thus leaving, they shall no longer hold their land; and should they not have previously disposed of the same, or should not the alienation be in conformity to Article 19, it shall become entirely vacant.

"ART.38. Decree No. 16 of the 24th of March, 1825, is hereby repealed."

For its fulfillment, the Governor of the State shall cause to be printed, published, and circulated.

"Given in the city of Leona Vicario on the 28th of April, 1832.

JOSE J. GRANDEA, President
MANUEL MUZQUIZ, D. S.
CESARIO FIGUEROA, D. S. ad
interim.

From
Decree 272

STATE OF COAHUILA AND TEXAS

March 26, 1834

(1 Gammel 357-362)

Executive Department of)
the State of Coahuila   )
and Texas   )

The Governor of the State of Coahuila and Texas, to all the inhabitants thereof: Be it known that the congress of said state has decreed as follows:

DECREE No. 272

"The Congress of the State of Coahuila and Texas has thought proper to decree:

Section 1.

"ART. 1. The vacant lands of the state shall be sold at public auction.

"ART. 2. A vara of three geometrical feet, and a mile consisting of a thousand varas, shall be the unit for lineal measure; and a millionada containing a million square varas, or what is the same thing, a square measuring a thousand varas on each side, shall be the unit for area measure.

"ART. 3. The lands shall be sold at public auction by order of the executive when he thinks proper to order those of any district to be surveyed and sold, or on notice from any person interested in purchasing any land, which he may point out, and of which he may request a survey.

"ART. 4. The lands in both cases shall be surveyed in parcels not exceeding a millionada, and after they are surveyed, the sale, and day whereon it is to be made, shall be advertised for three months, posting written slips for that object in all the municipalities of the department to which the lands belong, and in those of the two nearest departments, and should it be in Texas, in all those of the three departments; describing said land in general terms, and giving notice of the place where they lie.

"ART. 5. The day appointed for the sale having arrived, they shall be offered at public auction in millionadas, or fractions of millionada, and adjudged to the highest bidder, provided, that the bid does not fall short of the minimum price.

"ART. 6. The minimum price in Texas shall be ten dollars for each millionada, payable in three installments; the first in hand, the second at the expiration of the first, and the third at the expiration of the second year, under penalty of forfeiting what has been paid, and of the title becoming null in case of non-fulfillment; and the purchaser may pay the whole in advance should it thus suit his convenience.

"ART.11. The same person shall not be permitted to purchase more than two hundred and seventy-five millionadas, and no corporation or company shall be allowed to purchase.

"ART.12. For this object, every purchaser, on receiving title to his land, shall declare under oath that he has not purchased for another person, but for himself only, or as attorney of another, whom he shall make known by his entire name, and in that case, the title shall not be issued until the true purchaser appears to receive it in his own name, which shall do within one year under penalty of forfeiting his right, and what shall have been paid.

Section 2.

"ART.13. For the proper regulation, and better administration of this department, there shall be two general commissioners, to be appointed by the executive, one for Coahuila, the other for Texas.

"ART.14. There shall also be such number of subordinate commissioners as the executive shall deem proper, and he shall assign them in their commissions, the limits of the districts wherein they are to exercise their functions.

"ART.15. The attributes and duties of the subordinate commissioners shall be as follows: To fulfill the orders and instructions of the executive and the respective general commissioners; To appoint surveyors duly qualified on their

responsibility, and administer them the oath specified in
Article 19; To cause the lands to be surveyed in accordance
with the provisions of Articles 3 and 4; To keep a bound
book of common paper for carefully recording the surveys
therein, adding a map of the same, and signing the recital
with the surveyor who made the survey, and witness who
accompanied him; To form a general map of his district,
whereon the particular surveys, and sales that shall have
been made, shall be noted down; To furnish the advertisements
mentioned in Article 4, and direct them to the respective
Alcaldes that may cause them to be posted up in the most
public and usual place; To sell the lands as provided in
Articles 1, 3, 4, 5, 6, and 7; To keep another bound book,
wherein he shall specify all the sales he shall make,
minutely describing the lands and surveys thereof, with a map
and stating the price of the sale, which he shall sign with
the purchaser and witnesses; To furnish the purchaser, without delay, a certified copy of said recital, with a map, and
should the lands be in different places, a separate certificate for each; And to forward to the general commissioner the
map of his district, and give to said commissioner and to the
executive, such information as they shall request.

"ART.16. The powers and duties of the general commissioners
shall be as follows: To conform entirely to the orders and
instructions of the executive, and to submit to him whatever
information he requests, and what is proper with regard to
lands which, in his opinion, may be , and ought to be sold,
paying strict attention to the time specified, whereon the
colonization contracts entered into previous to the publication of this law, are to expire; To issue to purchasers in
the name of the state, the title to the land sold in accordance with the certificates they present him for the subordinate commissioners, describing the lands and surveys thereof,
and expressing the amount for which they were sold; To
administer the oath mentioned in Article 12, and, as the case
may be, that prescribed in Article 8, previous to issuing a
purchaser his titles, being a foreigner; To record said
titles in a bound book which they will keep for the purpose,
causing the person interested and witnesses also to sign the
registers; To require of the subordinate commissioners such
information as they think proper, and give them the necessary
instructions, receiving from them the maps of their districts
and to form Archives of the whole.

"ART.19. The surveyors shall make oath before the respective
commissioner truly and faithfully to discharge the duties of
their office.

"ART.20. The course of the lines shall be determined by the
magnetic needle, and care shall be taken to determine its
variation from the pole in the district where the surveys are
made.

"ART.21. The surveys shall be made with great caution with metalic chains made for the purpose, and care shall be taken that the place of beginning the survey of each parcel of land be established with certainty, taking the bearings and distances of two permanent objects at least.

"ART.22. Lands fronting on permanent creeks, rivers, large lakes, bays and the sea shore, shall run back double the extent of their front.

"ART.23. To avoid litigation and future difficulties, the respective authorities shall present to the subordinate commissioners as soon as he enters on the discharge of his duties, all the titles and grants of land heretofore made that he may note down the same in the respective book, and cause such surveys as should not be distinct, to be rectified so that they may not interfere with one another.

"ART.24. Should the documents mentioned in the preceding article be in possession of private individuals, they shall present the same for the aforesaid object within one year, under penalty of foreefeiting the right, should the lands be granted to other persons for want of this knowledge.

"ART.25. The surveyors shall receive from the purchasers of lands, twelve rials for every thousand varas of lineal measure.

"ART.29. All the instructions for commissioners issued prior to this decree, so far as they are opposed to the same, are hereby repealed, and Decrees Number 62 of the 15th day of May, 1828; 190 of the 28th of April, 1832, and 128 of the 7th day of April, 1830, are likewise repealed, with the exception of the last six articles of the latter, which shall continue in force.

"ART.30. Hereafter, no colonization contract shall be made, and those heretofore made shall be strictly fulfilled, and in entire accordance with the law of the 24th of March, 1825.

Section 3

"ART.31. No petition for prolonging the time in contracts shall be passed to congress by the executive, unless authenticated so as sufficiently to prove that the persons interested have expended ten thousand dollars at least for carrying their engagements into effect, and that the non-fulfillment thereof has consisted solely in insuperable obstacles interposed by the Mexican authorities.

"ART.32. To the inhabitants of the frontier of Nacogdoches, and those residing east of Austin's colonies, titles shall be issued to the lands they occupy according to Article 16 of the colonization law of the 24th of March, 1825, and the resolutions of the general government off April and August, 1828, and the executive shall appoint one or two commissioners for that object, who without any delay shall execute the same at the expense of the persons interested, and the titles heretofore legally issued are hereby confirmed.

"ART.33. The other colonists of the state, who, having emigrated separately, and at their own expense, within the first six years from the establishment of any colony, should not have received the augmentation conceded by said Article 16 of said colonization law, shall manifest the same to the executive through the channel of the political chief.

"ART.34. To resolve in regard to said claims, the executive shall appoint three commissioners, who, citing the respective empresario, shall give the colonists a verbal hearing, and decide by majority of vote whether the claimant be entitled to the augmentation. Should it be decided in the affirmative, they shall give the party the corresponding certicicate.

"ART.35. Said party shall present himself to the Ayuntamiento specifying the land which he solicits, and requesting a surveyor to be appointed to run off the same, and, that being done, the said Ayuntamiento shall issue him the title giving notice to the executive through the ordinary channel.

"ART.36. Settlers, who shall have received titles to their lands may sell them at any time, and the purchaser shall remain with the charge of fulfilling the duties of vendor to the state, and the land shall be liable for the responsibility.

"For its fulfillment, the Governor of the State shall cause it to be printed, published, and circulated.

> R. de la FUENTE, President
> J. Y. C. FALCON, D. S.
> J. J. GRANDE, D. D.

"Wherefore I command it to be printed, published, circulated and duly fulfilled.

"Given in the city of Monclova on the 26th of March, 1834."

> FRANCISCO V. y VILLASENOR.

Jose Miguel Falcon, Secretary.

CHAPTER 3

SPANISH TERMS USED IN LAND GRANTS AND EARLY DEEDS

MISCELLANEOUS MEXICAN MEASURES

Linear Measures

```
Vara- - - - - - - - - - - - - - - - - 3 geometrical feet
Cordel- - - - - - - - - - - - - - - - 50 varas
League- - - - - - - - - - - - - - - - 100 cordeles
Soloman Pace- - - - - - - - - - - - - 58 inches
Marco - - - - - - - - - - - - - - - - 2 7/8 varas
Roman or Mexican Foot - - - - - - - - 11.13 inches
```

Ancient Measures

```
League  - - - - - - - - - - - - - - - 5,000 varas
Palmo (hand)- - - - - - - - - - - - - 1/4 varas
Paja- - - - - - - - - - - - - - - - - 1/3 dedo (finger)
Dedo- - - - - - - - - - - - - - - - - 1/48 vara
16 dedos- - - - - - - - - - - - - - - 1 foot
Paso- - - - - - - - - - - - - - - - - 5 feet (1 double
                                             step)
```

Area Measurements

Caballeria = Land given to soldiers in victorious battle - 552 varas x 1104 varas = 609,408 square varas (value adapted by the Mexican Government).

Suerte = 1/4 Caballeria - 276 varas x 552 varas.

League or Sitio de Ganado Mayor (large cattle) = 5,000 varas square = 4,428.4 acres.

League or Sitio de Ganado Menor (small cattle) = 3,333 1/3 varas square = 1,968.18 acres.

Labor = 1,000 varas square = 177.14 acres.

Hacienda = 5 leagues.

Porcion = variable quanity or about 30,000,000 square vares. Sometimes defined as 2 Sitios Granada Mayor or 1 Caballeria.

Peonia = Land given to soldiers as spoils of war = 50 pies (roman foot) x 100 pies.

Huebra = about .55 acres.

Fanega = number of acres required to grow 1 bushel of grain varies with grain = about 1.6 acres.

SPANISH NAMES OF TREES AND THEIR ENGLISH EQUIVALENTS

(Compiled from names of witness trees appearing on old titles and deeds).

SPANISH	ENGLISH
Abedulo	Birch
Abeto	Fir
Acacia	Locust
Acano	Beach
Acebo	Holly
Agume	Sumac
Aile	Wild Peach
Alamo	Cottonwood or Elm
Alamo Blanco	Sycamore
Alamo Colorado	Cottonwood
Algarroba	Honey Mesquite
Anaqua	Anaqua, a kind of Hickory
Anora	Pawpaw
Arandano	Whortleberry, Huckleberry
Arce	Maple
Brasil	Brazilletto or Brazil Wood
Capulin Sylvestre	Wild Cherry
Carcomecatal	Green Briar
Carrasca	Evergreen Oak
Castano	Chestnut
Castano Sylvestre	Chinquapin
Castor	Bay Tree
Catalpa	Wild China
Cedro	Cedar
Chapaarro Prieto	Black Brush
Chapote	Persimmon
Chino Sylvestre-Jaboncillo	Wild China
Chiquetin	Chincapin
Chopo	Black Popular
Cipres	Cypress
Copal	Gum
Copal Dulce	Sweet Gum
Copal Prieto	Black Gum
Cornejo (membrillo)	Dogwood
Encina	Live Oak
Encina Aquatia or Acautica	Water Oak
Encina Blanca	White Oak (or Live Oak)
Encina China	Black Oak
Encina Colorado	Red Oak
Encina de Corteza Negra	Black Jack
Encina Prieta	Black Oak
Encina Roble	Pin Oak (or Burr Oak)
Encina Roma	Post Oak
Encina Verde	Live Oak

SPANISH	ENGLISH
Fresno	Ash
Fresno Espinoso	Prickly Ash
Fresno Picante	Toothache Tree
Frijollio	Bean
Guayacan	Lignum - Bitae
Guelde	Water Elder
Guindillo	Wild Cherry
Haya	Beech
Hayaguil	Beech
Huisache	Huisache
Jaboncillo	Soap Root
Jaboncillo Sylvestre	Wild China
Juncia	Sweet Cypress
Junco	Locust Rush
Lila Sylvestre	Wild China
Maaguey	Century Plant
Mascan	Sweet Maple
Membrillo (cornejo)	Dogwood
Mesquite	Mesquite
Mispero	Persimmon
Mogote or Magote	Thicket - Mott
Mora	Mulberry
Morera	White Mulberry
Nispero or Nispera	Persimmon
Nogal	Walnut
Nogal Blanco	White Walnut
Nogal de Castilla	Pecan
Nogal Encarcelado	Hickory
Nogal Prieto	Black Walnut
Ojaranza	Hornbeam
Olmo	Elm
Orgifa	Nettle
Pacana	Pecan
Palma	Palm, dagger
Palo Amarillo	Bois de' Arc
Palo Blanco	Hackberry
Palo de Azucar	Maple or Sugar Tree
Palo de Castor	Magnolia or Bay
Palo de Fruta	Black Gum
Palo de Hierro	Iron Wood
Palo Gacho	Leaning Tree
Palo Pinto	Spotted Oak
Pino	Pine
Pino de Ajote	Pitch Pine
Pita	Spanish Dagger
Pita Bravosa	Linwood Tree
Renueva	Sprout
Roble	Oak
Sabina	Cypress
Sasafrasa	Sassafras

SPANISH	ENGLISH
Sauce	Willow
Sauco	Alder (or Elder)
Sauco de Box	Box Elder
Sicomoro	Sycamore
Socososote	Spanish Dagger
Tehocote	Black Haw or Hawthorne
Tilo	Linwood Tree
Tuya	Cedar
Tronco	Stump
Zarza	Briar

MISCELLANEOUS SPANISH WORDS FOUND IN DEEDS, ETC.

Ancon	Small creek into which tidewater backs
Arroyo	Waterway, dry creek, stream
Bajio	Shoal, sand bank, flat
Bajita	Low ground
Banda	Side
Barranco	Gulley with steep bank, bluff, ravine
Bayuco	Slough
Bosque	Wood place (thicket)
Cadena	Chain
Cala or Caleta	Creek
Charco	Pool of standing water, small lake
Cienega	Marsh
Cordel	Cord (50 varas)
Corolel	5 pasos
Derramadero	Draw (bushy) like a jungle
Escarpa	Slope of a ditch or ravine
Eslabon	Link
Estante	Post
Estero	Marsh
Lado	Side
Laga	Lake
Laguna	Lake, Lagoon
Llano	Prairie
Mar	Ocean
Monte	Timber
Mota	Mott
Pantano	Marsh
Paso	1 double step
Resaca	Beach or overflow land
Sendero	Trail or path cut in brush
Sitio	Tract of land, also league

CHAPTER 4

ORIGINAL COLONIES OF TEXAS

In an effort to settle the area that became known as Texas,
the Mexican Government set up a procedure for families to
obtain land grants here. Under their program, contracts were
made with certain parties, known as empresarios, giving them
authority to settle a certain number of families within
designated areas of land. Upon satisfying all legal
requirements, the settlers were to receive grants of land
from the Mexican Government.

The "First Contract" was dated February 25, 1823, with
Stephen F. Austin. The boundaries under this contract were
not defined and the colonists scattered in settlements from
the coast to the old San Antonio road and from the Lavaca to
the San Jacinto Rivers.

The limits of Austin's Second Contract, dated May 20, 1825,
Third Contract, dated November 20, 1827, and Fourth Contract,
dated July 28, 1828, are shown on an attached map. His Third
Contract was known as "Austin's Little Colony ".

The contract for Austin and Williams' Colony, dated February
25, 1831, encompassed most of Austin's first four contracts
except the ten littoral leagues along the seacoast, which the
Mexican government now wished to retain, extending the
colony boundaries further to the northwest.

The contract for "Robertson's Colony" was made on April 15,
1824, with Robert Leftwich. This area was sometimes called
the "Leftwich Colony". After signing the contract to settle
this area Leftwich returned to Tennessee to recruit settlers
and died there. A company, known as the Nashville Company,
was formed to settle the colony which they renamed the
"Nashville Colony". The Nashville Company named Alex
Thompson and Sterling C. Robertson to be in charge of the new
settlement and the colony then became " Robertson's Colony."
Records for any of the three colonies refer to the same land.

Mexican officials revoked the privileges of the Nashville
Company in 1831 and assigned the territory to Austin and
Williams. By decree of the State of Coahuila and Texas, April
29, 1834, the colony was transferred to Robertson, but this
decree was revoked May 18, 1835. This action complicated the
title to certain lands during this period.

Martin DeLeon, in his first contract dated October 6, 1824,
was to receive the land between the Lavaca and Guadalupe

Rivers and between Colito Creek and the coast, including the littoral leagues next to the sea. The grant of the seacoast land was with the approval of the Federal Executive. In his second contract, dated April 30, 1829, the grant from the first contract was affirmed and augmented.

The colonies granted by the Mexican Government and the dates of the contracts prior to 1833, are as follows:

Austin's First Colony		February 25,	1823
Robertson's Colony		April 15,	1824
Martin DeLeon's Colony	1st Contract	October 6,	1824
Green De Witt's Colony		October,	1824
Frost Thorn's Colony		April 15,	1825
Austin's Second Colony		May 20,	1825
Haden Edwards' Colony		April 18,	1825
Purnell and Drakes' Colony		October 22,	1825
Benjamin R. Milam's Colony		January 12,	1826
Arthur Wavel's Colony		March 9,	1826
Stephen J. Wilson's Colony		May 29,	1826
John L. Woodbury's Colony		November 14,	1826
David G. Burnet's Colony		December 22,	1826
Jos. Vehlein's Colonies	1st Contract	December 21,	1826
	2nd Contract	November 11,	1828
Austin's Little Colony		November 20,	1827
Austin's Fourth Colony		July 28,	1828
John Cameron's Colonies	1st Contract	May 21,	1827
	2nd Contract	September 19,	1828
Hewitson and Power's	1st Contract	June 11,	1828
Colonies	2nd Contract	April 21,	1830
McMullen and McGloin's Colony		August 16,	1828
John Domingnez' Colony		February 6,	1829
Lorenzo de Zavala's Colony		March 12,	1829
Martin DeLeon's Colony	2nd Contract	April 30,	1829
Thos. J. Chambers' and			
J. A. Padillo's Colony		February 12,	1830
Austin and Williams' Colony		February 25,	1831
Filisola's Colony		October 15,	1831
J.C. Beale's Colonies	1st Contract	March 14,	1832
	2nd Contract	May 1,	1832

McMullen and McGloin's Colony granted August 16, 1828, covered the same territory as that issued to Purnell and Drake on October 22, 1825.

A colonization contract was issued to Ector (or Exeter) and Wilson on September 23, 1829, for a grant of land on the Arkansas River, but this grant was outside the present Texas boundaries.

In locating the boundaries of these colonies, every designated landmark that could be located was used. Despite all efforts, however, many boundary lines are indefinite.

Some boundaries represent the divides between two streams and others follow old roads or trails. Of course, over the years, streams as well as roads and trails change their courses and boundary lines become obscure. The boundaries we use, as well as the location of old roads, trails, and towns, is the best we can determine by use of old maps and descriptions.

The eastern boundary of Vehlein's, Burnet's, Filisola's, and Thorn's colonies was intended to be twenty leagues from the United States boundary in accordance with a provision of the Mexican Government to insulate the settlers in Texas from those of the United States. Later contracts were made with Cameron and DeZavala for settling these border leagues.

COLONY GRANTS BY THE REPUBLIC OF TEXAS

The Republic of Texas, in order to further immigration, also issued contracts for colonies to be settled in the new republic. These colonies and the contract dates are as follows:

H. Castro Colony   February 15, 1842
        Four tracts located along the Rio Grande
        River and North toward the interior.

Fisher and Miller's Colony   January 29, 1844
        Central Texas along the Colorado River.

Gen. Charles F. Mercer's Colony   January 29, 1844
        Northern Texas near Indian Territory

Peters' Colony   1st Contract   August 30,   1841

                      2nd Contract   November 20, 1841
                      3rd Contract   July 26,   1842
                      4th Contract   January 23,   1843

        Four Contracts signed between W.S.Peters,et
        al, and the Republic of Texas, on the dates
        indicated, were later ratified by the Act of
        February 10, 1852, for grants of land along
        Red River and the Indian Territory.

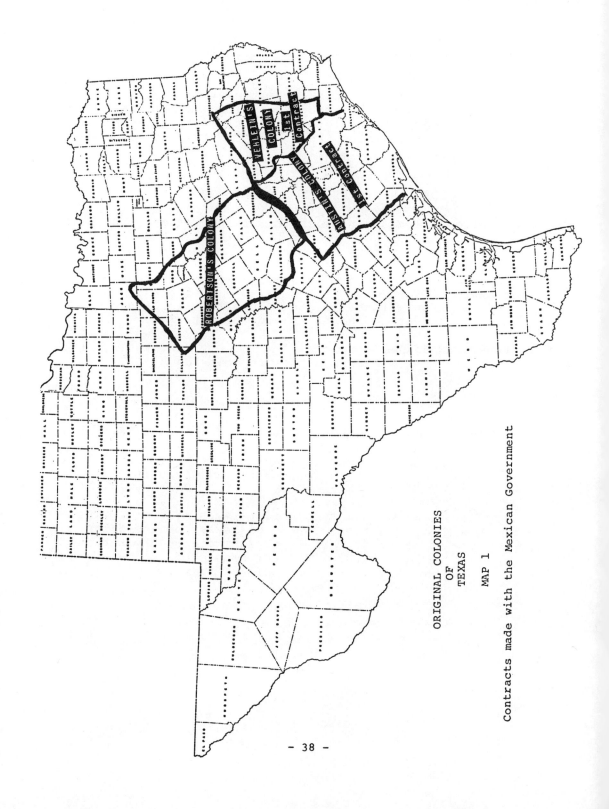

ORIGINAL COLONIES
OF
TEXAS

MAP 1

Contracts made with the Mexican Government

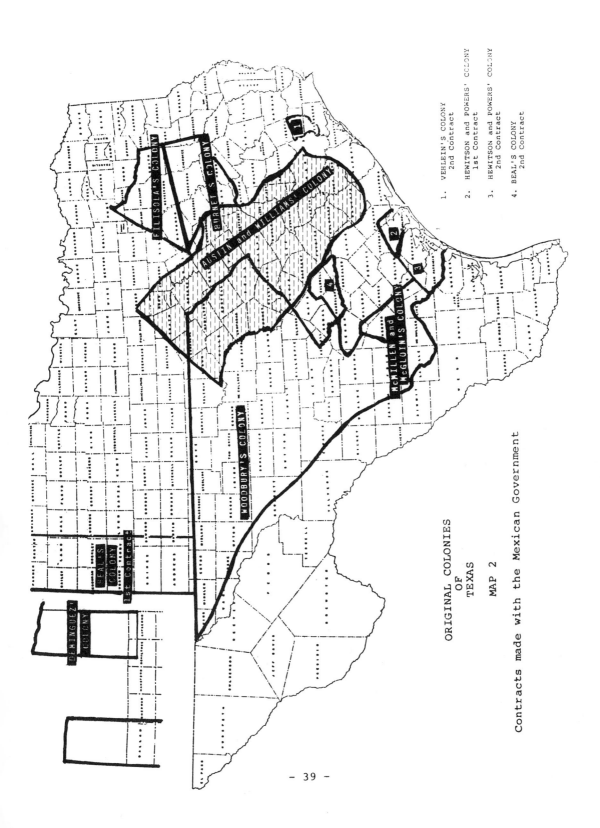

ORIGINAL COLONIES
OF
TEXAS

MAP 2

Contracts made with the Mexican Government

1. VEHLEIN'S COLONY
    2nd Contract

2. HEWITSON and POWERS' COLONY
    1st Contract

3. HEWITSON and POWERS' COLONY
    2nd Contract

4. BEAL'S COLONY
    2nd Contract

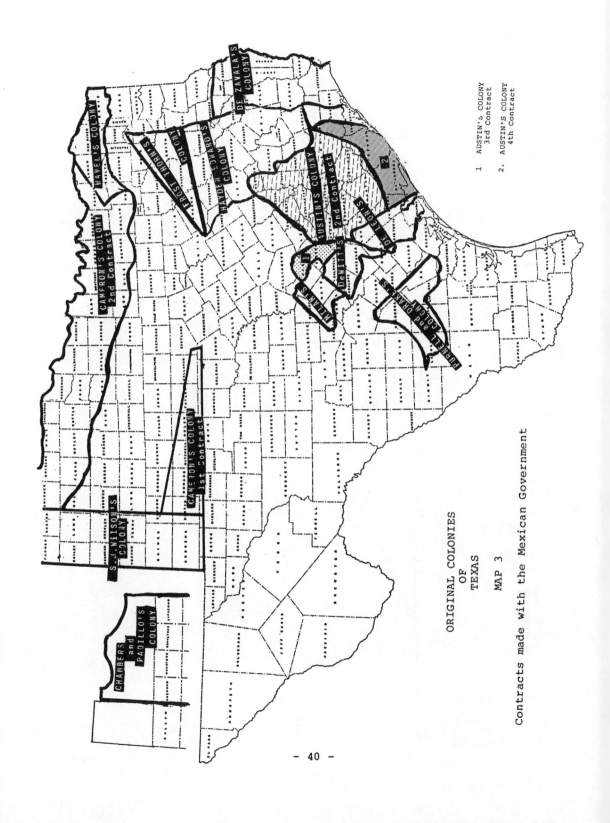

ORIGINAL COLONIES
OF
TEXAS

MAP 3

Contracts made with the Mexican Government

1. AUSTIN's COLONY
   3rd Contract

2. AUSTIN's COLONY
   4th Contract

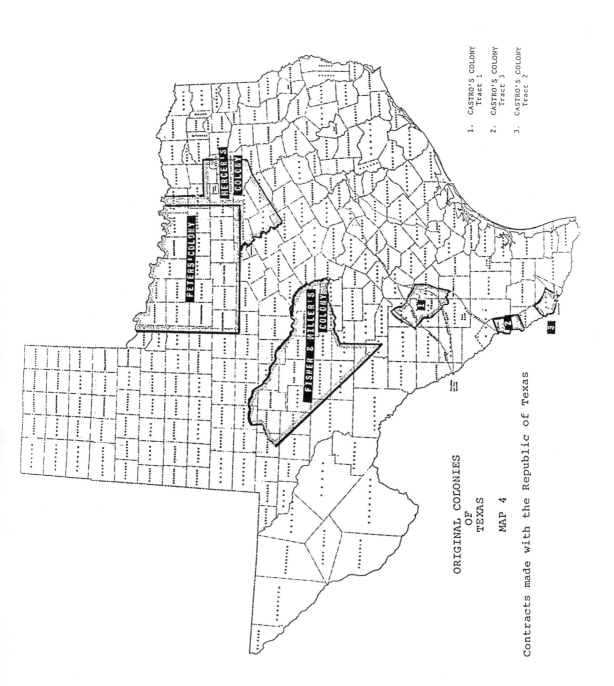

ORIGINAL COLONIES
OF
TEXAS

MAP 4

Contracts made with the Republic of Texas

1. CASTRO'S COLONY
   Tract 1

2. CASTRO'S COLONY
   Tract 3

3. CASTRO'S COLONY
   Tract 2

CHAPTER 5

LAND DISTRICTS OF TEXAS

The first Land Districts were established by the creation of
the General Land Office in 1836. The following maps show the
territory included within the various Land Districts which
were established by acts of the Republic of Texas and the
State of Texas. Descriptions of these Land Districts were
obtained from legislative statutes. Map 10 shows certain old
counties of Texas which no longer exist.

The early Land Districts depended for their locations on the
county boundaries as they formerly existed. These county
descriptions were also obtained from these statutes.

The purpose of these maps is to show the Land Districts in
which present counties, or any particular portions of present
counties, formerly lay. The maps, arranged chronologically,
are as follows:

    Map 1 - Land Districts established by the creation of
             the General Land Office in 1836. By this act, a
             General Land Office was established at the seat
             of government and eleven land offices designated
             for the eleven districts shown. The locations of
             the Land Offices were as follows:

             Land Office 1 - The house of George Wright on
                              the Red River.
             Land Office 2 - San Augustine.
             Land Office 3 - Liberty.
             Land Office 4 - Nacogdoches.
             Land Office 5 - Matagorda.
             Land Office 6 - Washington (now Washington-on
                              the Brazos).
             Land Office 7 - Cameron.
             Land Office 8 - Bastrop.
             Land Office 9 - Gonzales.
             Land Office 10 - San Antonio.
             Land Office 11 - Victoria.

    Map 2 - Land Districts established by the General
             Land Office Act of May 12, 1846. This act
             provided that "the several counties of the
             Republic of Texas as they existed February 15,
             1846" should constitute Land Districts, and
             provide also that no new county created by the
             legislature should be made a separate land
             district but should remain a part of the
             district from which it was taken.

The Land Districts are listed as follows:

Austin, Bastrop, Bexar, Bowie, Brazos, Brazoria, Colorado, Fayette, Fannin, Fort Bend, Galveston, Goliad, Gonzales, Harris, Harrison, Houston, Jackson, Jasper, Jefferson, Lamar, Liberty, Matagorda, Milam, Montgomery, Nacogdoches, Red River, Refugio, Robertson, Rusk, Sabine, Shelby, San Augustine, San Patricio (San Patricio and Nueces), Travis, Victoria, and Washington.

Map 3 - Land Districts established or redefined from 1852 to 1856 are listed as follows:

Cooke, Cameron, Denton, Hidalgo, Karnes, Nueces, Presidio and El Paso, San Patricio, Starr, and Webb.

Map 4 - Land Districts established or redefined in 1874 are listed as follows:

Brown, Clay, Eastland, Jack, Palo Pinto, San Saba, and Young.

Map 5 - Land Districts established or redefined by the 16th Legislature in 1879 are listed as follows:

Bexar, Brown, Clay, Eastland, Jack, Palo Pinto, Shackelford, San Saba and Young.

Map 6 - Land Districts established or redefined by Acts of March 11, 1881, and April 2, 1883 are listed as follows:

Baylor, Clay, Howard, Mitchell, Oldham, and Wheeler.

Map 7 - Land Districts established or redefined by Act of April 9, 1883 are listed as follows:

Donley, Oldham, Wheeler, and Wilbarger.

Map 8 - Land Districts established or redefined by Acts of February 27, and March 24, 1885 are listed as follows:

Hardeman, Nolan, and Webb.

Map 9 - Land Districts established by Act of April 1, 1887 are listed as follows:

Crosby, Knox, Martin, and Scurry.

Map 10 - Map shows certain former counties mentioned in
surveyors records and the former boundaries of
certain counties whose surveyors records may now
include surveys outside their present
boundaries. This may have a bearing on the
location of old records. They are listed as
follows:

Crockett, Edwards, Encinal, Greer, Hardeman,
Kinney, Nueces, Tom Green, and Wegefarth.

The following counties were attached for surveying purposes
by Act of February 3, 1909:

Loving and Winkler Counties attached to Reeves County.

Crane County attached to Ector County.

Andrews and Upton Counties attached to Midland County.

Data shown on Maps No. 1 and 2 were taken from the Acts of
the Congress of the Republic of Texas. Data shown on Maps
No. 3 thru 10 were taken from the Acts of the Legislature of
the State of Texas.

The Act of the 16th Legislature in 1879, which established
the Land Districts shown on Map 5, also provided that the
existing counties, having duly elected surveyors, should
constitute separate land districts. When a county that is
organized thereafter should elect a qualified surveyor, it
should become a separate land district.

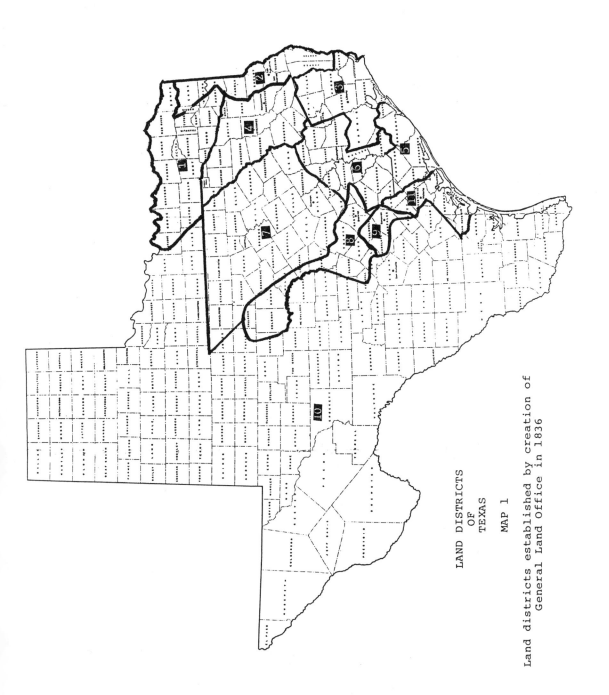

LAND DISTRICTS
OF
TEXAS

MAP 1

Land districts established by creation of
General Land Office in 1836

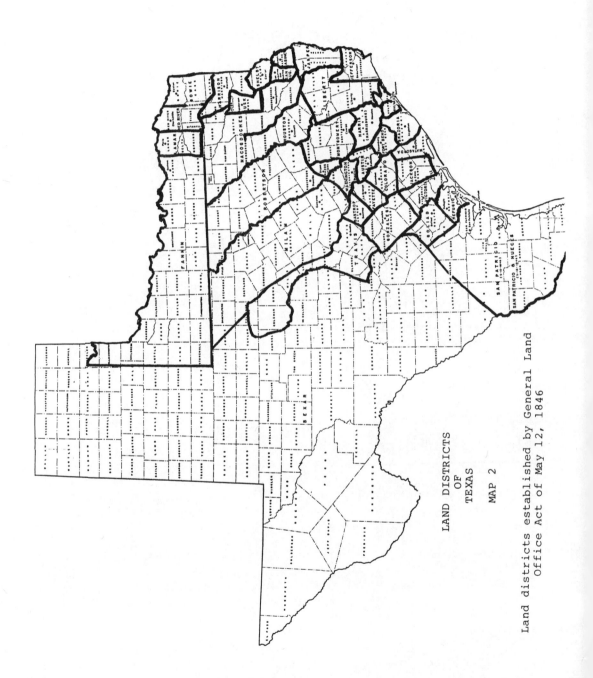

LAND DISTRICTS
OF
TEXAS

MAP 2

Land districts established by General Land
Office Act of May 12, 1846

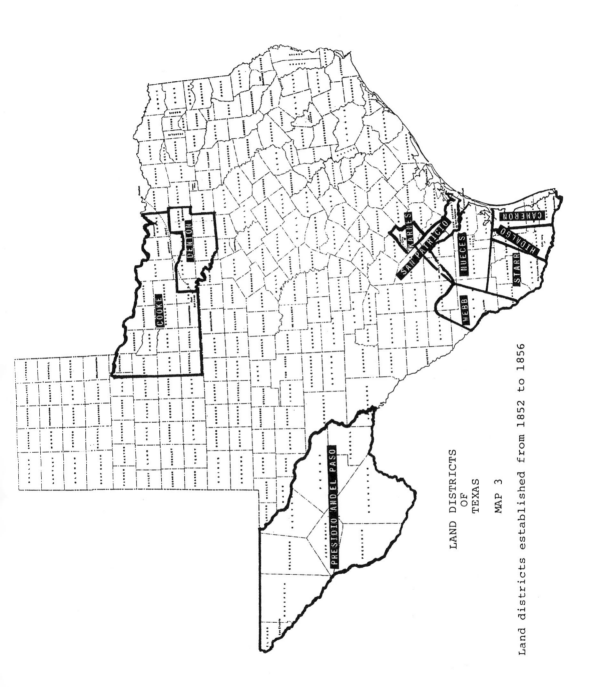

LAND DISTRICTS
OF
TEXAS

MAP 3

Land districts established from 1852 to 1856

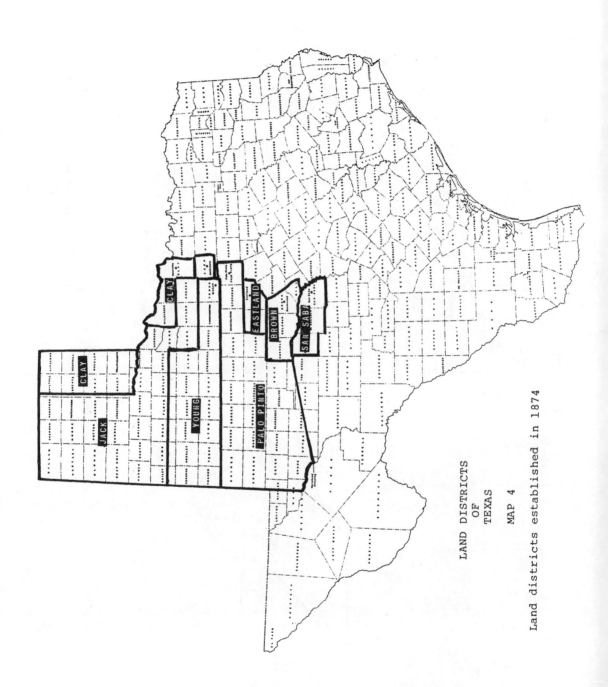

LAND DISTRICTS
OF
TEXAS

MAP 4

Land districts established in 1874

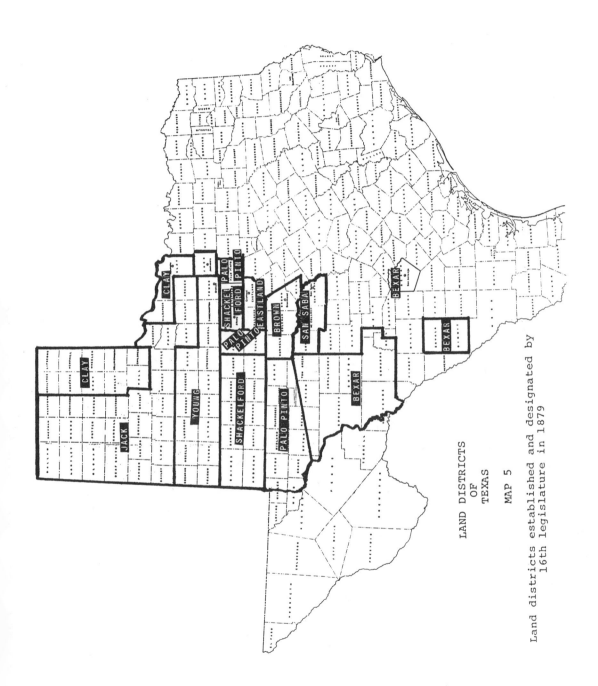

LAND DISTRICTS
OF
TEXAS

MAP 5

Land districts established and designated by
16th legislature in 1879

- 49 -

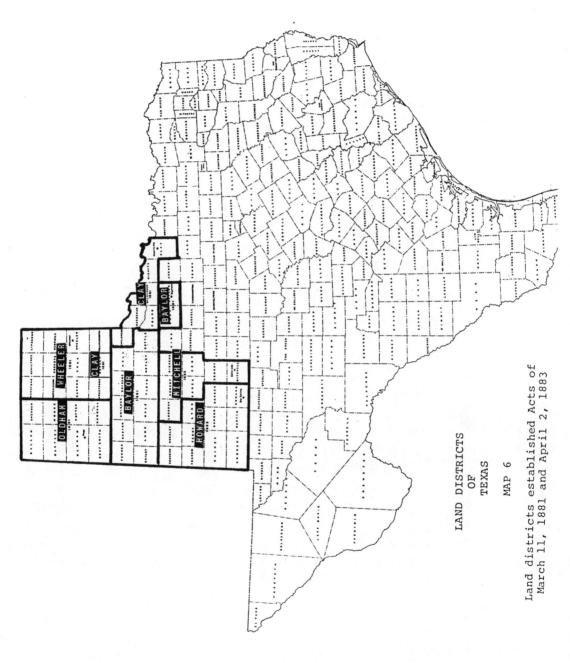

LAND DISTRICTS
OF
TEXAS

MAP 6

Land districts established Acts of
March 11, 1881 and April 2, 1883

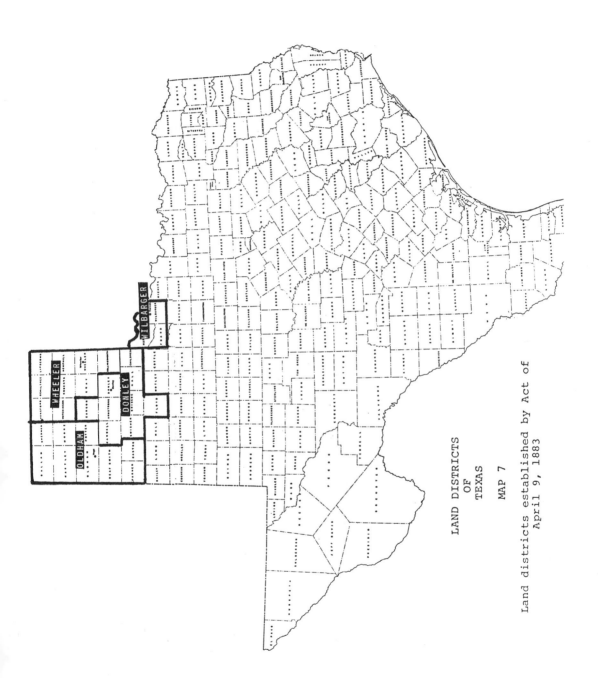

LAND DISTRICTS
OF
TEXAS

MAP 7

Land districts established by Act of
April 9, 1883

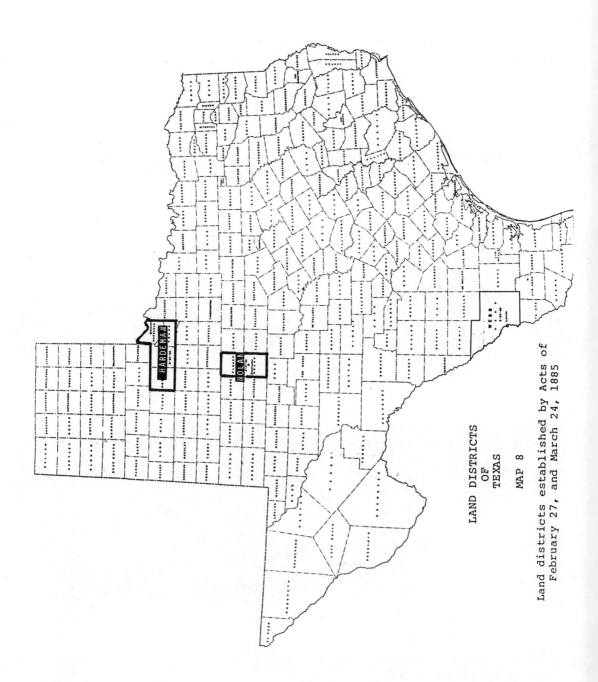

LAND DISTRICTS
OF
TEXAS

MAP 8

Land districts established by Acts of
February 27, and March 24, 1885

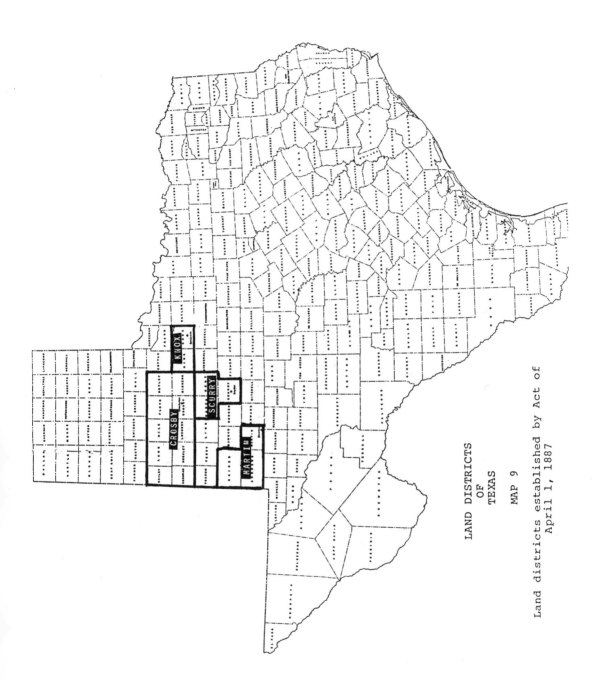

LAND DISTRICTS
OF
TEXAS

MAP 9

Land districts established by Act of
April 1, 1887

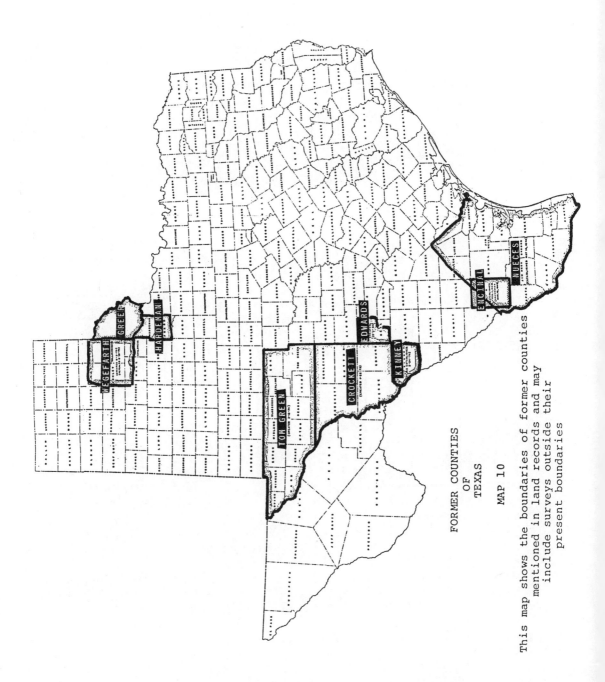

FORMER COUNTIES
OF
TEXAS

MAP 10

This map shows the boundaries of former counties
mentioned in land records and may
include surveys outside their
present boundaries

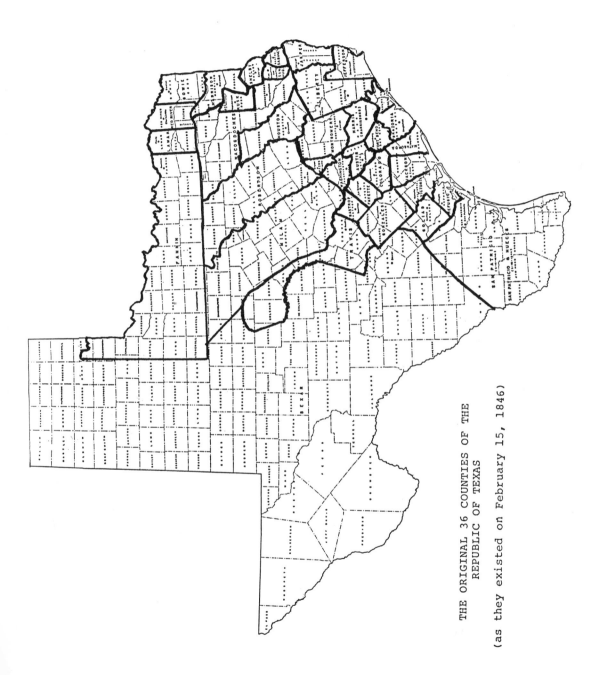

THE ORIGINAL 36 COUNTIES OF THE
REPUBLIC OF TEXAS

(as they existed on February 15, 1846)

LIST OF TEXAS COUNTIES IN WHICH RECORDS HAVE BEEN DESTROYED

Aransas	Most records prior to 1840 destroyed by fire.
Bowie	Records prior to 1889 destroyed by several fires.
Blanco	All records destroyed by fire in 1876.
Brown	All records destroyed by fire in 1880.
Chambers	All records destroyed by fire in Fall, 1875.
Clay	Records from 1858-1862 destroyed by fire.
Coke	All records 1889-1890 destroyed by fire in 1891.
Denton	Fire in December, 1975 destroyed records.
Edwards	Fire in 1888 destroyed most 1883-1888 records.
Garza	Records partially damaged by fire in 1911.
Goliad	Records destroyed in 1870 and have suffered considerable storm damage since.
Hamilton	Records destroyed by fire in 1870 and partially destroyed in 1885.
Hays	Records damaged by fires in 1855, 1864, and 1888.
Houston	Records have suffered from two destructive fires.
Hood	All records destroyed by fire in 1875.
Jasper	Records destroyed by fire about 1850.
Karnes	Records partially destroyed by fire about 1857.
Kimble	Records from 1876-1884 destroyed by fire in 1884.
Lamar	Some damage to records by two minor fires.
Lampasas	Most records destroyed by fire in 1875 and partially destroyed by flood in the 1880s.
Liberty	Records destroyed by fire in 1875 and damaged by storm in 1900.
Limestone	Records completely destroyed by fire in 1873.
Llano	Records from 1856 to October, 1888 totally destroyed by fire.
Madison	Records from 1853-1873 have vanished.
Mason	All records from 1858-1877 destroyed by fire.
Milam	All records destroyed by fire April, 1874.
Montague	Two fires almost completely destroyed all records before 1880.
Parker	Records destroyed by fire in 1874.
Rains	All records destroyed by fire in late 1879.
Refugio	Records have suffered fire and hurricane damage.
Sabine	All records prior to 1876 destroyed by fire.
San Patricio	Records destroyed by fire in 1846 and 1867.
San Saba	Fire in 1868 destroyed prior District Court records.
Shelby	Several fires have destroyed records prior to 1881.
Tarrant	Records destroyed by fire in 1864 and 1876.
Titus	Records prior to 1895 destroyed by fire.
Trinity	Records destroyed by fire in 1876.
Wise	Records for 1856-1881 destroyed by fire.
Wood	Records destroyed by fire in the winter of 1878.

CHAPTER 6

FORMATION AND ORGANIZATION OF THE COUNTIES IN TEXAS

Many Texas counties assembled their records in unusual and
varied means. Some records came from Spanish land grants,
some from Mexico, some from the Republic of Texas and a great
many from the counties from which they were formed.

The following information was gathered in order to make
research easier for the average genealogist.

PRONUNCIATION   Because Texian spelling and pronunciation is
unique, the phonetic pronunciation of the
county and the county seat is given.

ZIP CODE   The zip code + 4 digits will soon be required
in order to get mail delivered to the courthouses. The + 4 digit that is given is for
the county clerk's office.

CREATION DATE   This is the date given in The Laws of Texas
1822-1897, by H. P. N. Gammel, c1898, as the
date the county was created.

ORGANIZATION
DATE   The date which the county actually began
doing business as a county government.

PARENT COUNTY   Parent counties are determined as being the
county or counties from which the county
was made at the time of its creation.

COUNTY
DERIVATION   The derivation of each county was determined
by using Gammel's "Laws of Texas". This is
very important to the researcher in order
that he may be able to determine in which
county his ancestor resided in a given year.
One is often faced with the fact that a
county was not created until after a census
year, making it very difficult to find the
ancestor for that year. By using the county
derivation, one is able to locate the county
of residence for previous years.

MAPS   Only the counties which were created out of
several counties have maps. These maps show
the derivations of the separate areas of that
county.

```
COUNTY              COUNTY SEAT    ZIP        DATE CREATED
PRONUNCIATION                                 DATE ORGANIZED
==================================================================

ANDERSON           Palestine      78801      Created      3-24-1846
                                  -3097      Organized    7-13-1846
```

Parent county or territory: Houston.

Records in:
    <u>Area A</u>: Nacogdoches 1831-1837,
Houston 1837-1846. Includes
all of county except Area B.
<u>Area B</u>: Nacogdoches 1831-1837,
Houston 1837-1850. Includes
that part of the Box Leagues
in the southwestern corner of
the county and adjacent to the
Trinity River lying south of
an extension of the balance of
the county line running
westward from the Neches River.

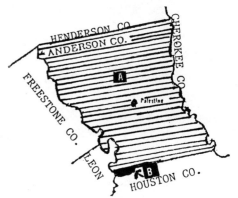

Records available:
    Deeds since 1846, marriages since 1846, probates since
1846, District Court minutes since 1846, index to
naturalization records 1874-1922, naturalization
records 1891-1922, petition for naturalization 1928,
records of declaration of intensions 1882-1901.

```
ANDREWS            Andrews        79714      Created      8-21-1876
                                  -6517      Organized      -1910
```

Parent county or territory: Young.

Records in:
    Bexar 1831-1858, Young 1858-1876, Shackelford 1876-1881,
Mitchel 1881-1883, Howard 1883-1885, Martin 1885-1889,
Midland 1889-1891, Martin 1891-1909, Midland 1909-1910.

Records available:
    Deeds since 1896, marriages since 1910, probates since
1910, District Court minutes since 1910.

```
ANGELINA           Lufkin         75901      Created      4-22-1846
                                  -0908      Organized    7-13-1846
```

Parent county or territory: Nacogdoches.

Records in:
    Nacogdoches County prior to 1846.

(continued)

===

Records available:
    Deeds since 1846, marriages since 1846, probates since
    1850, District Court minutes since 1847.

| ARANSAS | Rockport | 78382 | Created | 9-18-1871 |
| A ran' sas | | -9998 | Organized | -1871 |

Parent county or territory: Refugio.

Records in:
    Refugio County prior to 1871. Some early records
    originating in territory of Aransas County may be found in
    Bexar County.

Records available:
    Deeds since 1839; marriages since 1871, probates since
    1860, District Court minutes since 1872, declaration of
    intention 1908-1913.

Most Refugio County records before 1841 destroyed by fire.

| ARCHER | Archer City | 76351 | Created | 1-22-1858 |
| | | -0815 | Organized | 7-27-1880 |

Parent county or territory: Cooke.

Records in:
    Red River 1836-1838, Fannin 1838-1846, Grayson 1846-1849,
    Cooke 1849-1858, Young 1858-1866, Jack 1866-1870, Young
    1870-1873, Clay 1873-1880.

Records available:
    Deeds since 1884, marriages since 1880, probates since
    1880, District Court minutes since 1880.

| ARMSTRONG | Claude | 79019 | Created | 8-21-1876 |
| | | -0309 | Organized | 3-08-1890 |

Parent county or territory: Jack.

Records in:
    Bexar 1831-1854, Cooke 1854-1860, Montague 1860-1873, Clay
    1873-1874, Jack 1874-1879, Wheeler 1879-1883, Donley 1883-
    1890.

(continued)

Records available:
    Deeds since 1883, marriages since 1890, probates since
    1890, District Court minutes since 1890.

All records in Montague County, 1860-1873, destroyed by fire.

```
ATASCOSA        Jourdanton    78026    Created    1-25-1856
Ah tass co' sa                -3495    Organized  8-04=1856
```

Parent county or territory: Bexar.

Records in:
    Area A: Bexar 1731-1856.
    Includes all of county except the
    southwest corner southwest of the
    original boundary or San Miguel Creek.
    Area B: Bexar 1731-1834, San
    Patricio 1834-1838, Bexar 1838-1856.
    Includes all of the southwest corner
    southwest of the original boundary
    line or San Miguel Creek.

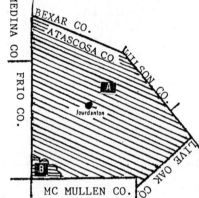

Records available:
    Deeds since 1856, marriages since 1856, probates since
    1873, District Court minutes since 1857, record of
    declaration 1888-1903.

All San Patricio County records destroyed by fire in 1870.

```
AUSTIN          Bellville     77418    Created    3-07-1827
                              -1551    Organized       1829
```

Parent county or territory: old Mexican Municipality.

Records in:
    Bexar 1731-1829. Austin County created and organized as a
    Municipality.

Records available:
    County records: Deeds since 1837, Spanish deeds since
    1825, marriages since 1838, probates and succession
    records since 1837, index to naturalization record
    1855-1936, record of declarations 1856-1906,
    naturalization records 1896-1906.

(continued)

District Court Records: Court minutes since 1837, index to
naturalization 1855-1936, naturalization records 1881-1906
application for citizenship 1854-1878, declaration of
intention 1881-1917.

```
BAILEY          Muleshoe      79347    Created    8-29-1876
                Mule' shoe    -0589    Organized      -1919
```

Parent county or territory: Young.

Records in:
   Bexar 1831-1854, Cooke 1854-1858, Young 1858-1876, Jack
   1876-1881, Baylor 1881-1887, Crosby 1887-1889, Hale 1889-
   1892, Castro 1892-1919.

Records available:
   Deeds since 1892, marriages since 1919, probates since
   1919, District Court minutes since 1919.

```
BANDERA         Bandera       78003    Created    1-26-1856
Band'era                      -0823    Organized  3-10-1856
```

Parent county or territory: Bexar.

Records in:
   Bexar 1831-1856.

Records available:
   Deeds since 1856, marriages since 1856, probates since
   1856, District Court minutes since 1857.

```
BASTROP         Bastrop       78602    Created    4-24-1834
Bass' trop                    -3889    Organized      -1836
```

Parent county or territory: Municipality of Mina.
(The name was changed from Mina to Bastrop on 12-18-1837)

Records in:
   Area A: Austin 1827-1834. Includes territory south of the
   old San Antonio road on both sides of the Colorado River.
   Area B: Austin 1832-1834. Includes the territory north of
   the old San Antonio road and north of the Colorado River,
   except the area north of the Brazos-Colorado divide.
   Area C: Bexar 1831-1834. Includes the territory north of
   the old San Antonio road and south of the Colorado River.

(continued)

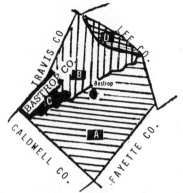

Area D: Milam 1835-1846,
Burleson 1846-1856. Includes
the territory north of the
Brazos-Colorado divide.

Records available:
   Deeds since 1837, marriages
   since 1851, probates since
   1937, naturalization records
   1892-1906, District Court
   minutes since 1837, record
   of declaration 1889-1906.

Milam County records were destroyed by fire April, 1874.

BAYLOR   Seymour   76380   Created   2-01-1858
Bay' lor   See' more   -2566   Organized   4-12-1879

Parent county or territory: Cooke.

Records in:
   Bexar 1831-1838, Fannin 1838-1846, Grayson 1846-1849,
   Cooke 1849-1858, Young 1858-1866, Jack 1866-1870, Young
   1870-1873, Clay 1873-1879.

Records available:
   Deeds since 1879, marriages since 1879, probates since
   1879, District Court minutes since 1881.

BEE   Beeville   78102   Created   12-08-1857
                               -5635   Organized   -1858

Parent county or territory: Live Oak, Goliad, Refugio, San
                             Patricio, Karnes.

Records in:
   Area A: Bexar 1831-1834, San
   Patricio 1834-1856, Live Oak
   1856-1858. Includes most of
   the county west of U.S. 181.
   Area B: Goliad 1829-1858.
   Includes most of the county east
   of U. S. Highway 181.
   Area C: Refugio 1825-1858.
   Includes the territory adjacent
   to Refugio County.
   Area D: Bexar 1831-1834, San
   Patricio 1834-1858. Includes

- 62 -

(continued)

the territory adjacent to San Patricio County.
Area E: Bexar 1831-1834, San Patricio 1834-1854, Karnes
1854-1857. Includes the territory adjacent to Karnes
County.

Records available:
    Deeds since 1858, marriages since 1860, probates since
    1859, District Court minutes since 1858, naturalization
    record 1891-1906, record of declaration 1894-1906.

BELL   Belton   76513   Created   1-22-1850
                Bell' ton   Organized   -1850

Parent county or territory: Milam.

Records in:
    Entire county in Bexar 1831-1834.
    Area A: Milam 1834-1850. Includes
    the area included in the original
    definition of the county, being
    the area southwest of an
    extension of the McLennan-Coryell
    line and northwest of an extension
    of the south line of Falls County.
    Area B: Milam 1834-1851, Falls
    1851-1856. Includes the strip
    six miles wide adjacent to Falls
    County.

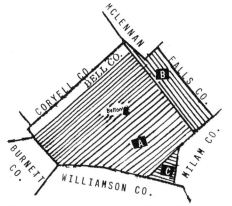

    Area C: Milam 1834-1861. Includes the territory south of
    an extension of the south line of Falls County.

Records available:
    Deeds since 1850, marriages since 1850, probates since
    1850, District Court minutes since 1852.

BEXAR   San Antonio   78204   Created   -1731
Bay' er   San An tone'eo -2715   Organized   -1837

Parent county or territory: Municipality of San Fernando de
                            Bexar.

Records in:
    Bexar 1820. The Municipality of San Fernando de Bexar was
    populated in 1731 and some sort of political organization
    began to function at that time. The boundaries were not
    defined but for all practical purposes embraced most of
    the present Texas. Records originating in present Bexar
                                                    (continued)

COUNTY   COUNTY SEAT   ZIP   DATE CREATED
PRONUNCIATION   DATE ORGANIZED
===

County territory and throughout Texas for the period of
1791-1841 may be found at Austin, Texas in the General
Land Office, University of Texas Library, or at Mexico
City in Biblioteca de Mexico.

Records available:
County Records: Deeds since 1837, marriages since 1837,
probates since 1836, land and probates since 1736, lands
outside of Bexar County 1736-1836, land grants 1736-1836,
Mission records 1736-1836, index to naturalization 1860-
1906, naturalization records 1851-1906, declaration of
intention 1852-1906.
District Court Records: Court minutes since 1841, index to
naturalization records 1855-1906, naturalization papers
1851-1906, declaration of intention record 1884-1892.

BLANCO   Johnson City 78636   Created   2-12-1858
Blaw' n ko   -0065   Organized   4-12-1858

Parent county or territory: Gillespie, Burnet, Comal, Hays.

Records in:

Area A: Bexar 1831-1834, Bastrop
1834-1837, Bexar 1837-1848,
Gillespie 1848-1858. Includes
the triangular area in the northwest part of the county lying
northwest of a line running
northeast from the southeast
corner of present Gillespie
County.
Area B: Bexar 1831-1834, Bastrop
1834-1840, Travis 1840-1854, Burnet
1854-1858. Includes the northern portion of the county
taken from Burnet County being approximately the north
one-fourth of the county.
Area C: Bexar 1831-1834, Bastrop 1834-1840, Travis 1840-
1846, Comal 1846-1858. Includes the territory in the
southern triangle of the county taken from Comal County.
Area D: Bexar 1831-1834, Bastrop 1834-1840, Travis 1840-
1846, Hays 1846-1858. Includes the area in the center of
the county taken from Hays County in 1858.
Area E: Bexar 1831-1834, Bastrop 1834-1840, Travis 1840-
1846, Hays 1846-1862. Includes the area adjacent to
present Hays County taken from Hays County in 1862.

(continued)

```
COUNTY            COUNTY SEAT    ZIP      DATE CREATED
PRONUNCIATION                             DATE ORGANIZED
=========================================================
```

Records available:
    Deeds since 1876, marriages since 1876, probates since
    1876, index to naturalization records 1884-1930, natural-
    ization records 1910-1925, declaration of intention 1910-
    1922, record of declaration 1896-1902, final naturalizat-
    ion record 1892-1901, District Court minutes since 1877.

```
BORDEN          Gail           79738    Created    8-21-1876
Bawrd'n         Gale           -9998    Organized  3-17-1891
```

Parent county or territory: Young.

Records in:
    Bexar 1831-1858, Young 1858-1876, Shackelford 1876-1881,
    Mitchell 1881-1883, Howard 1883-1891.

Records available:
    Deeds since 1883, marriages since 1891, probates since
    1891, District Court minutes since 1891.

```
BOSQUE          Meridian       76665    Created    2-04-1854
Baws'key                       -9998    Organized  8-07-1854
```

Parent county or territory: McLennan.

Records in:
    Brazos 1831-1834, Milam 1834-1850, McLennan 1850-1854.

Records available:
    Deeds since 1854, marriages since 1860, probates since
    1855, naturalization record 1903-1906, District Court
    minutes since 1856.

```
BOWIE           Boston         75557    Created    12-17-1840
Boo'ee                         -0186    Organized     -1841
```

Parent county or territory: Red River.

Records in: Nacogdoches 1831-1835, Red River 1835-1841.

Records available:
    All records prior to 1889 destroyed by several courthouse
    fires. The territory north of the Sulpher River and east
    of the south extension of the Oklahoma line was claimed by
    Arkansas prior to 1847. Some land records in this area

                                              (continued)

prior to 1847 may be found in Miller and Hempstead
Counties, Arkansas although fires may have destroyed most
of these early records. The Arkansas State Library at
Little Rock may contain some early records. Deeds since
1889, marriages since 1889, probates since 1889, District
Court minutes since 1889.

BRAZORIA   Angleton   77515   Created   5-01-1832
Bruh zor'e ah Angle' ton   -4642   Organized   -1837

Parent county or territory: Austin.

Records in:
  Area A: Austin 1829-1832.
  Includes all the present territory
  of the county south of the original
  lower line of Austin's First Colony
  except the Deer Island and San Luis
  Islands.
  Area B: Austin 1827-1832.
  Includes the territory north of
  of the original line of Austin's
  Colony except Areas C and D
  described below.
  Area C: Austin 1827-1832, Fort Bend 1832-1846. Includes
  the territory in the northeastern portion of the county
  east of the San Bernard River.
  Area D: Austin 1827-1832, Harrisburg 1832-1837. Includes
  the territory in the northern portion of the county east
  of the Brazos River.
  Area E: Austin 1829-1832, Galveston 1832-1839. Includes
  the Deer Islands and San Luis Islands.

Records available:
  Deeds since 1837, records of Spanish deeds 1831-1893,
  marriages since 1829, probates since 1837, County Court
  minutes include naturalization proceedings 1867-1887,
  District Court minutes since 1837.

  Brazoria County was organized as a municipality in 1832;
  records still existing from that date prior to the
  organization as a county in 1837.

BRAZOS   Bryan   77801   Created   1-30-1841
Braz' uhs   -5237   Organized   2-06-1843

Parent county or territory: Washington, Robertson.

(continued)

```
COUNTY           COUNTY SEAT    ZIP      DATE CREATED
PRONUNCIATION                            DATE ORGANIZED
======================================================
```

Records in:
    <u>Area A</u>: Austin 1829-1835,
    Washington 1835-1843. Includes
    the territory south of the old
    San Antonio road, being taken
    from Washington County.
    <u>Area B</u>: Austin 1829-1834, Milam
    1834-1838, Robertson 1838-1843.
    Includes the territory north of
    the old San Antonio road along
    the Brazos River, being taken
    from Robertson County.

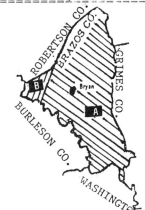

Records available:
    Deeds since 1841, marriages since 1844, probates since
    1844, District Court minutes since 1841, index to natural-
    iation unknown -1941, naturalization records 1903-1906,
    declaration of intention 1903-1906, naturalization minutes
    1890-1906.

All Milam County records destroyed by fire in April 1874.

```
BREWSTER        Alpine         79830    Created      2-02-1887
Broo' stir                     -0119    Organized    2-26-1887
```

Parent county or territory: Presidio.

Records in:
    Bexar 1831-1866, El Paso 1866-1875, Presidio 1875-1887.

Records available:
    Deeds since 1887, marriages since 1887, probates
    since 1887, District Court minutes since 1887.

```
BRISCOE         Silverton      79257    Created      8-21-1876
Bris'ko                        -9998    Organized    1-11-1892
```

Parent county or territory: Jack.

Records in:
    Bexar 1831-1854, Cooke 1854-1858, Young 1858-1874, Jack
    1874-1879, Wheeler, 1879-1883, Donley 1883-1892.

Records available:
    Deeds since 1883, marriages since 1892, probates since
    1892, District Court minutes since 1892.

```
COUNTY          COUNTY SEAT    ZIP      DATE CREATED
PRONUNCIATION                           DATE ORGANIZED
=====================================================================
```

BROOKS   Falfurrias   78355   Created   3-11-1911
                Fal fyou' ree us -9998 Organized   -1911

Parent county or territory: Starr, Hidalgo.

Records in:
  All County records prior to 1846
  in Municipalities of Matamoros,
  Reynosa, or Camargo.
  Area A: Nueces 1846-1848, Starr
  1848-1911. Includes the
  territory taken from Starr
  County, being the area lying
  northwest of a line running from
  a point on the Rio Grande River
  dividing the jurisdiction of
  Reynosa and Camargo.
  Area B: Nueces 1846-1848, Starr 1848-1852, Hidalgo 1852-
  1911. Includes the territory taken from Hidalgo, being the
  area southeast of the above described line.

Records available:
  Deed records since 1911, marriages since 1911, probates
  since 1911, District Court minutes since 1911.

All county prior to 1846 in Municipalities of Matamoros,
Reynosa, or Camargo.

```
---------------------------------------------------------------
```

BROWN   Brownwood   76801   Created   8-27-1856
                               -3188   Organized   3-02-1857

Parent county or territory: Travis, Coryell.

Records in:
  Area A: Bexar 1831-1848, Travis
  1848-1857. Includes the territory west of the Brazos-Colorado
  divide and south of the line of
  1856, which was a line drawn
  southwest across the county from
  a point due east of the town of
  May on the present Brown-Comanche
  line, being most of the present
  County.
  Area B: Bexar 1831-1848, Travis
  1848-1858. Includes the territory
  west of the Brazos-Colorado divide and north of the above
  mentioned line of 1856.

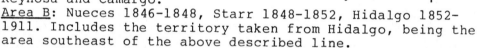

(continued)

Area C: Milam 1834-1850, Bell 1850-1854, Coryell 1854-1857. Includes the territory east of the Brazos-Colorado divide and south of the above mentioned line of 1856.
Area D: Milam 1834-1850, Bell 1850-1854, Coryell 1854-1858 Includes the territory east of the Brazos-Colorado divide and north of the above mentioned line of 1856.

Records available:
    Deeds since 1880, marriages since 1880, probates since 1880, District Court minutes since 1884.

Milam County records destroyed by fire in April 1874.

Brown County records destroyed by fire in 1880.

```
BURLESON        Caldwell       77836    Created      3-24-1846
Burr'luh son                   -9998    Organized    7-13-1846
```

Parent county or territory: Milam.

Records in:
    Area A: Austin 1829-1834, Milam
    1834-1846. Includes the area
    north of the old San Antonio
    Road.
    Area B: Austin 1829-1835,
    Washington 1835-1840, Milam 1840-
    1846. Includes the area south
    of the old San Antonio Road.

Records available:
    Deeds since 1846, marriages since
    1846, probates since 1847,
    District Court minutes since 1880.

Milam County records destroyed by fire April 1874.

```
BURNET          Burnet         78611    Created      2-05-1852
Burr'net                       -3136    Organized    8-07-1854
```

Parent county or territory: Bell, Williamson, Travis.

Records in:
    Area A: Milam 1834-1850, Bell 1850-1854. Includes the territory east of the Brazos-Colorado divide, except the small area taken from Williamson County.
    Area B: Milam 1834-1848, Williamson 1848-1854. Includes the territory east of the Brazos-Colorado divide, taken from Williamson County in 1852.   (continued)

==

Area C: Austin 1831-1838,
Bastrop 1838-1840, Travis 1840-
1854. Includes the territory
south of the Brazos-Colorado
divide, southeast of the old
Travis Land District line and
north of the original
Municipality of Mina line.
Area D: Austin 1831-1834,
Bastrop 1834-1840, Travis 1840-
1854. Includes the territory
north of the Colorado River,
south of the original line of the Municipality of Mina,
and east of the old Travis Land District line.
Area E: Bexar 1787-1834, Bastrop 1834-1840, Travis 1840-
1854. Includes the territory south of the Colorado River.
Area F: Bexar 1831-1834, Bastrop 1834-1838, Bexar 1838-
1848, Travis 1848-1854. Includes the territory north and
east of the Colorado River, west of the old Travis Land
District line and south of the original line of the
Municipality of Mina.
Area G: Bexar 1831-1848, Travis 1848-1854. Includes the
territory between the Colorado River and the Colorado-
Brazos divide southward from the Lampasas County line to
the old Travis Land District line and the original line
of the Municipality of Mina.

Records available:
Deeds since 1852, marriages since 1852, probates since
1852, District Court minutes since 1867, record of
declarations 1886-1906.

Milam County records destroyed by fire April 1874.

CALDWELL   Lockhart   78644   Created   3- 6-1848
                                  -2758   Organized   8- 7-1848

Parent county or territory: Gonzales, Bastrop.

Records in:
Area A: Bexar 1787-1832, Gonzales 1832-1834, Bastrop
1834-1837, Gonzales 1837-1848. Includes the central
portion of the county southwest of the old San Antonio
road and between the Bastrop County lines of 1834 and
1848, being the area taken from Gonzales County.
Area B: Bexar 1787-1832, Gonzales 1832-1848. Includes the
southwest portion of the county northwest of San Marcos
River above Plum Creek, being a part of the territory

(continued)

taken from Gonzales County
in 1848 which was not included
in Mina (Bastrop) in 1834.
Area C: Bexar 1787-1832,
Gonzales 1832-1850.
Includes the area southwest of
the old Bastrop-Gonzales line
and southeast of the Caldwell-
Gonzales line as defined in
1848, being a part of the
territory taken from Gonzales
County in 1850.

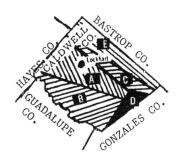

Area D: Bexar 1787-1832, Gonzales 1832-1834, Bastrop 1834-
1837, Gonzales 1837-1850. Includes the territory northwest
of the present line, between the Gonzales-Bastrop line of
1834 and the Gonzales-Bastrop line of 1840, and southeast
of the Caldwell-Gonzales line of 1848, being a part of
the territory taken from Gonzales County in 1850.
Area E: Austin 1821-1834, Bastrop 1834-1850. Includes the
territory about seven miles wide adjacent to Bastrop
County which remained in Bastrop County until 1850.

Records available:
    Deeds since 1846, marriages since 1848, probates since
    1849, District Court minutes since 1848, record of
    declaration 1898-1906, index to naturalization 1850-1920,
    naturalization minutes 1892-1902.

CALHOUN   Port Lavaca   77979   Created   4-04-1846
                   Port La va' kuh -4298   Organized   7-13-1846

Parent county or territory: Jackson, Victoria.

Records in:
    Area A: Austin 1821-1834,
    Matagorda 1834-1835, Jackson 1835-
    1846. Includes the territory
    between Lavaca Bay and Carancaha
    Bay, being the territory taken
    from Jackson County.
    Area B: Bexar 1787-1832, Victoria
    1832-1846. Includes the territory
    between Lavaca and San Antonio Bay,
    being the territory taken from
    Victoria County in 1846.
    Area C: Bexar 1787-1832, Victoria
    1832-1856. Includes the Juan N.
    Sismeros League in the

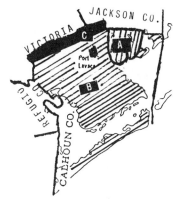

(continued)

- 71 -

COUNTY   COUNTY SEAT   ZIP   DATE CREATED
PRONUNCIATION   DATE ORGANIZED
==

   northwestern corner of the county which was transferred
   from Victoria to Calhoun County in 1856.

Records available:
   Deeds since 1846, marriages since 1846, probates since
   1846, index to probates (also indexes naturalization
   records) 1849-1968, District Court Minutes since 1847.

CALLAHAN   Baird   79504   Created   2-01-1858
Kal' uh han   -5305   Organized   7-03-1877

Parent county or territory: Travis, Comanche, Bosque.

Records in:
   Area A: Bexar 1831-1848, Travis
   1848-1860, Comanche 1860-1870,
   Palo Pinto 1870-1875, Shackelford
   1875-1876, Eastland 1876-1877.
   Includes the territory drained by
   the Colorado River, being the
   southwestern one-half of the
   county.
   Area B: Bexar 1831-1834, Milam
   1834-1850, Bell 1850-1854,
   Coryell 1854-1856, Comanche
   1856-1870, Palo Pinto 1870-1875,Shackelford 1875-1876,
   Eastland 1876-1877.   Includes the territory drained by the
   Leon River, being the territory in the southeast corner of
   the county.
   Area C: Bexar 1831-1834, Milam 1834-1850, McLennan 1850-
   1854, Bosque 1854-1860, Comanche 1860-1870, Palo Pinto
   1870-1875, Shackelford 1875-1876, Eastland 1876-1877.
   Includes the territory drained by the Brazos River, being
   most of the northeastern one-half of the county.

Records available:
   Deeds since 1878, marriages since 1878, probates since
   1879, District Court minutes since 1879.

Milam County records destroyed by fire April 1874.

CAMERON   Brownsville   78520   Created   2-12-1848
                                -7198   Organized   8-07-1848

Parent county or territory: Nueces.Records in:
    Municipality of Matamoros 1792-1846, Nueces 1846-1848.

Records available:
    Deeds since 1848, marriages since 1848, probates since
    1848, declaration of intention 1876-1906, declaration
    record 1895-1906, naturalization record 1900-1904,
    District Court minutes since 1849, declaration of citizen-
    ship 1871-1890.

CAMP   Pittsburg   75686   Created   4-06-1874
                                -1342   Organized   6-20-1874

Parent county or territory: Upshur.

Records in:
    Area A: Nacogdoches 1831-1846,
    Upshur 1846-1874. Includes the
    western one-third of the county
    lying west of the old Jones-
    borough road which ran along the
    western bank of the northern fork
    of Little Cypress Creek.
    Area B: Nacogdoches 1831-1837,
    Shelby 1837-1839, Harrison 1839- 1846, Upshur 1846-1874.
    Includes the eastern two-thirds of the county lying east
    of Jonesborough Road.

Records available:
    Deeds since 1874, marriages since 1874, probates since
    1874, District Court minutes since 1874.

Most of Shelby County records prior to 1881 destroyed by
fire.

CARSON   Panhandle   79068   Created   8-21-1876
                                -0487   Organized   6-26-1888

Parent county or territory: Jack.

Records in:
    Bexar 1831-1854, Cooke 1854-1860, Montague 1860-1873, Clay
    1873-1874, Jack 1874-1879, Wheeler 1879-1883, Donley 1883-
    1888.

                                            (continued)

Records available:
    Deeds since 1883, marriages since 1888, probates since
    1888, District Court minutes since 1888.

Records in Montague County 1860-1873, destroyed by fire.

CASS   Linden   75563   Created   4-25-1846
                                  -0468   Organized   7-13-1846
(Name changed to Davis (named for Jefferson Davis) in
1861, renamed Cass in 1871)

Parent county or territory: Bowie.

Records in:
    Nacogdoches 1831-1835, Red River 1835-1840, Bowie
    1840-1846.

Records available:
    Deeds since 1846, marriages since 1847, probates since
    1846, District Court minutes since 1847.

All records in Bowie County prior to 1889 were destroyed
by several fires.

CASTRO   Dimmitt   79027   Created   8-21-1876
Cass' tro   Dim' it   -2643   Organized   -1891

Parent county or territory: Jack.

Records in:
    Bexar 1831-1854, Cooke 1854-1858, Young 1858-1874, Jack
    1874-1879, Wheeler 1879-1881, Oldham 1881-1891.

Records available:
    Deeds since 1887, marriages since 1891, probates since
    1891, District Court minutes since 1892.

CHAMBERS   Anahuac   77514   Created   2-11-1858
                  An' ah wack   -9998   Organized   8-02-1858

Parent county or territory: Liberty, Jefferson.

Records in:
    Area A: Liberty 1831-1835, Harrisburg 1835-1837, Liberty
    1837-1858. Includes the strip of territory about 5 miles
    wide along the western border between Cedar Bayou and the
                                               (continued)

Cedar Bayou-Trinity River divide.
Area B: Liberty 1831-1858.
Includes the central part of the
county east of the said divide
and west of the southward
extension of the present east
line of Liberty County.
Area C: Liberty 1831-1837,
Jefferson 1837-1858. Includes
eastern part of county about 6
miles wide east of Area B.

Records available:
    Deeds since 1875, marriages since 1876, probates since
    1876, District Court minutes since 1876.

All records in Chambers County destroyed by fire in 1875.

Liberty County records were destroyed by fire in 1875 and
damaged by storm in 1900.

CHEROKEE   Rusk   75785   Created   4-11-1846
                                -1396   Organized   7-13-1846

Parent county or territory: Nacogdoches.

Records in:
    Nacogdoches 1831-1846.

Records available:
    Deeds since 1846, marriages since 1846, probates since
    1868, District Court minutes since 1846.

CHILDRESS   Childress   79201   Created   8-21-1876
Chilld' res   -9998   Organized   4-11-1887

Parent county or territory: Jack, Clay.

Records in:
    Area A: Fannin 1838-1846, Grayson 1846-1849, Cooke 1849-1858,
    Young 1858-1874, Jack 1874-1876. Includes that part of the
    county south of the Prairie Dog Fork of the Red River.
                                                    (continued)

<u>Area B</u>: Bexar 1831-1854, Cooke
1854-1860, Montague 1860-1873,
Clay 1873-1876. Includes that part
of the county north of the
Prairie Dog Fork of the Red River.

Records available:
   Deeds since October, 1891, marriages
   since 1887, probates since 1888,
   District Court minutes since 1887.

Records for Montague County, 1860-1873, destroyed by fire.

CIBILO   (see Wilson County)

CLAY   Henrietta   76365   Created   12-24-1857
                              -2858   Organized   11-24-1873

Parent county or territory: Cooke.

Records in:
   Fannin 1838-1846, Grayson 1846-1849, Cooke 1849-1860,
   Montague 1860-1873.

Records available:
   Deeds since 1870, marriages since 1873, probates since
   1873, District Court records since 1874.

Records for 1860-1873, Montague County, destroyed by fire.

COCHRAN   Morton   79346   Created   8-21-1876
                              -2598   Organized   -1924

Parent county or territory: Lubbock.

Records in:
   Bexar 1831-1854, Cooke 1854-1858, Young 1858-1881, Baylor
   1881-1887, Crosby 1887-1889, Hale 1889-1891, Lubbock
   1891-1924.

Records available:
   Deeds since 1890, marriages since 1924, probates since
   1924, District Court minutes since 1925.

```
COUNTY                 COUNTY SEAT   ZIP       DATE CREATED
PRONUNCIATION                                  DATE ORGANIZED
==============================================================

COKE                   Robert Lee    76945     Created    3-07-1889
                                     -9998     Organized  4-23-1889
```

Parent county or territory: Tom Green.

Records in:
   Bexar 1831-1875, Tom Green 1875-1889.

Records available:
   Deeds since 1891, marriages since 1891, probates since
   1891, District Court minutes since October, 1891.

In 1891, a fire destroyed all records for years 1889-1890.

```
COLEMAN                Coleman       76834     Created    2-01-1858
                                     -4219     Organized    -1876
```

Parent county or territory: Brown, Travis.

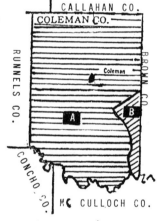

Records in:
   Area A: Bexar 1831-1848, Travis
   1848-1860, Brown 1860-1876.
   Includes most of the present
   county, being the area west of
   Muckwater Creek and north of the
   Brown County line of said creek.
   Area B: Bexar 1831-1848, Travis
   1848-1857, Brown 1857-1876.
   Includes area east of Muckwater Creek
   and south of the Brown County line.

Records available:
   Deeds since 1876, marriages since 1876, probates since
   1876, District Court minutes 1876-1880 and since 1883.

   Coleman County was temporarily organized in 1858, and
   again in 1864, but permanent organization was not
   perfected until 1876.

```
COLLIN                 McKinney      75069     Created    4-03-1846
                                     -5698     Organized  7-13-1846
```

Parent county or territory: Fannin.

Records in:
   Nacogdoches 1831-1838, Fannin 1838-1846.

                                                   (continued)

Records available:
  Deeds since 1846, marriages since 1846, probates since
  1855, District Court minutes since 1846.

COLLINGSWORTH   Wellington   79095   Created   8-21-1876
                                -3092   Orgaznized 9-30-1890

Parent county or territory: Clay.

Records in:
  Bexar 1831-1854, Cooke 1854-1860, Montague 1860-1873, Clay
  1873-1879, Wheeler 1879-1889, Childress 1889-1890.

Records available:
  Deeds since 1890, marriages since 1890, probates since
  1890, District Court minutes 1891.

All records 1860-1873, Montague County, destroyed by fire.

COLORADO   Columbus   78934   Created   1-08-1836
                                -2456   Organized   -1837

Parent county or territory: Austin, Jackson.

Records in:
  Area A: Austin 1829-1836.
  Includes all the county except
  the strip between Lavaca and
  Wharton Counties.
  Area B: Austin 1829-1834,
  Matagorda 1834-1835, Jackson
  1835-1846. Includes the strip
  described above.

Records available:
  Deeds since 1836, marriages since 1837, probates since
  1837, District Court minutes since 1837, index to
  naturalizations 1851-1905, naturalization records
  1856-1906, record of declarations of intent 1891-1906.

COMAL   New Braunsfels 78130   Created   3-24-1846
Ko'mall   New Bronz'fels -0329   Organized 7-13-1846

Parent county or territory: Bexar, Travis, Guadalupe,
                            Gonzales.

                                        (continued)

Records in:
  Area A: Bexar 1787-1846.
  Includes the area between the
  Guadalupe and Cibolo Rivers
  except Area E described below.
  Area B: Bexar 1787-1838, Bastrop
  1838-1840, Travis 1840-1846.
  Includes the area north of
  Guadalupe River and northwest
  of a line running from a point
  on the Guadalupe River approximately
  8 miles upstream from New Braunfels.
  Area C: Bexar 1787-1838, Bastrop 1838-1840, Travis 1840-
  1846, Guadalupe 1846-1858. Includes the area northeast of
  the Guadalupe River, north of the old San Antonio road and
  southeast of the line described in Area B.
  Area D: Bexar 1787-1832, Gonzales 1832-1846, Guadalupe
  1846-1858. Includes the area east of the Guadalupe River
  and south of the old San Antonio road, being a part of the
  area taken from Guadalupe County in 1858.
  Area E: Bexar 1787-1832, Gonzales 1832-1846. Includes
  the area west of the Guadalupe River and south of the old
  San Antonio road southwest to the old Gonzales County
  line, which was located about 4 miles southwest of New
  Braunfels.

Records available:
  Deeds since 1847, marriages since 1846, probates since
  1860, District Court minutes since 1846, index to
  naturalizations 1847-1921.

| COMANCHE | Comanche | 76442 | Created | 1-25-1856 |
| Kuh man' chee | | -3297 | Organized | 3-17-1856 |

Parent county or territory: Coryell.

Records in:
  Bexar 1787-1834, Milam 1834-1850, Bell 1850-1854, Coryell
  1854-1856.

Records available:
  Deeds since 1856, marriages since 1856, probates since
  1856, District Court minutes since 1858.

Milam County records destroyed by fire in 1874.

===

| CONCHO | Paint Rock | 76866 | Created | 2-01-1858 |
| Kawn'cho | | -0098 | Organized | 3-11-1879 |

Parent county or territory: Bexar.

Records in:
  Bexar 1831-1860, San Saba 1860-1879, McCullough 1879.

Records available:
  Deeds since 1879, marriages since 1879, probates since
  1879, District Court minutes since 1880.

| COOKE | Gainsville | 76240 | Created | 3-20-1848 |
| | | -4781 | Organized | 3-10-1849 |

Parent county or territory: Grayson.

Records in:
  Nacogdoches 1831-1838, Fannin 1838-1846, Grayson
  1846-1849.

Records available:
  Deeds since 1850, marriages since 1858, probates since
  1849, record of declarations 1882-1904, District Court
  minutes 1872, index to naturalizations 1868-1926,
  naturalization service and petition records 1897-1930,
  naturalization records 1884-1915.

| CORYELL | Gatesville | 76528 | Created | 2-04-1854 |
| Core yell' | | -1301 | Organized | 3-04-1854 |

Parent county or territory: Bell, McLennan.

Records in:
  Area A: Bexar 1831-1834, Milam
  1834-1850, Bell 1850-1854.
  Includes the territory drained by
  the Leon River being most of the
  county.
  Area B: Bexar 1831-1834, Milam
  1834-1850, McLennan 1850-1854.
  Includes the northeast corner of
  the county that is drained by the
  middle Bosque River.

(continued)

```
COUNTY             COUNTY SEAT   ZIP      DATE CREATED
PRONUNCIATION                             DATE ORGANIZED
==================================================================
```

Records available:
    Deeds since 1854, marriages since 1854, probates since
    1854, District Court minutes since 1856.

Milam County records destroyed by fire in April 1874.

```
COTTLE             Paducah       79248    Created    8-21-1876
Kah' tul           Puh dyou' ka  -0729    Organized  3-11-1892
```

Parent county or territory: Young.

Records in:
    Fannin 1838-1846, Grayson 1846-1849, Cooke 1849-1858,
    Young 1858-1876, Jack 1876-1881, Baylor 1881-1883,
    Wilbarger 1883-1885, Hardeman 1885-1889, Childress 1889-
    1892.

Records available:
    Deeds since 1892, marriages since 1892, probates since
    1892, District Court minutes since 1892.

```
CRANE              Crane         79731    Created    2-26-1887
                                 -2527    Organized     -1927
```

Parent county or territory: Tom Green.

Records in:
    Bexar 1831-1875, Tom Green 1875-1887, Midland 1887-1903,
    Ector 1903-1927.

Records available:
    Deeds since 1927, marriages since 1927, probates since
    1927, District Court minutes since 1927.

```
CROCKETT           Ozona         76943    Created    1-22-1875
Krah'kit           O zone'a      -0076    Organized  7-14-1891
```

Parent county or territory: Bexar.

Records in:
    Bexar 1831-1875, Kinney 1875-1887, Val Verde 1887-1891.

Records available:
    Deeds since 1891, marriages since 1891, probates since
    1891, District Court minutes since 1892.

```
CROSBY            Crosbyton     79322    Created      8-21-1876
Cross'bee         Cross'bee ton -2543    Organized    9-11-1886
```

Parent county or territory: Young.

Records in:
   Bexar 1831-1854, Cooke 1854-1858, Young 1858-1881, Baylor
   1881-1886.

Records available:
   Deeds since 1887, marriages since 1887, probates since
   1887, District Court minutes since 1887.

```
CULBERSON         Van Horn      79855    Created      3-10-1911
Cull'ber son                    -9998    Organized      -1911
```

Parent county or territory: El Paso.

Records in:
   Bexar 1831-1866, El Paso 1866-1911.

Records available:
   Deeds since 1911, marriages since 1911, probates since
   1911, District Court minutes since 1911.

```
DALLAM            Dalhart       79022    Created      8-21-1876
Dal'uhm           Dal' hahrt    -2736    Organized    8-09-1891
```

Parent County or Territory: Jack.

Records in:
   Bexar 1831-1854, Cooke 1854-1860, Montague 1860-1873, Clay
   1873-1874, Jack 1874-1879, Wheeler 1879-1881, Oldham 1881-
   1891, Hartley 1891.

Records available:
   Deeds since 1877, marriages since 1891, probates since
   1891, District Court minutes since 1892.

All records 1860-1873, Montague County, destroyed by fire.

```
DALLAS            Dallas        75202    Created      1-30-1846
                                         Organized    7-10-1846
```

Parent county or territory: Nacogdoches, Robertson.

(continued)

Records in:
    Area A: Nacogdoches 1831-1846.
    Includes the territory east of
    the main Trinity River and the
    Elm Fork of the Trinity River.
    Area B: Nacogdoches 1831-1838,
    Roberton 1838-1846. Includes
    the territory west of the above
    mentioned rivers.

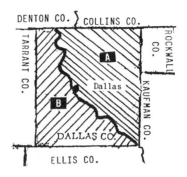

Records available:
    Deeds since 1846, marriages
    since 1846, probates since
    1846, District Court minutes
    since 1846.

DAVIS   Cass County changed name to Davis County (in
    honor of Jefferson Davis) in 1861, renamed
    Cass in 1871.

DAWSON (Defunct)   Created   2-1-1858
    Include the western portion of the present Kinney County
    and the eastern portion of Uvalde County; it included no
    part of the present Dawson County.

DAWSON   Lamesa   79331   Created   8-21-1876
               Luh mee' suh -1268   Organized   -1905

Parent county or territory: Young.

Records in:
    Bexar 1831-1858, Young 1858-1876, Shackelford 1876-1881,
    Mitchell 1881-1883, Howard 1883-1905.

Records available:
    Deeds since 1879, marriages since 1905, probates since
    1905, District Court minutes since 1905.

DEAF SMITH   Hereford   79045   Created   8-21-1876
               Her' furd   -5593   Organized   12-01-1890

Parent county or territory: Jack.

Records in:
    Bexar 1831-1854, Cooke 1854-1860, Montague 1860-1873, Clay
    1873-1874, Jack 1874-1879, Wheeler 1879-1881, Oldham 1881-
    1890.   (continued)

| COUNTY | COUNTY SEAT | ZIP | DATE CREATED |
| PRONUNCIATION | | | DATE ORGANIZED |

===

Records available:
    Deeds since 1878, marriages since 1890, probates since
    1890, District Court minutes since 1890.

All records 1860-1873 in Montague County destroyed by fire.

| DELTA | Cooper | 75432 | Created | 8-26-1868 |
| Recreated 7-13-1870 | | -1726 | Organized | 10-06-1870 |

Parent county or territory: Lamar, Hopkins.

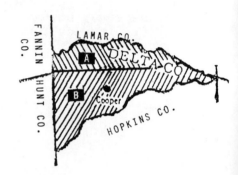

Records in:
Area A: Nacogdoches 1831-1835,
Red River 1835-1840, Lamar
1840-1870. Includes the territory
north of a line due east from the
southwest corner of Fannin County.
Area B: Nacogdoches 1831-1835,
Red River 1835-1840, Lamar
1840-1846, Hopkins 1846-1870.
Includes the territory south of
the above mentioned line.

Records available:
    Deeds since 1856, marriages since 1871, probates since
    1871, District Court minutes since 1872.

| DENTON | Denton | 76201 | Created | 4-11-1846 |
| | | -9024 | Organized | 7-13-1846 |

Parent county or territory: Fannin.

Records in:
    Nacogdoches 1831-1838, Fannin 1838-1846.

Records available:
    Deeds since 1875, marriages since 1875, probates since
    1876, District Court minutes since 1877, Naturalizations
    1910-1919.

All records destroyed by fire in 1875.

| DEWITT | Cuero | 77954 | Created | 3-24-1846 |
| | Kway'ro | -2970 | Organized | 7-13-1846 |

Parent county or territory: Gonzales, Goliad, Victoria.

(continued)

```
COUNTY            COUNTY SEAT    ZIP      DATE CREATED
PRONUNCIATION                             DATE ORGANIZED
================================================================
```

Records in:
    Area A: Bexar 1787-1832,
    Gonzales 1832-1846. Includes
    the area taken from Gonzales,
    being the area northeast of a
    southeast extension of the
    present Gonzales-Karnes County
    line and northwest of a line
    running from where the old
    La Bahia road crosses the
    Guadalupe River (about 3 miles
    below Cuero).

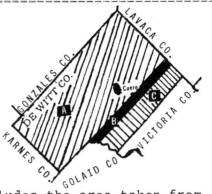

    Area B: Goliad 1829-1846. Includes the area taken from
    Goliad, being the area southwest of a southeast extension
    of the present Gonzales-Karnes County line.
    Area C: Bexar 1787-1832, Victoria 1832-1846. Includes
    the area taken from Victoria County being a strip about 8
    miles wide along the present Victoria County line.

Records available:
    Deeds since 1846, marriages since 1847, probates since
    1846, index to naturalizations 1851-1925, naturalizations
    and declarations 1892-1903, final naturalizations 1904-
    1906, records of declarations 1904-1906, District Court
    minutes since 1852.

```
DICKENS           Dickens        79229    Created    8-21-1876
                                 -0038    Organized  3-14-1891
```

Parent county or territory: Young.

Records in:
    Bexar 1831-1854, Cooke 1854-1858, Young 1858-1881, Baylor
    1881-1887, Crosby 1887-1891.

Records available:
    Deeds since 1877, marriages since 1891, probates since
    1891, District Court minutes since 1891.

```
DIMMIT         Carrizo Springs 78834  Created     2-01-1858
Dim'it         Kuh ree'zuh      -3198  Orgaanized  11-02-1880
```

Parent county or territory: Bexar, Webb.

Records in:
    Area A: Bexar 1831-1860, Webb 1860-1871, Maverick
    1871-1880. Includes the area southwest of the Nueces
                                                    (continued)

River and northwest of the
Webb County line of 1850 which
ran northeast from a point on
the Rio Grande River 10 miles
above Palafox.

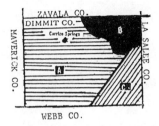

Area B: Bexar 1831-1834, San
Patricio 1834-1838, Bexar 1838-
1860, Webb 1860-1871, Maverick
1871-1880. Includes the area
northeast of the Nueces River.
Area C: Bexar 1831-1848, Webb
1848-1860, Maverick 1871-1880.
Includes the area southwest of the Nueces River and
southeast of the Webb County line of 1850 described above.

Records available:
  Deeds since 1881, marriages since 1881, probates since
  1881, District Court minutes since 1881, declaration of
  intention 1908-1926, record of declaration 1886-1906,
  petition of record 1908-1922.

San Patricio records destroyed by fire in 1846 and 1867.

DONLEY   Clarendon   79226   Created   8-21-1876
                  Klar'in dn   -2020   Organized   3-22-1882

Parent county or territory: Clay.

Records in:
  Bexar 1831-1854, Cooke 1854-1860, Montague 1860-1873, Clay
  1873-1879, Wheeler 1879-1882.

Records available:
  Deeds since 1882, marriages since 1882, probates since
  1882, District Court minutes since 1882.

All Montague County records, 1860-1873, destroyed by fire.

DUVAL   San Diego   78384   Created   2-01-1858
Doo'vawl   -0248   Organized   11-07-1876

Parent county or territory: Nueces, Live Oak, Hidalgo.

Records in:
  Area A: Nueces 1846-1876. Includes most of the county,
  being all the area lying north of the Nueces County line
  of 1848 except Area B; said line extended northwest from
                                              (continued)

the mouth of Olmos Creek.
Area B: Nueces 1846-1856, Live
Oak 1856-1858, Nueces 1858-1876.
Includes a small triangular area
in the northeast corner of the
county formerly included in
Live Oak County.
Area C: Nueces 1846-1848,
Cameron 1848-1852, Hidalgo 1852-
1870, Nueces 1870-1876.
Includes the area in the south-
east portion of the county
lying south of the Nueces County

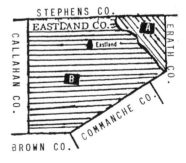

line of 1848 and east of the Starr-Cameron County line of
1848 which ran northeast from a point about 10 miles west
of the present southeast corner of Duval County.
Area D: Nueces 1846-1848, Starr 1848-1870, Nueces 1870-
1876. (The extreme western part of this area was included
in Zapata County from 1858-1870). Includes the area in the
southwest portion of the county lying south of the Nueces
County line of 1848 and west of the Starr-Cameron County
line of 1848 described above.

Records available:
    Deeds since 1877, marriages since 1877, probates since
    1877, District Court minutes since 1879.

```
EASTLAND        Eastland        76448    Created      2-01-1858
                                -9998    Organized    12-02-1873
```

Parent county or territory: Bosque, Comanche.

Records in:
    Area A: Bexar 1831-1834, Milam
    1834-1850, McLennan 1850-1854,
    Bosque 1854-1860, Comanche 1860-
    1870, Palo Pinto 1870-1873.
    Includes the territory drained by
    the Brazos River.
    Area B: Bexar 1831-1834, Milam
    1834-1850, Bell 1850-1854,
    Coryell 1854-1856, Comanche 1856-
    1870, Palo Pinto 1870-1873.
    Includes the territory drained
    by the Leon River.

(continued)

Records available:
    Deeds since 1870, marriages since 1873, probates since
    1874, District Court minutes since 1874.

EDWARDS   Rocksprings   78880   Created   2-01-1858
                               -0184   Organized 4-10-1883

Parent county or territory: Bexar.

Records in:
    Area A: Bexar 1831-1875, Kinney
    1875-1887. Includes the area
    west of a southern extension of
    the present west line of Kimble
    County.
    Area B: Bexar 1831-1860, Bandera
    1860-1861, Uvalde 1861-1866,
    Bandera 1866-1870, Kerr 1870-
    1883. Includes all the county
    except Area A.

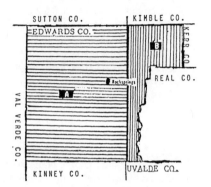

Records available:
    Deeds since 1888, marriages since 1888, probates since
    1888, District Court records since 1888.

Most of Edwards County records for the period 1883-1888 were
destroyed by fire.

ECTOR   Odessa   79760   Created   2-26-1887
Ek'ter   -5162   Organized 1-06-1891

Parent county or territory: Tom Green.

Records in:
    Bexar 1831-1875, Tom Green 1875-1887, Midland 1887-1891.

Records available:
    Deeds since 1886, marriages since 1891, probates since
    1891, District Court minutes since 1891.

ELLIS   Waxahachie   75165   Created   12-20-1849
                Wawks uh ha'chee -3759 Organized   8-05-1850

Parent county or territory: Navarro.

Records in:
    Nacogdoches 1829-1838, Robertson 1838-1846, Navarro 1846-
    1850.

                                              (continued)

Records available:
  Deeds since 1845, marriages since 1850, probates since
  1849, guardianship records 1867-1894, District Court
  minutes since 1850, naturalization records 1878-1926.

All Milam County records destroyed by fire in 1874.

```
EL PASO          El Paso       79901     Created     1-03-1850
L Pass' o                      -2496     Organized      -1866
```

Parent county or territory: Bexar.

Records in:
  Bexar 1846-1866.

Records available:
  Deeds since 1850, marriages since 1866, probates since
  1866, District Court minutes since 1861.

  Presidio-El Paso Land District organized in 1854 and the
  County organized in 1866 under the supervision of the
  United States Military forces.

```
ENCINAL                        was created in February 1, 1856; it included
                               the western part of the present Webb County.
                               It was never organized and was abolished on
                               March 12, 1899 by incorporating it into Webb
                               County.
```

```
ERATH            Stephenville  76401     Created     1-25-1856
Ee'rath                        -4280     Organized      -1866
```

Parent county or territory: Bosque, Coryell.

Records in:
  Area A: Milam 1834-1850, McLennan 1850-1854, Bosque
  1854-1860. Includes the area drained by the Bosque River
  lying south of a northeast extension of the present
  Comanche-Eastland County line.
  Area B: Milam 1834-1850, Bell 1850-1854, Coryell 1854-
  1856, Bosque 1856-1866. Includes the area drained by the
  Leon River.

(continued)

Area C: Milam 1834-1850,
McLennan 1850-1854, Bosque
1854-1857, Palo Pinto 1857-1866.
Includes the north part of the
county, being the area north
of the line described in Area A.

Records available:
    Deeds since 1847, marriages
    since 1869, probates since
    1866, naturalization records
    1886-1910, District Court
    minutes since 1866, naturalization records 1892-1905.

All Milam County records destroyed by fire in 1874.

FALLS   Marlin   76661   Created   1-28-1850
                  Mahr'lin   -0458   Organized   -1851

Parent county or territory: Milam, Limestone.

Records in:
    Area A: Austin 1831-1834, Milam
    1834-1850, Bell 1850-1851.
    Includes the territory west of
    the Brazos River.
    Area B: Austin 1831-1834, Milam
    1834-1838, Robertson 1838-1846,
    Limestone 1846-1851.   Includes
    the territory east of the Brazos
    River except Area C.
    Area C: Austin 1831-1834, Milam
    1834-1838, Robertson 1838-1846,
    Limestone 1846-1863. Includes the
    narrow strip transferred from Limestone County to Falls
    County in 1863 as a result of county line survey.

Records available:
    Deeds since 1850, marriages since 1854, probates since
    1851, record of declarations 1887-1906, naturalization
    petitions and records 1907, final naturalization records
    1904-1906, record of petition and affidavit 1874-1903,
    District Court minutes since 1851.

All Milam County records destroyed by fire in 1874.

All Limestone County records completely destroyed in 1873.

```
COUNTY           COUNTY SEAT   ZIP      DATE CREATED
PRONUNCIATION                           DATE ORGANIZED
==========================================================

FANNIN           Bonham        75418    Created    12-14-1837
Fan'in           Bah'nm        -4395    Organized  1-    1838
```

Parent county or territory: Nacogdoches.

Records in:
  Nacogdoches 1831-1838.

Records available:
  Deeds since 1838, marriages since 1852, probates since
  1838, District Court minutes since 1840.

```
FAYETTE          La Grange     78945    Created    12-14-1837
Fay' et          Luh Graang'   -2204    Organized  1-   -1838
```

Parent county or territory: Colorado, Bastrop.

Records in:
  Area A: Austin 1829-1836,
  Colorado 1836-1838.
  Includes the southeast of the
  county, lying southeast of the
  old upper La Bahia road.
  Area B: Austin 1829-1834,
  Bastrop 1834-1836, Colorado
  1836-1838. Includes the area
  south of Buckner's Creek,
  west of La Bahia road, and east
  of a line due north from the

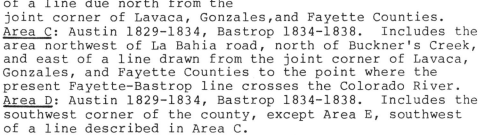

  joint corner of Lavaca, Gonzales,and Fayette Counties.
  Area C: Austin 1829-1834, Bastrop 1834-1838. Includes the
  area northwest of La Bahia road, north of Buckner's Creek,
  and east of a line drawn from the joint corner of Lavaca,
  Gonzales, and Fayette Counties to the point where the
  present Fayette-Bastrop line crosses the Colorado River.
  Area D: Austin 1829-1834, Bastrop 1834-1838. Includes the
  southwest corner of the county, except Area E, southwest
  of a line described in Area C.
  Area E: Austin 1829-1834, Bastrop 1834-1836, Colorado
  1836-1838. Includes the small area lying between two
  lines, one line described in Area B and the other line
  described in Area C.

Records available:
  Deeds since 1838, marriages since 1838, probates since
  1838, naturalization civil minutes 1855-1861, application
  for naturalization 1876-1896, application for minors
  naturalization records 1882-1906, naturalization minutes
                                                   (continued)
```
```

==

1855-1890, naturalization records 1873-1903, minors
naturalization records 1880-1910, petition and record
1906-1910, record of declaration 1906-1912, District
Court minutes since 1838.

| FISHER | Roby | 79543 | Created | 8-21-1876 |
| | Roo' bee | -9998 | Organized | 4-27-1886 |

Parent county or territory: Young.

Records in:
   Bexar 1831-1854, Young 1854-1876, Shackelford 1876-1881,
   Nolan 1881-1886.

Records available:
   Deeds since 1884, marriages since 1886, probates since
   1886, District Court minutes since 1886.

| FLOYD | Floydada | 79235 | Created | 8-21-1876 |
| | Floy day' da | -2749 | Organized | 5-28-1890 |

Parent county or territory: Young.

Records in:
   Bexar 1831-1854, Cooke 1854-1858, Young 1858-1876, Jack
   1876-1881, Baylor 1881-1883, Donley 1883-1887, Crosby
   1887-1890.

Records available:
   Deeds since 1873, marriages since 1890, probates since
   1890, District Court minutes since 1890.

| FOARD | Crowell | 79227 | Created | 3-03-1891 |
| Ford | Crow' uhl | -0597 | Organized | 4-27-1891 |

Parent county or territory: Hardeman, Knox, Childress.

Records in:
   Entire County was in Fannin 1838-1846, Grayson 1846-1849,
   Cooke 1849-1858, Young 1858-1860.
   Area A: Montague 1860-1873, Clay 1873-1881, Baylor 1881-
   1883, Wilbarger 1883-1885, Hardeman 1885-1891. Includes
   most of the county, being that part lying north and east
   of the northwest corner of Knox County.

(continued)

===

Area B: Jack 1860-1870, Young
1870-1879, Clay 1879-1881,
Baylor 1881-1886, Knox 1886-
1891. Includes that part lying
south and west of the northwest
corner of Baylor County.
Area C: Young 1860-1876, Jack
1876-1881, Baylor 1881-1883,
Wilbarger 1883-1885, Hardeman
1885-1889, Childress 1889-1891.
Includes the west three miles
of the county.

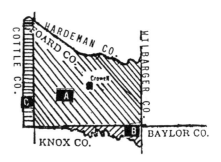

Records available:
Deeds since 1891, marriages since 1891, probates since
1891, District Court minutes since 1891.

All Montague County records, 1860-1873, destroyed by fire.

| FORT BEND | Richmond | 77469 | Created | 12-29-1837 |
| | | -9998 | Organized | 1- -1838 |

Parent county or territory: Austin, Harris, Brazoria.

Records in:

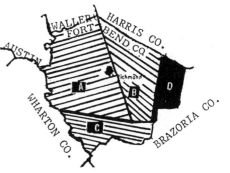

Area A: Austin 1829-1837.
Includes the northwest part of
the county, lying north of a line
running from the mouth of Turkey
Creek in the San Bernard River
to a point 4 miles north of the
mouth of Big Creek on the Brazos
and then to the head of Clear
Creek, and west of a southerly
extension of the present Harris-
Waller County line.
Area B: Austin 1829-1834, Harris 1834-1837. Includes the
northeastern part of the county lying north of the line
described in Area A and east of the Harris-Waller County
line extended southerly.
Area C: Austin 1829-1832, Brazoria 1832-1837. Includes
the area between the Brazos and San Bernard Rivers and
south of the line described in Area A.
Area D: Austin 1829-1832, Brazoria 1832-1837, Harris 1837.
Includes the area east of the Brazos River and south of
the line described in Area A.

(continued)

Records available:
  Deeds since 1838, marriages since 1838, probates since
  1838, District Court minutes since 1838, index to
  naturalizations 1854-1929, declaration records 1896-1906,
  naturalization records 1895-1903.

  Fort Bend County maintained 2 different types of books
  relating to probate matters. The first was a record of
  the proceedings of the Probate Court, containing copies of
  official orders issued by the court and minutes of the
  proceedings. The second set, usually recorded only after
  the estate was settled, consisted of recorded copies
  of instruments filed in probate cases. In most
  counties these were called Probate Records or Record of
  Estates.

FRANKLIN   Mt. Vernon   75457   Created   3-08-1875
                              -0573   Organized   4-30-1875

Parent County or Territory: Titus.

Records in:
  Nacogdoches 1831-1835, Red River 1835-1846, Titus 1846-
  1875.

Records available:
  Deeds since 1846, marriages since 1875, probates since
  1875, District Court minutes since 1875.

FREESTONE   Fairfield   75840   Created   9-06-1850
                              -1595   Organized   7-06-1851

Parent county or territory: Limestone.

Records in:
  Area A: Austin 1829-1838,
  Robertson 1838-1846, Limestone
  1846-1851. Includes the area
  west of the Brazos-Trinity
  divide.
  Area B: Nacogdoches 1829-1838,
  Robertson 1838-1846, Limestone
  1846-1851. Includes the area
  east of the Brazos-Trinity divide.

Records available:
  Deeds since 1852, marriages since 1851, probates since
  1851, District Court minutes since 1852.

(continued)

Limestone County records were completely destroyed by fire in 1873.

```
FRIO             Pearsall       78061    Created     2-01-1858
Free' oh         Peer'sawl      -9998    Organized   7-20-1871
```

Parent county or territory: Uvalde, Bexar, Atascosa.

Records in:
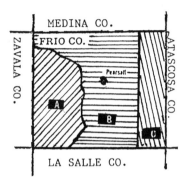
Entire County: Bexar 1831-1834, San Patricio 1834-1838.
Area A: Bexar 1838-1856, Uvalde 1856-1860, Atascosa 1860-1870, Medina 1870-1871. Includes the area west of the Frio River and north of a line running southwest from the mouth of the Leona River.
Area B: Bexar 1838-1860, Atascosa 1860-1870, Medina 1870-1871. Includes all of the county except Areas A and C.
Area C: Bexar 1838-1856, Atascosa 1856-1870, Medina 1870-1871. Includes an area approximately 7-1/2 miles wide, 23 miles long running north and south situated in the northeast portion of the county and lying mostly north and east of San Migel Creek.

Records available:
Deeds since 1871, applications to purchase homesteads 1873-1908, marriages since 1871, probates since 1873, District Court minutes since 1873, declaration records 1900.

San Patricio County records destroyed in 1846 and in 1867.

```
GAINS            Seminole       79360    Created     8-21-1876
                                -4397    Organized   10-24-1905
```

Parent county or territory: Young.

Records in:
Bexar 1831-1858, Young 1858-1876, Shackelford 1876-1881, Mitchell 1881-1883, Howard 1883-1885, Martin 1885-1905.

Records available:
Deeds since 1884, marriages since 1905, probates since 1905, District Court minutes since 1906.

```
COUNTY              COUNTY SEAT    ZIP        DATE CREATED
PRONUNCIATION                                 DATE ORGANIZED
=================================================================

GALVESTON           Galveston      77550      Created      5-15-1838
Gal' ves ton                       -2317      Organized        -1838
```

Parent county or territory: Harrisburg, Brazoria, Liberty,
                             Jefferson.

Records in:
    Area A: Austin 1829-1832, Brazoria
    1832-1836, Harrisburg 1836-1838.
    Includes all of Galveston Island
    Area B: Austin 1829-1832, Brazoria
    1832-1839. Includes the Mainland
    northeast of Highland Bayou and
    east of a line drawn north from
    the head of said Bayou to Clear
    Creek; this line passes along the
    east edge of League City townsite.
    Area C: Austin 1829-1832,
    Brazoria 1832-1841. Includes the territory southwest of
    Highland Bayou and west of the north-south line described
    above.
    Area D: Liberty 1831-1838. Includes the Red Fish Reef and
    Galveston Bay south of said reef, all of East Bay, and
    Bolivar Peninsula west of a southern extension of the
    present Liberty-Jefferson County line.
    Area E: Liberty 1831-1837, Jefferson 1837-1838. Includes
    that portion of Bolivar Peninsula east of Area D.

Records available:
    Deeds since 1838, marriages since 1838, probates since
    1838, index to declaration of intentions and final papers
    1867-1908, declaration of intentions 1876-1906, District
    Court minutes since 1839, index to naturalization 1860-
    1890, declaration of intentions 1860-1906.

    Liberty County records destroyed by fire in 1875 and
    damaged by storm in 1900.

```
GARZA               Post           70356      Created      8-21-1876
Gahr'zuh                           -3242      Organized    6-15-1907
```

Parent county or territory: Young.

Records in:
    Bexar 1831-1854, Cooke 1854-1858, Young 1858-1881,
    Throckmorton 1881-1883, Mitchell 1883-1885, Scurry
    1885-1897, Borden 1897-1907.

                                            (continued)

Records available:
    Deeds since 1882, marriages since 1907, probates since
    1907, District Court minutes since 1911.

Garza County records partially damaged by fire in 1911.

GILLESPIE   Fredricksburg 78624   Created   2-23-1848
Guh les' pe   -0551   Organized   6-03-1848

Parent county or territory: Bexar.

Records in:
    Area A: Bexar 1831-1834, Bastrop
    1834-1837, Bexar 1837-1848.
    Includes the area lying north
    east of the old Mina line which
    ran northwest from the present
    southeast corner of the county.
    Area B: Bexar 1831-1848. Includes
    the area lying southwest of the
    above line.

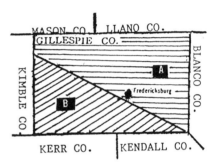

Records available:
    Deeds since 1850, marriages since 1850, probates since
    1850, record of declaration 1885-1906, index to
    naturalization minutes 1850-1936, naturalization minutes
    1891-1906, District Court minutes since 1849.

GLASSCOCK   Garden City   79739   Created   4-04-1887
                               -9998   Organized   3-28-1893

Parent county or territory: Tom Green.

Records in:
    Bexar 1831-1875, Tom Green 1875-1887, Martin 1887-1889,
    Howard 1889-1893.

Records available:
    Deeds since 1889, marriages since 1893, probates since
    1893, District Court minutes since 1893.

GOLIAD   Goliad   77963   Created   3-17-1836
Go' lee add   -9998   Organized   -1837

Goliad Municipality   Created   1827 or 1829

                                           (continued)

COUNTY   COUNTY SEAT   ZIP   DATE CREATED
PRONUNCIATION   DATE ORGANIZED
==

Parent county or territory: old Mexican Municipality.

Records in:
  Goliad County.

Records available:
  Deeds since 1870, marriages since 1870, probates since
  1871, District Court minutes 1855.

  Goliad records destroyed in 1870 and since damaged by
  storm.

  Records for period 1846-1848 for area north of extension
  of the present southeast and southwest lines of DeWitt
  County to intersection in Goliad County went to DeWitt
  County.

GONZALES   Gonzales   78629   Created   -1832
Guhn zahl' s   -4069   Organized   -1837

Gonzales created as municipality in 1832 and organized as a
county in 1837.

Parent county or territory: old Mexican Municipality.

Records in:
  Gonzales County.

Records available:
  Deeds since 1848, marriages since 1892, probates since
  1838, naturalization records 1887-1906, petition for
  naturalization 1892-1911, declaration of intention 1906-
  1929, final record 1838-1845, District Court minutes since
  1876.

  For period 1834-1838, records for area north of a line
  running northwest from the common west corner of Lavaca
  and Fayette Counties may be found in Bastrop County.

Gonzales County records damaged by 2 fires and by storm.

GRAY   Pampa   79065   Created   8-21-1876
               Pam' puh   -1902   Organized   5-27-1902

Parent county or territory: Clay.

```
COUNTY              COUNTY SEAT    ZIP      DATE CREATED
PRONUNCIATION                               DATE ORGANIZED
=================================================================
```

Records available:
  Deeds since 1902, marriages since 1902, probates since
  1902, District Court minutes since 1903.

```
GRAYSON          Sherman        75090    Created      2-17-1846
                                -5958    Organized    7-13-1846
```

Parent county or territory: Fannin.

Records in:
  Nacogdoches 1831-1838, Fannin 1838-1846.

Records available:
  Deeds since 1846, marriages since 1846, probates since
  1846, District Court minutes since 1836, index to
  naturalizations 1853-1903, declaration of intention 1892-
  1913, naturalization records 1892-1906.

```
GREER (Now Okla.) Mangum        73554    Created      2-08-1860
                                         Organized    7-  -1886
```

Parent county or territory: Young.

  Greer County was organized as a county of Texas; it was
  developed and administered by Texas for thirty-five years.
  Greer County became a territory of the United States in
  1896 by the ruling of the Supreme Court, and finally in
  1906, it became a county in Oklahoma.

Records in:
  Fannin 1838-1846, Grayson 1846-1849, Cooke 1849-1858,
  Young 1858-1860, Montague 1860-1873, Clay 1873-1881,
  Baylor 1881-1883, Wilbarger 1883-1884, Wheeler 1884-1886.

Records available:
  Deeds since 1901, marriages since 1901, probates since
  1901.

```
GREGG            Longview       75601    Created      4-12-1873
                                -9998    Organized    6-28-1873
```

Parent county or territory: Upshur, Rusk.

                                             (continued)

==

Records in:

  Area A: Nacogdoches 1831-1846,
  Upshur 1846-1873. Includes the area
  west of the old Cherokee trace and
  north of the Sabine River.
  Area B: Nacogdoches 1831-1837,
  Shelby 1837-1840, Harrison 1840-
  1846, Upshur 1846-1873.
  Includes the area east of the said
  trace and north of the Sabine River.
  Area C: Nacogdoches 1831-1843,
  Rusk 1843-1873. Includes the area south of the Sabine
  River.

Records available:
  Deeds since 1873, marriages since 1873, probates since
  1873, District Court minutes since 1873.

Shelby County records prior to 1881 destroyed by fire.

GRIMES   Anderson   77830   Created   4-06-1846
                                 -9998   Organized   7-15-1846

Parent county or territory: Montgomery.

Records in:
  Austin 1827-1835, Washington 1835-1837, Montgomery 1837-
  1846.

Records available:
  Deeds since 1846, marriages since 1849, probates since
  1847, declaration of intention and naturalization records
  1890-1925. District Court minutes since 1844.

GUADALUPE   Sequin   78155   Created   3-30-1846
Gwah duh loop'e See geen'   -5727   Organized   7-13-1846

Parent county or territory: Gonzales, Bexar.

Records in:
  Area A: Bexar 1787-1832, Gonzales 1832-1846. Includes the
  area northeast of a northwest extension of the present
  Karnes-Gonzales County line.
  Area B: Bexar 1787-1846. Includes the area southwest of
  the above described line except Area C.

                                                   (continued)

- 100 -

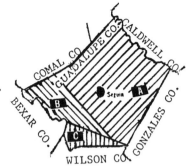

Area C: Bexar 1787-1846,
Guadalupe 1846-1869, Wilson 1869-
1874. Includes the area south of
a line from the present corner of
Gonzales-Wilson Counties to Cibolo
Creek at the mouth of Martinez Creek.

Records available:
Deeds since 1840, marriages since
1846, probates since 1846,
naturalization records 1892-1903,
District Court minutes since 1846,
declaration records 1884-1906, final naturalization
1891-1942.

HALE	Plainview	79072	Created	8-21-1876
		-9998	Organized	8-13-1888

Parent county or territory: Young.

Records in:
Bexar 1831-1854, Cooke 1854-1858, Young 1858-1876, Jack
1876-1881, Baylor 1881-1884, Donley 1884-1887, Crosby
1887-1888.

Records available:
Deeds since 1881, marriages since 1888, probates since
1888, District Court minutes since 1888.

HALL	Memphis	79245	Created	8-21-1876
		-3343	Organized	6-23-1890

Parent county or territory: Clay, Jack.

Records in:
Entire county in Clay 1876-1879,
Wheeler 1879-1883, Donley 1883-1890.
Area A: Bexar 1831-1854, Cooke
1854-1860, Montague 1860-1873,
Clay 1873-1876. Includes that
part of the county north of the
Red River.
Area B: Bexar 1831-1854, Cooke
1854-1858, Young 1858-1874,
Jack 1874-1876. Includes that
part of the county south of the
Red River.

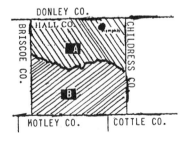

(continued)

Records available:
   Deeds since 1882, marriages since 1890, probates since
   1890, District Court minutes since 1890.

Records for Montague County, 1860-1873, destroyed by fire.

HAMILTON   Hamilton   76531   Created   1-22-1858
                                -1993   Organized   8-02-1858

Parent county or territory: Comanche, Bosque, Lampasas.

Records in:
   Entire County in Milam 1834-1850.
   Area A: Bell 1850-1854, Coryell
   1854-1856, Comanche 1856-1858.
   Includes the area drained by the
   Leon River except Area D.
   Area B: McLennan 1850-1854,
   Bosque 1854-1856, Comanche
   1856-1858. Includes the area
   drained by the Bosque River
   except Area C.
   Area C: McLennan 1850-1854,
   Bosque 1854-1858. Includes
   a strip 2-1/2 miles wide
   southwest of and adjacent to Bosque County.
   Area D: Bell 1850-1854, Coryell 1854-1856, Lampasas 1856-
   1858. Includes a triangular area in the south corner of
   the county south of U. S. Highway 84.

Records available:
   Deeds since 1866, marriages since 1876, probates since
   1870, District Court minutes since 1871.

Fires destroyed records of Hamilton County in 1870, Milam
County in 1874, and Lampasas County in 1875.

HANSFORD   Spearman   79081   Created   8-21-1876
                                -0397   Organized   3-11-1889

Parent county or terrritory: Jack.

Records in:
   Bexar 1831-1854, Cooke 1854-1860, Montague 1860-1873, Clay
   1873-1874, Jack 1874-1879, Wheeler 1879-1889, Lipscomb
   1889.

                                                  (continued)

Records available:
    Deeds since 1877, marriages since 1889, probates since
    1889, District Court minutes since 1889.

Records in Montague County 1860-1873 destroyed by fire.

HARDEMAN   Quanah   79252   Created   2-21-1858
                  Kwah'nuh   -0510   Organized   12-31-1884

Parent county or territory: Cooke.

Records in:
    Fannin 1838-1846, Grayson 1846-1849, Cooke 1849-1858,
    Young 1858-1860, Montague 1860-1873, Clay 1873-1881,
    Baylor 1881-1883, Wilbarger 1883-1884.

Records available:
    Deeds since 1884, marriages since 1885, probates since
    1885, District Court minutes since 1885.

All records in Montague County 1860-1873 destroyed by fire.

HARDIN   Kountze   77625   Created   1-22-1858
                  Koon'z   -9998   Organized   8-02-1858

Parent county or territory: Liberty, Jefferson, Tyler.

Records in:
    Area A: Liberty 1831-1858.
    Includes the the area south of
    Village Creek and west of a
    northerly extension of the
    present Liberty-Jefferson
    County line.
    Area B: Liberty 1831-1837,
    Jefferson 1837-1858. Includes
    the area south of Village
    Creek and east of the above
    described line.
    Area C: Liberty 1831-1846, Tyler 1846-1858. Includes the
    area north of Village Creek.

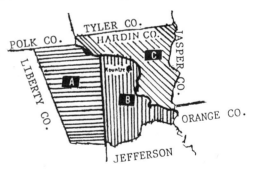

Records available:
    Deeds since 1858, marriages since 1862, probates since
    1887, District Court minutes since 1871.

Liberty County records destroyed by fire in 1875 and damaged
by storm in 1900.

```
COUNTY              COUNTY SEAT    ZIP        DATE CREATED
PRONUNCIATION                                 DATE ORGANIZED
================================================================

HARRIS              Houston        77002      Created     12-30-1835
                                   -1899      Organized       -1836
(Organized as Municipality of
 Harrisburg in 1836 and as a county in 1837)

Parent County or Territory: Austin and Liberty.
```

Records in:
    <u>Area A</u>: Austin 1827-1835.
    Includes all the county west of
    the San Jacinto River except
    Area C.
    <u>Area B</u>: Liberty 1831-1835.
    Includes the area east of the
    San Jacinto River.
    <u>Area C</u>: Austin 1825-1837, Fort
    Bend 1837-1846. Includes the

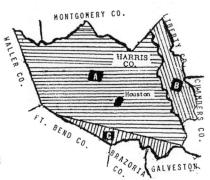

area around the head of Brays
Bayou, west of a line drawn from
the head of Clear Creek to the
head of Brays Bayou at the point
where the present line crosses Buffalo Bayou.

Records available:
    Deeds since 1836, marriages since 1837, probates since
    1836, District Court minutes since 1837.

```
HARRISON            Marshall       75670      Created     1-28-1839
                                   -4053      Organized       -1840

Parent County or Territory: Shelby.
```

Records in:
    Nacogdoches 1831-1837, Shelby 1837-1840.

Records available:
    Deeds since 1840, marriages since 1839, probates since
    1839, District Court minutes since 1840.

Shelby County records 1837-1840 destroyed by fire.

```
HARTLEY             Channing       79018      Created     8-21-1876
                                   -9998      Organized   2-09-1891

Parent county or territory: Jack.
```

(continued)

Records in:
    Bexar 1831-1854, Cooke 1854-1860, Montague 1860-1873, Clay
    1873-1874, Jack 1874-1879, Wheeler 1879-1881, Oldham 1881-
    1891.

Records available:
    Deeds since 1882, marriages since 1891, probates since
    1891, District Court minutes since 1891.

Records for Montague County, 1860-1873, destroyed by fire.

HASKELL   Haskell   79521   Created   2-01-1858
                                -5917   Organized   1-13-1885

Parent county or territory: Cooke.

Records in:
    Fannin 1838-1846, Collin 1846-1849, Cooke 1849-1858, Young
    1858-1866, Jack 1866-1870, Young 1870-1876, Shackelford
    1876-1881, Throckmorton 1881-1885.

Records available:
    Deeds since 1873, marriages since 1885, probates since
    1885, District Court minutes since 1885.

HAYS   San Marcos   78666   Created   3-01-1848
                 San mahr'cus   -5683   Organized   8-07-1848

Parent county or territory: Travis, Guadalupe.

Records in:
    Area A: Bexar 1831-1834, Bastrop
    1834-1840, Travis 1840-1848.
    Includes all of the county
    northwest of the old San Antonio
    road except Area B.
    Area B: Bexar 1787-1832, Gonzales
    1832-1846, Guadalupe 1846-1858.
    Includes the area south of a
    line running southeast from the
    present southeast corner of
    Gillespie County.

Records available:
    Deeds since 1848, marriages since 1848, probates since
    1839, District Court minutes from 1850-1864; 1874-1876;
    and since 1881.

(continued)

- 105 -

===

Hays County records considerably damaged by fires in 1855, 1864, 1888.

HEMPHILL   Canadian   79014   Created   8-21-1876
                               -9998   Organized   7-05-1887

Parent county or territory: Clay.

Records in:
    Bexar 1831-1854, Cooke 1854-1860, Montague 1860-1873, Clay 1873-1879, Wheeler 1879-1887.

Records available:
    Deeds since 1881, marriages since 1887, probates since 1887, District Court minutes since 1887.

Records in Montague County 1860-1873 destroyed by fire.

Clay County records 1873-1876 partially complete.

HENDERSON   Athens   75751   Created   4-27-1846
                               -9998   Organized   7-13-1846

Parent county or territory: Houston, Nacogdoches.

Records in:
    Area A: Nacogdoches 1831-1837, Houston 1837-1846. Includes the area south of the original Houston-Nacogdoches County line (which ran west from the northwest corner of the Neches-Saline league in Smith County to the Trinity River) and west of a north-south line through a point 43 miles due east of the southeast corner of present Dallas County.

    Area B: Nacogdoches 1831-1846. Includes the area north of said old Houston-Nacogdoches County line and west of said north-south line.
    Area C: Nacogdoches 1831-1846, Henderson 1846-1848, Van Zandt 1848-1850. Includes the area north of said old Houston-Nacogdoches County line and east of said north-south line.

(continued)

- 106 -

Area D: Nacogdoches 1831-1837, Houston 1837-1846, Henderson 1846-1848, Van Zandt 1848-1850. Includes the area south of said old Houston-Nacogdoches County line and east of said north-south line.

Records available:
Deeds since 1839, marriages since 1846, probates since 1846, District Court minutes since 1847.

All Houston County records 1837-1846 destroyed by fire.

```
HIDALGO          Edinburg      78539    Created      1-24-1852
He dal'go        Edd'n burg    -3563    Organized    8-07-1852
```

Parent county or territory: Cameron.

Records in:
Municipality of Reynosa 1780-1846, Nueces 1846-1848, Cameron 1848-1852.

Records available:
Deeds since 1852, marriages since 1852, probates since 1852, District Court minutes since 1887.

```
HILL             Hillsboro     76645    Created      1-07-1853
                               -0398    Organized    5-14-1853
```

Parent county or territory: Navarro.

Records in:
Area A: Austin 1831-1834, Milam 1834-1838, Robertson 1838-1846, Navarro 1846-1853. Includes area west of the Brazos-Trinity divide.
Area B: Nacogdoches 1831-1838, Robertson 1838-1846, Navarro 1846-1853. Includes the area east of the said divide except Area C.
Area C: Nacogdoches 1831-1838, Robertson 1838-1846, Navarro 1846-1858. Includes the strip 3 miles wide adjoining Navarro County.

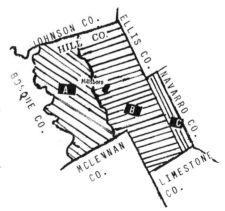

Records available:
Deeds since 1857, marriages since 1873, probates since 1853, District Court minutes since 1867.

(continued)

All Milam County records destroyed by fire 1874.

HOCKLEY   Levelland   79336   Created   8-21-1876
                Le'vel land   -4529   Organized   -1921

Parent county or territory: Young.

Records in:
   Bexar 1831-1854, Cooke 1854-1858, Young 1858-1881, Baylor
   1881-1887, Crosby 1887-1889, Hale 1889-1891, Lubbock 1891-
   1921.

Records available:
   Deeds since 1908, marriages since 1921, probates since
   1921, District Court minutes since 1921.

HOOD   Grandbury   76048   Created   11-02-1866
                               -2493   Organized   12-25-1866

Parent county or territory: Johnson, Bosque.

Records in:
   Area A: Milam 1834-1850, McLennan
   1850-1854, Johnson 1854-1866.
   Includes the area west of the
   Brazos River and east of the old
   Johnson County line.
   Area B: Milam 1834-1838,
   Robertson 1838-1846, Navarro 1846-
   1853, Hill 1853-1854, Johnson 1854-
   1866. Includes the area east of
   the Brazos River.
   Area C: Milam 1834-1850, McLennan 1850-1854, Bosque
   1854-1866, Erath 1866. Includes the area west of the old
   Johnson County line as previously described.

Records available:
   Deeds since 1871, marriages since 1875, probates since
   1876, District Court minutes since 1875.

All Hood County records were destroyed by fire in 1875.

Milam County records destroyed by fire in 1874.

```
COUNTY            COUNTY SEAT   ZIP      DATE CREATED
PRONUNCIATION                            DATE ORGANIZED
================================================================

HOPKINS           Sulphur Springs 75482  Created    3-25-1846
                               -2682  Organized    7-13-1846

Parent county or territory: Lamar.

Records in:
    Nacogdoches 1831-1835, Red River 1835-1840, Lamar 1840-
    1846.

Records available:
    Deeds since 1846, marriages since 1846, probates since
    1846, District Court minutes since 1846.
-----------------------------------------------------------

HOUSTON           Crockett      75835    Created    6-12-1837
                               -2034    Organized      -1837

Parent county or territory: Nacogdoches.

Records in:
    Nacogdoches 1831-1837.

Records available:
    Deeds since 1865, marriages since 1882, probates since
    1859, District Court minutes since 1878, Index to
    naturalizations 1880-1925.

Houston County records have suffered from two distructive
fires.
-----------------------------------------------------------

HOWARD            Big Spring    79720    Created    8-21-1876
                                         Organized   6-15-1882

Parent county or territory: Young.

Records in:
    Bexar 1831-1858, Young 1858-1876, Shackelford 1876-1882.

Records available:
    Deeds since 1882, marriages since 1882, probates since
    1882, District Court minutes since 1882.
-----------------------------------------------------------

HUDSPETH          Sierra Blanco 79851    Created    2-16-1917
Hud'spth          Sier'ah Blan'ko -9998  Organized      -1917

Parent County or territory: El Paso.
                                        (continued)
```

Records in:
  Bexar 1846-1866, El Paso 1866-1917.

Records available:
  Deeds since 1917, marriages since 1917, probates since
  1917, District Court minutes since 1917.

```
HUNT                Greenville     75401     Created      4-11-1846
                                   -1097     Organized    7-12-1846
```

Parent county or territory: Fannin, Nacogdoches.

Records in:
  Area A: Nacogdoches 1831-1837,
  Fannin 1837-1846. Includes the
  territory north of a due east
  and west line drawn through a
  point on a southward extension
  of the present Hunt-Hopkins line
  60 miles south of the present
  northeast corner of Fannin
  County on the Red River, except
  Area C, described below.
  Area B: Nacogdoches 1831-1846.
  Includes area south of east-west line described above.
  Area C: Nacogdoches 1831-1837, Fannin 1837-1846, Hunt
  1846-1868, Delta 1868-1870. Includes the area east of the
  96th meridian and north of the Middle Sulphur River.

Records available:
  Deeds since 1846, marriages since 1858, probates since
  1847, District Court minutes since 1857, index to
  naturalizations 1851-1926, record of declaration 1889-
  1903.

```
HUTCHINSON          Stinnett       79083     Created      8-21-1876
                    Stin net'      -9998     Organized       -1901
```

Parent county or territory: Jack.

Records in:
  Bexar 1831-1854, Cooke 1854-1860, Montague 1860-1873, Clay
  1873-1874, Jack 1874-1879, Wheeler 1879-1889, Carson
  1889-1891, Roberts 1891-1901.

                                        (continued)

===

Records available:
    Deeds since 1901, marriages since 1901, probates since
    1901, District Court minutes since 1901.

Records in Montague County 1860-1873 destroyed by fire.

| IRION | Mertzon | 76941 | Created | 3-07-1889 |
| Ir'e on | Merts'n | -9998 | Organized | 4-16-1889 |

Parent county or territory: Tom Green.

Records in:
    Bexar 1831-1875, Tom Green 1875-1889.

Records available:
    Deeds since 1887, marriages since 1889, probates since
    1889, District Court minutes since 1889.

| JACK | Jacksboro | 76056 | Created | 8-27-1856 |
| | | -2119 | Organized | 7-01-1857 |

Parent county or territory: Cooke.

Records in:
    Fannin 1838-1846, Collin 1846-1849, Cooke 1849-1857.

Records available:
    Deeds since 1858, marriages since 1858, probates since
    1858, District Court minutes since 1858.

| JACKSON | Edna | 77957 | Created | 12-03-1835 |
| | | -2799 | Organized | -1835 |

(Created as the Municipality of Jackson;
the county was organized in 1836)

Parent county or territory: Matagorda, Victoria.

Records in:
    Area A: Austin 1821-1834, Matagorda 1834-1835. Includes
    the area east of Lavaca River.
    Area B: Bexar 1787-1832, Victoria 1832-1837, Jackson
    1837-1844, Victoria 1844-1846. Includes the area west of
    the Lavaca River and east of a line running northwest from
    the mouth of the Lavaca River.

(continued)

Area C: Bexar 1787-1832,
Victoria 1832-1846. Includes
the area west of the Lavaca
River and west of the line
described in Area B.

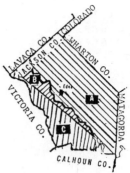

Records available:
  Deeds since 1836, marriages
  since 1840, probates since
  1836, District Court minutes
  since 1838, naturalization
  1903-1906.

JASPER   Jasper   75951   Created   3-17-1835
                               -4193   Organized   -1835
(Created as the Municipality of Bevi in 1835;
the county was created in 1836 and organized in 1837).

Parent county or territory: Liberty, San Augustine.

Records in:
  Area A: Liberty 1831-1835. Includes the area east of the
  Angelina River except Areas C and D.
  Area B: Liberty and Nacogdoches? 1831-1837. Includes the
  area northwest of the Angelina River and northwest of
  Bear Creek.
  Area C: Nacogdoches 1831-1834,
  San Augustine 1834-1835, Sabine
  1835-1837. Includes the area
  north of a line drawn from the
  head of Little Cow Creek westerly
  to the mouth of Ayish Bayou on
  Bear Creek.

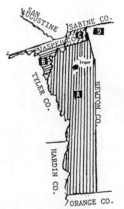

  Area D: Liberty 1831-1835, Jasper
  1835-1846, Newton 1846-1852.
  Includes the area east of a line
  running southeast from the
  present northeast corner of
  Jasper County.

Records available:
  Deeds since 1849, marriages since 1849, probates since
  1849, District Court minutes since 1850.

Liberty County records destroyed by fire in 1875.

All Sabine records prior to 1876 destroyed by fire.

Jasper records destroyed by fire in about 1850.

===

| JEFF DAVIS | Fort Davis | 79734 | Created | 3-15-1887 |
| | | -0788 | Organized | 5-24-1887 |

Parent county or territory: Presidio.

Records in:
Bexar 1846-1866, El Paso 1866-1875, Presidio 1875-1887.

Records available:
Deeds since 1887, marriages since 1887, probates since 1887, District Court minutes since 1887.

| JEFFERSON | Beaumont | 77704 | Created | 3-17-1836 |
| | Bow'mahnt | -2268 | Organized | -1837 |

(Created as municipality on 12-5-1835 coinciding with present Orange County)

Parent county or territory: Liberty.

Records in:
Liberty 1831-1837.

Records available:
Deeds since 1837, marriages since 1837, probates since 1838, District Court minutes since 1844.

| JIM HOGG | Hebbronville | 78361 | Created | 3-31-1913 |
| | Heb'rn vil | -0729 | Organized | -1913 |

Parent county or territory: Brooks, Duval, Starr.

Records in:
Entire county records prior to 1846 may be found in Mexican Municipalities of Guerrero, Mier, Camargo, or Reynosa.
Area A: Nueces 1846-1848, Starr 1848-1858, Zapata 1858-1870, Webb 1870-1887, Zapata 1887-1911, Brooks 1911-1913. Includes the area in the northwest corner of the county northwest of the Zapata County line of 1858, which was a line northeast from the present southwest corner of Jim Hogg County.

(continued)

Area B: Nueces 1846-1848, Starr 1848-1911, Brooks
1911-1913. Includes the area east of the above described
Zapata County line, south of a west extension of the
present north boundary of Brooks County and west of the
Starr-Cameron line of 1848 which ran northeast from a
point about 4 miles west of the present southeast corner
of Jim Hogg County.
Area C: Nueces 1846-1876, Duval 1876-1913. Includes the
area in the north offset taken from Duval County.
Area D: Nueces 1846-1848, Cameron 1848-1852, Hidalgo 1852-
1870, Starr 1870- 1913. Includes a strip about 3 miles
wide and lying east of the Starr-Cameron County line
described above.

Records available:

Deeds since 1913, marriages since 1913, probates since
1913, District Court minutes since 1913.

JIM WELLS   Alice   78332   Created   3-25-1911
                                  -1459   Organized   -1911

Parent county or territory: Nueces.

Records in:
    Entire county records prior to
    1846 may be found in Mexican
    Municipalities of Guerrero,
    Mier, Camargo, Reynosa or
    Matamoros.
    Area A: Nueces 1846-1911.
    Includes most of the county
    except Areas B and C.
    Area B: Nueces 1846-1856, Live
    Oak 1856-1863, Nueces 1863-1911.
    Includes the area lying northwest
    of a southwest extension of the
    present Live Oak-San Patricio
    County line, being the area
    included in Live Oak County in 1856.
    Area C: Nueces 1846-1848, Cameron 1848-1852, Hidalgo 1852-
    1870, Nueces 1870-1911. Includes a strip from 4 to 6
    miles wide across the extreme south end of the county.

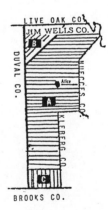

Records available:
    Deeds since 1911, marriages since 1911, probates since
    1911, District Court minutes since 1911.

COUNTY PRONUNCIATION	COUNTY SEAT	ZIP	DATE CREATED DATE ORGANIZED

==

JOHNSON	Cleburne	76031	Created	2-13-1854
	Klee'burn	-0662	Organized	8-07-1854

Parent county or territory: Hill, Ellis, McLennan.

Records in:
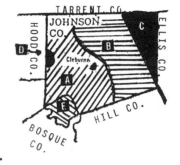

    Area A: Austin 1831-1834, Milam 1834-1838, Robertson 1838-1846, Navarro 1846-1853, Hill 1853-1854. Includes the area west of the Brazos-Trinity divide and east of the Brazos River except Area E.

    Area B: Nacogdoches 1831-1838, Robertson 1838-1846, Navarro 1846-1853, Hill 1854-1854. Includes the area east of the Brazos-Trinity divide except Area C.

    Area C: Nacogdoches 1831-1838, Robertson 1838-1846, Navarro 1846-1850, Ellis 1850-1871. Includes the area east of a northwest extension of the present Hill-Ellis County line.

    Area D: Austin 1831-1834, Milam 1834-1850, McLennan 1850-1854, Bosque 1854. Includes area west of the Brazos River.

    Area E: Austin 1831-1834, Milam 1834-1838, Robertson 1838-1846, Navarro 1846-1853, Hill 1853-1881. Includes the area along the Brazos River adjacent to Hill County.

Records available:
    Deeds since 1850, marriages since 1854, probates since 1950, District Court minutes since 1856.

Milam County records destroyed by fire in 1874.

JONES	Anson	79501	Created	2-01-1858
		-4396	Organized	6-13-1881

Parent county or territory: Bexar, Bosque.

Records in:
    Area A: Bexar 1831-1858, Young 1858-1860, Palo Pinto 1868-1876, Shackelford 1876-1881. Includes the area north of the Clear Fork of the Brazos River.

(continued)

Area B: Bexar 1831-1837, Milam
1837-1859, McLennan 1850-1854,
Bosque 1854-1858, Young 1858-
1860, Palo Pinto 1860-1876,
Shackelford 1876-1881. Includes
the area south of the Clear Fork
of the Brazos River.

Records available:
  Deeds since 1876, marriages since
  1881, probates since 1881,
  District Court minutes since 1881.

All Milam County records destroyed by fire in April 1874.

KARNES   Karnes City   78118   Created   2-04-1854
                               -2959   Organized   2-27-1854

Parent county or territory: Bexar, San Patricio, Goliad,
                            DeWitt.

Records in:
  Area A: Bexar 1782-1834, San
  Patricio 1834-1838, Bexar 1838-
  1857. Includes the area northwest of an extension of the
  Atascosa-Live Oak County line.
  Area B: Bexar 1782-1834, San
  Patricio 1834-1857. Includes
  the area southeast of said
  county line extension and west
  of U. S. Highway 181.
  Area C: Goliad 1829-1857.
Includes the area southeast of Karnes City along both
sides of the San Antonio River.
Area D: Goliad 1829-1846, DeWitt 1846-1854. Includes a
strip about 4 miles wide adjoining present southwest line
of DeWitt County and northeast of Runge, Texas.

Records available:
  Deeds since 1855, marriages since 1865, probates since
  1865, District Court minutes since 1858, naturalization
  record 1887-1906, final record 1854-1870.

```
COUNTY           COUNTY SEAT    ZIP      DATE CREATED
PRONUNCIATION                            DATE ORGANIZED
=========================================================
```

```
KAUFMAN          Kaufman        75142    Created      1-26-1848
                                -9998    Organized    8-07-1848
```

Parent county or territory: Henderson.

Records in:
  Area A: Nacogdoches 1831-1846,
  Henderson 1846-1848. Includes
  the territory north of a line
  running northeast from a point
  8 miles down the Trinity River
  on a due course from the southeast corner of Dallas County, to
  a point due east of the southeast
  corner of Dallas County, and then
  due east to the present eastern
  line of Kaufman County.
  Area B: Nacogdoches 1831-1846,
  Henderson 1846-1850. Includes the area south of the above
  described line.

Records available:
  Deeds since 1849, marriages since 1849, probates since
  1849, naturalization and declaration papers 1892-1893,
  District Court minutes since 1849.

```
KENDALL          Boerne         78006    Created      1-10-1862
                 Burn'e         -0806    Organized    1-18-1862
```

Parent county or territory: Kerr, Blanco.

Records in:
  Area A: Bexar 1787-1856, Kerr
  1856-1862. Includes the area
  taken from Kerr County, being
  most of the county.
  Area B: Bexar 1787-1838, Bastrop
  1838-1849, Travis 1840-1846,
  Comal 1846-1858, Blanco 1858-
  1862. Includes the area north
  of the Guadalupe River and east
  of the old Travis-Bexar line,
  which ran southwest from the
  present southeast corner of Gillespie County.
  Area C: Bexar 1787-1846, Comal 1846-1858, Blanco 1858-
  1862. Includes area south of the Guadalupe River adjacent
  to Comal County.

(continued)

```
COUNTY           COUNTY SEAT    ZIP       DATE CREATED
PRONUNCIATION                             DATE ORGANIZED
========================================================================
```

Records available:
   Deeds since 1862, marriages since 1862, probates since
   1862, District Court minutes since 1869, index to
   naturalizations 1876-1906, declaration records 1904-1906.

All Blanco County records destroyed by fire in 1876.

```
KENEDY           Sarita         78385     Created      3-11-1911
                 Suh reet'ah    -9998     Organized        -1911
```
(Created under the name of Willacy and re-created as Kenedy
county on April 1, 1921)

Parent county or territory: Cameron, Hidalgo.

Records in:
   Some records for entire county
   prior to 1846, may be found in
   the Municipalities of Reynosa or
   Matamoros.
   Area A: Nueces 1846-1848, Cameron
   1848-1911. Includes all of the
   county except Area B.
   Area B: Nueces 1846-1848, Cameron
   1848-1852, Hidalgo 1852-1911.
   Includes that part of
   the county taken from Hidalgo
   County, being approximately the west 8 miles of the
   county.

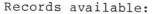

Records available:
   Deeds since 1911, marriages since
   1911, probates since 1911,
   District Court minutes since 1811.

```
KENT             Jayton         79528     Created      8-21-1876
                 Jay' tn        -9998     Organized   11-08-1892
```

Parent county or territory: Young.

Records in:
   Bexar 1831-1854, Cooke 1854-1858, Young 1858-1881,
   Throckmorton 1881-1883, Mitchell 1883-1885, Scurry 1885-
   1892.

Records available:
   Deeds since 1884, marriages since 1892, probates since
   1892, District Court minutes since 1892.

- 118 -

```
COUNTY              COUNTY SEAT    ZIP      DATE CREATED
PRONUNCIATION                               DATE ORGANIZED
==========================================================

KERR                Kerrville      78028    Created      1-26-1856
                                   -5389    Organized    3-22-1856

Parent county or territory: Bexar.

Records in:
    Bexar prior to 1856.

Records available:
    Deeds since 1856, marriages since 1856, probates since
    1857, District Court minutes since 1856.
-----------------------------------------------------------

KIMBLE              Junction       76849    Created      1-22-1858
                    Juhngk'shn     -4798    Organized    1-03-1876

Parent county or territory: Bexar.
```

Records in:
    Area A: Bexar 1831-1860,
Gillespie 1860-1876. Includes
all the county except Area B.
Area B: Bexar 1831-1834, Bastrop
1834-1837, Bexar 1837-1860,
Gillespie 1860-1876. Includes
the area east of the main Llano
River (below Junction) and north
of the old Mina line, which ran
southeast from the junction of
the North and South Llano Rivers.

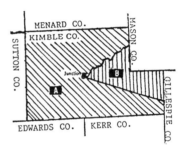

Records available:
    Deeds since 1884, marriages since 1884, probates since
    1884, District Court minutes since 1884.

Kimble County records 1876-1884 destroyed by fire.

```
KING                Guthrie        79236    Created      8-21-1876
                    Guhth'ree      -9998    Organized    6-25-1891

Parent county or territory: Young.

Records in:
    Fannin 1838-1846, Grayson 1846-1849, Cooke 1849-1858,
    Young 1858-1881, Baylor 1881-1887, Knox 1887-1891.
```
(continued)

Records available:
    Deeds since 1877, marriages since 1914, probates since
    1914, District Court minutes since 1914. Deed records
    1877-1914 are transcribed.

All records were destroyed by fire in 1914.

KINNEY   Brackettville 78832   Created   1-28-1850
                            -0009   Organized   -1873

Parent county or territory: Bexar.

Records in:
    Area A: Bexar 1846-1860, Ulvalde
    1860-1871, Maverick 1871-1873.
    Includes the area west of the
    west line of the "ghost county"
    of Dawson, which was a north-
    south line of 60 miles west of
    the present west line of Medina
    County.
    Area B: Bexar 1846-1858, Uvalde
    1858-1871, Maverick 1871-1873.
    Includes the area included in
    said "ghost county" which
    included approximately the east 16 miles of Kinney County.

Records available:
    Deeds since 1852, marriages since 1872, probates since
    1872, District Court minutes since 1873, declaration
    records 1887-1906.

KLEBURG   Kingsville   78363   Created   2-27-1913
Klee'burg   -9998   Organized   -1913

Parent county or territory: Nueces.

Records in:
    Nueces 1846-1913.

Records available:
    Deeds since 1913, marriages since 1913, probates since
    1913, District Court minutes since 1914.

    Prior to 1846 some records may be found in the
    Municipalities of Matamoros and Reynosa.

                                              (continued)

===

Records in a small area in the southwest corner of the
county south of a line northwest from the mouth of Olmos
Creek may be found in Cameron from 1848-1852 and in
Hidalgo from 1852-1870.

| KNOX | Benjamin | 79505 | Created | 2-01-1858 |
| | | -0196 | Organized | 3-20-1886 |

Parent county or territory: Cooke.

Records in:
    Fannin 1838-1846, Grayson 1846-1849, Cooke 1849-1858,
    Young 1858-1866, Jack 1866-1870, Young 1870-1879, Clay
    1879-1881, Baylor 1881-1886.

Records available:
    Deeds since 1886, marriages since 1886, probates since
    1886, District Court minutes since 1886.

| LAMAR | Paris | 75460 | Created | 12-17-1840 |
| | | -4265 | Organized | -1841 |

Parent county or territory: Red River.

Records in:
    Area A: Nacogdoches 1831-1835,
    Red River 1835-1840. Includes
    all the county except Area B.
    Area B: Nacogdoches 1831-1835,
    Red River 1835-1840, Lamar
    1840-1846, Hopkins 1846-1871.
    Includes a small area in the
    southeast corner lying north
    of the North Sulphur River,
    and south of a line running
    east from the present southeast
    corner of Fannin County.

Records available:
    Deeds since 1836, marriages since 1851, probates since
    1841, District Court minutes since 1887, index to
    naturalizations 1855-1925, declaration of intention 1907-
    1914.

Some damage to records by two minor fires.

```
COUNTY               COUNTY SEAT   ZIP      DATE CREATED
PRONUNCIATION                               DATE ORGANIZED
===============================================================

LAMB                 Littlefield   79339    Created      8-21-1876
                                   -3302    Organized       -1908
```

Parent county or territory: Young.

Records in:
   Bexar 1831-1854, Cooke 1854-1858, Young 1858-1876, Jack
   1876-1881, Baylor 1881-1887, Crosby 1887-1889, Hale 1889-
   1892, Castro 1892-1908.

Records available:
   Deeds since 1888, marriages since 1909, probates since
   1909, District Court minutes since 1909.

```
LAMPASAS             Lampasas      76550    Created      2-01-1856
Lam'pass us                        -9998    Organized    3-10-1956
```

Parent county or territory: Travis, Coryell, Bell.

Records in:
   <u>Area A</u>: Bexar 1831-1848, Travis
   1848-1856. Includes the area
   west of the Brazos-Colorado
   divide.
   <u>Area B</u>: Milam 1834-1850, Bell
   1850-1854, Coryell 1854-1856.
   Includes the area east of said
   divide except Area C.
   <u>Area C</u>: Milam 1834-1850, Bell
   1850-1858. Includes the area in
   the southeast corner lying southeast
   of an extension of the present
   Coryell-Bell County line.

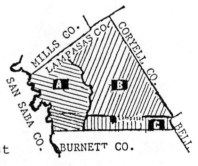

Records available:
   Deeds since 1851, marriages since 1856, probates since
   1856, District Court minutes since 1877.

Most Lampasas records destroyed by fire in 1875 and damaged
by flood in the 1880's.

Milam County records destroyed by fire in 1874.

```
LA SALLE             Cotulla       78014    Created      2-01-1858
                     Ca tulla'     -0340    Organized    11-02-1880
```

Parent county or territory: Bexar, Webb.

(continued)

Records in:
  Area A: Bexar 1831-1834, San
  Patricio 1834-1838, Bexar 1838-
  1860, Nueces 1860-1866, Live Oak
  1866-1870, Webb 1870-1871. Live Oak
  1871-1873, Webb 1873-1879, McMullen
  1879-1880.Includes the area
  northeast of the Nueces River.
  Area B: Webb 1784-1860, Nueces 1860-
  1866, Live Oak 1866-1870, Webb 1870-
  1871, Live Oak 1871-1873, Webb 1873-
  1879, McMullen 1879-1880. Includes
  the area southwest of the Nueces River.

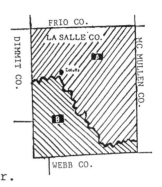

Records available:
  Deeds since 1880, marriage since 1880, probates since
  1881, District Court minutes since 1881, Records of
  declaration 1882-1906.

San Patricio records destroyed by fire in 1846 and 1867.

LAVACA   Hallettsville 77964   Created   4-06-1846
Luh va'ca   -0326   Organized   7-13-1846

Parent county or territory: Colorado, Gonzales, Fayette,
                            Jackson, Victoria.

Records in:
  Area A: Austin 1829-1836,
  Colorado 1836-1846. Includes the
  area east of the Lavaca River,
  south of a southwest extension
  of the present Fayette-Colorado
  line to the Colorado River, and
  north of the original line of
  Jackson Municipality which ran
  southeast of the mouth of Rocky
  (Smithers) Creek on the Lavaca
  River.
  Area B: Bexar 1787-1832,
  Victoria 1832-1837, Gonzales
  1837-1846. Includes the area
  west of the Lavaca River, east of the old upper La Bahia
  road, and north of the Gonzales line of 1837 which ran
  southwest from the lower corner of the Andrew Kent League
  #2 on the Lavaca River about 10 miles below Hallettsville
  to the crossing of the La Bahia road on the Guadalupe
  River about 3 miles below Cuero. The La Bahia road crossed
                                                  (continued)

the north line of Lavaca County about 3.5 miles east of
its northwest corner and ran southerly crossing the Lavaca
River about 2 miles below Moulton, passing about 3 miles.
east of Shiner, and crossing the southwest line of Lavaca
County about 3 miles northwest of Yoakum.
Area C: Bexar 1787-1832, Gonzales 1832-1846. Includes the
area north and west of the old upper La Bahia road except
Areas E and F.
Area D: Austin 1829-1836, Colorado 1836-1837, Fayette
1837-1854. Includes the area northeast of the Lavaca River
and northwest of a southwest extension of the present
Fayette-Colorado line to said river, except Area E.
Area E: Austin 1829-1834, Bastrop 1834-1836, Colorado
1836-1837, Fayette 1837-1854. Includes the area in the
northwest part of the county east of the Lavaca River and
west of La Bahia road.
Area F: Bexar 1787-1832, Gonzales 1832-1856. Includes the
area northwest of the present Gonzales-Lavaca line
extended northeast from the north corner of DeWitt County.
Area G: Austin 1829-1835, Jackson 1835-1846. Includes
the area east of the Lavaca River and south of the
original line of Jackson Municipality as described in
Area A.
Area H: Bexar 1787-1832, Victoria 1832-1837, Jackson 1837-
1844, Victoria 1844-1846. Includes the area west of the
Lavaca River, southeast of the Gonzales line of 1837, as
described in Area B, and northeast of the Jackson County
line of 1837 which ran southeast from a point on the
Gonzales line of 1837, six miles southwest from the Lavaca
River.
Area I: Bexar 1787-1832, Victoria 1832-1846. Includes the
the area southeast of the Gonzales line of 1837, and
southwest of Area H.

Records available:
  Deeds since 1846, marriages since 1847, probates since
  1846, naturalization minutes 1890-1906, District Court
  minutes since 1847, declaration of imigration 1882-1911,
  petition for naturalization 1906-1909.

COUNTY	COUNTY SEAT	ZIP	DATE CREATED	
LEE	Giddings	78942	Created	4-14-1874
		-9998	Organized	6-02-1874

Parent county or territory: Burleson, Washington, Williamson,
                            Bastrop and Fayette.

(continued)

Records in:

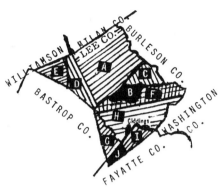

Area A: Austin 1829-1835, Milam
1835-1846, Burleson 1846-1874.
Includes the area north of the
old San Antonio road except the
area northwest of a southwest
extension of the present Lee-
Milam county line. Old San
Antonio ran northeasterly
bisecting Lee County.

Area B: Austin 1829-1835,
Washington 1835-1874. Includes
the area southeast of the old
San Antonio road, south of
Middle Yegua Creek, and northeast of the Brazos-Colorado
river divide.

Area C: Austin 1829-1835, Washington 1835-1840, Milam
1840-1846, Burleson 1846-1874. Includes the area
southeast of the old San Antonio road, and between Middle
Yegua and First Yegua Creeks.

Area D: Austin 1829-1835, Milam 1835-1848, Williamson
1848-1883. Includes the area northwest of an extension
of the present Lee-Milam line and east of the Brazos-
Colorado divide.

Area E: Austin 1829-1838, Bastrop 1838-1856, Williamson
1856-1883. Includes the extreme northwest portion of the
county west of the Brazos-Colorado divide.

Area F: Austin 1829-1834, Bastrop 1834-1838, Washington
1838-1874. Includes the area south of the old San
Antonio road and northeast of the Brazos-Colorado divide
which was included in the Municipality of Bastrop in 1834.
The Bastrop line of 1834 ran southeast from the present
corner of Lee County near Manheim, Texas.

Area G: Austin 1829-1835, Washington 1835-1838, Bastrop
1838-1856, Washington 1856-1874. Includes the small area
southwest of the Brazos-Colorado divide and northeast of
the Bastrop line of 1834.

Area H: Austin 1829-1834, Bastrop 1834-1856, Washington
1856-1874. Includes the area near Giddings southwest of
the Brazos-Colorado divide (excepting area G), northeast
of a southeast extension of the middle portion of the e
present southwest line of Lee County and northwest of a
northeast extension of the present Bastrop-Fayette line.

(continued)

COUNTY PRONUNCIATION	COUNTY SEAT	ZIP	DATE CREATED DATE ORGANIZED

===

Area I: Austin 1829-1834, Bastrop 1834-1874. Includes the area southwest of a southeast extension of the middle portion of the present southwest line of Lee County, and northwest of a northeast extension of the present Bastrop-Fayette line.

Area J: Austin 1829-1934, Bastrop 1834-1838, Fayette 1838-1874. Includes the area southeast of a northeast extension of the present Bastrop-Fayette line and southwest of the Brazos-Colorado divide.

Records available:
Deeds since 1874, marriages since 1874, probates since 1874, naturalization records 1891-1906, records of declaration 1890-1906, District Court minutes since 1874.

Milam County records destroyed by fire in April 1874.

LEON	Centerville	75833 -9998	Created 3-17-1846 Organized 7-13-1846

Parent county or territory: Robertson.

Records in:
Area A: Nacogdoches 1831-1838, Robertson 1838-1846. Includes the area east of the Navasota-Trinity river divide.
Area B: Austin 1829-1838, Robertson 1838-1846. Includes the area west of the Navasota-Trinity river divide.

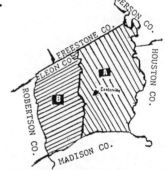

Records available:
Deeds since 1846, marriages since 1885, probates since 1846, District Court minutes since 1846.

LIBERTY	Liberty	77575 -0369	Created -1831 Organized -1831

(The Municipality of Liberty was organized in 1831 and the county in 1837)

Parent county or territory: old Mexican Municipality.

Records in:
Liberty since 1831.

(continued)

- 126 -

Records available:
Deeds since 1875, marriages since 1875, probates since 1873, District Court minutes since 1874.

Records from the area west of the Trinity divide went to Harris County for the period of December, 1835 to December 1837.

Liberty County records destroyed by fire in 1875 and damaged by storm in 1900.

```
LIMESTONE         Groesbeck      76642    Created      4-11-1846
                  Gross'beck     -1783    Organized    8-18-1846
```

Parent county or territory: Robertson.

Records in:
Area A: Milam 1834-1838, Robertson 1838-1846. Includes most of the county being the area southeast of the 1846 Limestone County line which was a southwest extension of the present Navarro-Freestone County line.
Area B: Milam 1834-1838, Robertson 1838-1846, Navarro 1846-1848. Includes the triangular area adjacent to McLennan County north of the Limestone County line of 1846 and south of the Navarro County line of 1848 which ran northeast from a point on the present southwest line of Limestone about one mile southeast from the west corner of said county.
Area C: Milam 1834-1838, Robertson 1838-1846, Navarro 1846-1850. Includes the area north of the Navarro County line and northwest of the Limestone County line of 1846 except Area D.
Area D: Milam 1834-1838, Robertson 1838-1846, Navarro 1846-1858. Includes the area adjacent to Navarro County lying northwest of the Limestone County line of 1846 and northeast of a line running northwest from a point about 1-1/2 miles west of Datura, Texas.

Records available:
Index to deeds since 1833, deeds since 1877, marriages since 1873, probates since 1874, District Court minutes since 1870.

(continued)

Limestone County records completely destroyed by fire in
1873.

Milam County records destroyed by fire in April 1874; but a
few records for this area prior to 1834 may be found in
Austin County.

LIPSCOMB	Lipscomb	79056	Created	8-21-1876
Lips'come		-9998	Organized	6-06-1887

Parent county or territory: Clay.

Records in:
    Bexar 1831-1854, Cooke 1854-1860, Montague 1860-1873, Clay
    1873-1879, Wheeler 1879-1887.

Records available:
    Deeds since 1887, marriages since 1887, probates since
    1887, District Court minutes since 1887.

Records in Montague County 1860-1873 destroyed by fire.

LIVE OAK	George West	78022	Created	2-02-1856
		-9998	Organized	8-04-1856

Parent County or territory: San Patricio, Nueces.

Records in:
    Area A: San Patricio 1834-1856.
    Includes the area north and east
    of the Nueces River.
    Area B: Nueces 1846-1856.
    Includes the area south and west
    of the Nueces River.

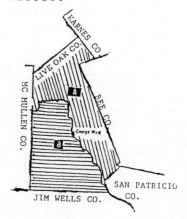

Records available:
    Deeds since 1857, marriages since
    1857, probates since 1860,
    District Court minutes since 1857.

All San Patricio records prior to 1848
destroyed by fire.

| COUNTY | COUNTY SEAT | ZIP | DATE CREATED |
| PRONUNCIATION | | | DATE ORGANIZED |

==

| LLANO | Llano | 78643 | 2-01-1856 |
| La'no | | -1998 | 8-04-1856 |

Parent county or territory: Bexar, Gillespie, Burnet.

Records in:
  Area A: Bexar 1831-1856.
  Includes the area north of the
  Llano River.
  Area B: Bexar 1831-1834, Bastrop
  1834-1837, Bexar 1837-1848,
  Gillespie 1848-1856. Includes
  the area south of the Llano
  River except Area C.
  Area C: Bexar 1831-1834, Bastrop
  1834-1840, Travis 1840-1854,
  Burnet 1854-1858. Includes an
  area about 4 miles square in the
  extreme southeast corner of the county.

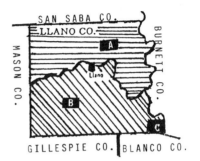

Records available:
  Deeds since 1880, marriages since 1880, probates since
  1880, District Court minutes since 1882.

Llano County records from 1856 to 1880 destroyed by fire

| LOVING | Mentone | 79754 | Created | 2-26-1887 |
| | Men tone' | -9998 | Organized | -1931 |

Parent county or territory: Tom Green.

Records in:
  Bexar 1831-1875, Tom Green 1875-1887, Reeves 1887-1931.

Records available:
  Deeds since 1931, marriages since 1931, probates since
  1931, District Court minutes since 1932.

| LUBBOCK | Lubbock | 79408 | Created | 8-21-1876 |
| | Luh'b k | -3424 | Organized | 3-10-1891 |

Parent county or territory: Young.

Records in:
  Bexar 1831-1854, Cooke 1854-1858, Young 1858-1881, Baylor
  1881-1887, Crosby 1887-1891.

(continued)

```
COUNTY            COUNTY SEAT    ZIP       DATE CREATED
PRONUNCIATION                              DATE ORGANIZED
==========================================================
```

Records available:
  Deeds since 1881, marriages since 1891, probates since
  1891, District Court minutes since 1891.

```
LYNN              Tahoka         79373     Created      8-21-1876
                  Tuh ho' kuh    -9998     Organized        -1903
```

Parent county or territory: Young.

Records in:
  Bexar 1831-1854, Cooke 1854-1858, Young 1858-1881,
  Throckmorton 1881-1883, Howard 1883-1884, Mitchell 1884-
  1885, Howard 1885-1889, Crosby 1889-1891, Lubbock 1891-
  1903.

Records available:
  Deeds since 1879, marriages since 1903, probates since
  1903, District Court minutes since 1903.

```
McCULLOCH         Brady          76825     Created      8-27-1856
                                 -4593     Organized        -1876
```

Parent county or territory: Bexar.

Records in:
  Bexar 1831-1860, McCulloch 1860-1879.

Records available:
  Deeds since 1874, marriages since 1876, probates since
  1876, District Court minutes since 1876.

```
McLENNAN          Waco           76703     Created      1-22-1850
                  Way'ko         -1301     Organized    8-05-1850
```

Parent county or territory: Milam, Navarro, Limestone.

Records in:
  Area A: Austin 1831-1834, Milam 1834-1850. Includes the
  area west of the Brazos River.
  Area B: Austin 1831-1834, Milam 1834-1838, Robertson
  1838-1846, Navarro 1846-1850. Includes the area east of
  the Brazos River and north of a line drawn northeast from
  the mouth of Aquilla Creek on the Brazos River.
  Area C: Austin 1831-1834, Milam 1834-1838, Robertson
  1838-1846, Navarro 1846-1848, Limestone 1848-1850.
                                              (continued)

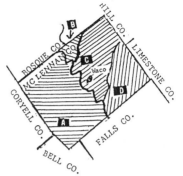

Includes the area east of the
Brazos river, south of Area B,
and north of a line drawn
northeast from the mouth of
Tehuacana Creek.
Area D: Austin 1831-1834, Milam
1834-1838, Robertson 1838-1846,
Limestone 1846-1850. Includes the
area east of the Brazos River and
south of Area C.

Records available:
    Deeds since 1850, marriages since 1850, probates since
    1861, Declaration of intentions 1887-1906, District Court
    minutes since 1851.

Milam County records destroyed by fire in 1874.

Limestone County records destroyed by fire in 1873.

McMULLEN   Tilden   78072   Created   2-01-1858
                   Til'd n   -9998   Organized   -1877

Parent county or territory: Bexar, Atascosa, Live Oak.

Records in:

    Entire county 1858-1877 in Live Oak.
    Area A: Bexar 1831-1834, San
    Patricio 1834-1838, Bexar 1838-
    1858. Includes the area north of
    the Nueces River, except Areas B
    and C, which were taken from Bexar.
    Area B: Bexar 1831-1834, San
    Patricio 1834-1838, Bexar 1838-
    1856, Atascosa 1856-1858. Includes
    the area in the northeast corner taken from Atascosa.
    Area C: Bexar 1831-1834, San Patricio 1834-1856, Live Oak
    1856-1858. Includes the area north of the Nueces River
    included in Live Oak County in 1856.
    Area D: Nueces 1846-1856, Live Oak 1856-1858. Includes the
    area south of the Nueces River and east of the Live Oak
    County line of 1856 which ran northwest from the present
    southeast corner of McMullen.
    Area E: Bexar 1831-1834, San Patricio 1834-1846, Nueces
    1846-1856, Live Oak 1856-1858. Includes the area south of
    the Nueces River and west of the Live Oak County line of
    1856 described above.
                                            (continued)

COUNTY   COUNTY SEAT   ZIP   DATE CREATED
PRONUNCIATION   DATE ORGANIZED
===

Records available:
   Deeds since 1877, marriages since 1877, probates since
   1877, District Court minutes since 1879, declaration
   records 1892.

San Patricio records for 1834-1848 were destroyed by fire
in 1848, but records for Area C for that period exist.

MADISON   Madisonville 77864   Created   1-27-1853
                          -1901   Organized   -1853

Parent county or territory: Grimes, Walker, Leon.

Records in:
   Area A: Austin 1829-1835,
   Washington 1835-1837,
   Montgomery 1837-1846, Grimes
   1846-1853. Includes the area
   west of the Brazos-Trinity
   divide.
   Area B: Nacogdoches 1829-1835,
   Washington 1835-1837,
   Montgomery 1837-1846, Walker
   1846-1853. Includes the area
   east of the said divide and
   south of the old San Antonio Road.
   Area C: Nacogdoches 1829-1838, Robertson 1838-1846, Leon
   1846-1853. Includes the area east of the said divide and
   north of the old San Antonio Road.

Records available:
   Deeds since 1873, marriages since 1873, probates since
   1873, District Court minutes since 1873.

MARION   Jefferson   75657   Created   2-08-1860
                          -2202   Organized   3-15-1860

Parent county or territory: Cass, Harrison, Titus.

Records in:
   Area A: Nacogdoches 1831-1835, Red River 1835-1840, Bowie
   1840-1846, Cass 1846-1860. Includes the area north of
   Big Cypress Bayou and Caddo Lake, except Area C and D.
   Area B: Nacogdoches 1831-1837, Shelby 1837-1840, Harrison
   1840-1874. Includes the area south of Big Cypress Bayou,
   except Area E.

(continued)

===

Area C: Nacogdoches 1831-1835,
Red River 1835-1840, Bowie
1840-1846, Titus 1846-1860.
Includes the area north of
Big Cypress Bayou and west of
a southerly extension of the
present Cass-Morris County line.
Area D: Nacogdoches 1831-1835,
Red River 1835-1837, Shelby
1837-1840, Harrison 1840-1844,
Bowie 1844-1846, Cass 1846-
1860. Includes the area north

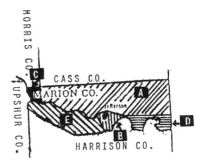

of Caddo and Ferry Lakes and south of
a line running east from the mouth of Big Cypress Bayou.
Area E: Nacogdoches 1831-1837, Shelby 1837-1840, Harrison
1840-1863. Includes the area between Big and Little
Cypress Bayous lying east of a line running southeast from
the northeast corner of the Alexander Johnson survey just
west of Jefferson.

Records available:
   Deeds since 1845, marriages since 1860, probates since
   1860, District Court minutes since 1860.

All Bowie records prior to 1889 destroyed by fire.

Titus records prior to 1895 destroyed by fire.

Shelby records destroyed by several fires, the last in 1881.

| MARTIN | Stanton
Stant'n | 79782
-9998 | Created   8-21-1876
Organized 11-04-1884 |

Parent county or territory: Young.

Records in:
   Bexar 1831-1858, Young 1858-1876, Shackelford 1876-1881,
   Mitchell 1881-1883, Howard 1883-1884.

Records available:
   Deeds since 1885, marriages since 1885, probates since
   1885, District Court minutes since 1885.

MASON   Mason   76856   Created   1-22-1858
                                -0702   Organized   8-02-1858

Parent county or territory: Bexar, Gillespie.

Records in:
   <u>Area A</u>: Bexar 1831-1858.
   Includes the area north of the
   Llano River.
   <u>Area B</u>: Bexar 1831-1834, Bastrop
   1834-1837, Bexar 1837-1848,
   Gillespie 1848-1858. Includes
   the area south of the Llano
   River.

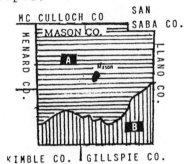

Records available:
   Deeds since 1877, marriages since 1877,
   probates since 1877, District Court minutes since 1877.

All Mason County records from 1858-1877 destroyed by fire.

MATAGORDA   Bay City   77414   Created   3-06-1834
Mat uh Gawr'duh   -0487   Organized   -1834
(Created and organized as a
Municipality in 1834; the county was organized in 1837)

Parent county or territory: old Mexican Municipality.

Records in:
   <u>Area A</u>: Austin 1827-1832,
   Brazoria 1832-34. Includes
   the area east of Tres Palacios
   Creek, west of Caney Creek,
   and south of Austin's 1st
   Colony line which followed
   the 10 Littoral League line.
   <u>Area B</u>: Austin 1829-1834,
   Matagorda 1834-1844, Jackson
   1844-1848. Includes the area
   west of Tres Palacios Creek.
   <u>Area C</u>: Austin 1829-1832, Brazoria 1832-1835. Includes
   the area east of Caney Creek and south of Austin's Colony
   as mentioned above.
   <u>Area D</u>: Austin 1827-1832, Brazoria 1832-1834. Includes
   the area west of Caney Creek, north of Austin's Colony
   line as mentioned above, and south of a due east-west line
   passing through the point where the present Matagorda-
   Wharton line crosses the Colorado River.

(continued)

- 134 -

Area E: Austin 1827-1832, Brazoria 1832-1835. Includes the area in the northeast corner of the county, north of the east-west line described above, except Area F.
Area F: Austin 1827-1832, Brazoria 1832-1846. Includes the area in the extreme northeast corner northeast of a line running northwest from the head of Linnville Bayou.

Records available:
Deeds since 1837, marriages since 1837, probates since 1837, District Court minutes since 1837, naturalization proceedings in Civil Court minutes 1837-1907.

| MAVERICK
Mav' rik | Eagle Pass | 78852
-9998 | Created
Organized | 2-02-1856
7-13-1871 |

Parent county or territory: Bexar.

Records in:
Bexar 1831-1866, Uvalde 1866-1871.

Records available:
Deeds since 1871, marriages since 1871, probates since 1876, District Court minutes since 1871, index to naturalization proceedings 1871-1924.

| MEDINA
Muh Dee'nuh | Hondo
Hahn'dough | 78861
-1897 | Created
Organized | 2-12-1848
8-07-1848 |

Parent county or territory: Bexar.

Records in:
Bexar prior to 1848.

Records available:
Deeds since 1848, marriages since 1848, probates since 1848, District Court minutes since 1849, all records of citizenship 1849-1909.

| MENARD
Muh nahrd' | Menard | 76859
-1028 | Created
Organized | 1-22-1858
5-08-1871 |

Parent county or territory: Bexar.

Records in:
Bexar 1831-1860, Mason 1860-1871.

(continued)

Records available:
  Deeds since 1860, marriages since 1871, probates since
  1871, District Court minutes since 1871.

All Mason County records from 1853-1877 destroyed by fire.

| MIDLAND | Midland | 79701 | Created | 2-21-1885 |
| Mid' lund | | -4512 | Organized | 6-15-1885 |

Parent county or territory: Tom Green.

Records in:
  Bexar 1831-1875, Tom Green 1875-1885.

Records available:
  Deeds since 1885, marriages since 1885, probates since
  1885, District Court minutes since 1886.

| MILAM | Cameron | 76520 | Created | -1834 |
| | | -9998 | Organized | -1834 |

(Created as the Municipality of
Viesca; named changed to Milam on December 27, 1835)

Parent county or territory: old Mexican Municipality.

Records in:
  Bexar 1731-1827, Austin 1827-1834.

Records available:
  Deeds since 4-22-1874, marriages since 1874, probates
  since 1874, old wills 1868-1875, District Court minutes
  since 5-19-1874, petition for naturalization 1906-1911,
  naturalization records 1882-1924, records of declaration
  1887-1906.

  Partial and scattered records from 1834-1837 may be found
  in Robertson County and Bexar County for the period 1731-
  1835.

Milam County records destroyed by fire in 1874.

```
COUNTY            COUNTY SEAT    ZIP       DATE CREATED
PRONUNCIATION                              DATE ORGANIZED
=============================================================

MILLS             Goldthwaite    76844     Created      3-15-1887
                  Gol'th wait    -0446     Organized    9-12-1887
```

Parent county or territory: Brown, Lampasas, Hamilton,
                            Comanche.

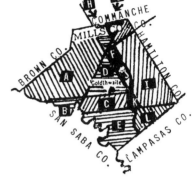

Records in:
  Area A: Bexar 1831-1848, Travis
  1848-1857, Brown 1857-1887.
  Includes the area north of a
  line due west from the present
  west corner of Coryell to the
  Colorado river (hereafter called
  Line 1) northwest of a line northeast from the mouth of Pecan
  Bayou (hereafter called Line 2)
  and southwest of a southeast
  extensionof the Brown-Comanche
  line (hereafter called Line 3).
  Area B: Bexar 1831-1848, Travis
  1848-1856, Lampasas 1856-1857, Brown 1857-1887. Includes
  the area south of Line 1 and west of Line 2.
  Area C: Bexar 1831-1848, Travis 1848-1856, Lampasas 1856-
  1858, Brown 1858-1887. Includes the area west of the
  Brazos-Colorado divide, south of Line 1, and north of a
  due east line from the mouth of Pecan Bayou (hereafter
  called Line 4).
  Area D: Bexar 1831-1848, Travis 1848-1858, Brown 1858-
  1887. Includes the area west of said divide, north of
  Line 2, and southwest of Line 3.
  Area E: Bexar 1831-1848, Travis 1848-1856, Lampasas 1856-
  1887. Includes the area west of said divide and south of
  Line 4.
  Area F: Bexar 1831-1848, Travis 1848-1856, Comanche 1856-
  1858, Hamilton 1858-1887. Includes the area west of said
  divide, northeast of Line 3, and southeast of a southwest
  extension of the present Hamilton-Comanche line (hereafter
  called Line 5.
  Area G: Bexar 1831-1848, Travis 1848-1856, Comanche 1856-
  1887. Includes the area west of said divide, northeast of
  Line 3, and northwest of Line 5.
  Area H: Milam 1834-1850, Bell 1850-1854, Coryell 1854-
  1856, Comanche 1856-1887. Includes the area east of said
  divide, and northwest of Line 5.
  Area I: Milam 1834-1850, Bell 1850-1854, Coryell 1854-
  1856, Comanche 1856-1858, Hamilton 1858-1887. Includes
  the area east of said divide and east of Line 3.
  Area J: Milam 1834-1850, Bell 1850-1854, Coryell 1854-
  1858, Brown 1858-1887. Includes the area east of said
                                                   (continued)

===

divide, west of Line 3, and north of Line 1.
<u>Area K</u>: Milam 1834-1850, Bell 1850-1854, Coryell 1854-1856, Lampasas 1856-1858, Brown 1858-1887. Includes the area east of said divide, south of Line 1, southwest of Line 3, and north of Line 4.
<u>Area L</u>: Milam 1834-1850, Bell 1850-1854, Coryell 1854-1856, Lampasas 1856-1887. Includes the area east of said divide, southwest of Line 3, and south of Line 4.

Records available:
  Deeds since 1887, marriages since 1887, probates since 1887, District Court minutes since 1887.

Milam records destroyed by fire April 1874.

Lampasas records destroyed by fire in 1875 and by flood in 1880's.

Brown County records were destroyed by fire in 1880.

MITCHELL   Colorado City 79512   Created   8-21-1876
                  Kah luh ra'duh 1166   Organized   1-10-1881

Parent county or territory: Young.

Records in:
  Bexar 1831-1858, Young 1858-1876, Shackelford 1876-1881.

Records available:
  Deeds since 1881, marriages since 1881, probates since 1881, District Court minutes since 1881.

MONTAGUE   Montague   76251   Created   12-24-1857
Mahn Tag'   -9998   Organized   8-02-1858

Parent county or territory: Cooke.

Records in:
  Nacogdoches 1831-1838, Fannin 1838-1846, Grayson 1846-1849, Cooke 1849-1858.

Records available:
  Deeds since 1873, marriages since 1873, probates since 1876, District Court minutes since 1873, declaration of intention 1907-1927.

Two fires almost destroyed all records prior to 1880.

```
COUNTY            COUNTY SEAT   ZIP      DATE CREATED
PRONUNCIATION                            DATE ORGANIZED
=======================================================


MONTGOMERY        Conroe        77301    Created    12-14-1837
                  Kahn' row     -2802    Organized      -1837
```

Parent county or territory: Washington, Harris, Liberty.

Records in:

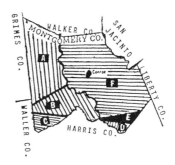

Area A: Austin 1827-1835,
Washington 1835-1837. Includes
the area west of the West Fork
of the San Jacinto River and
north of a line southwest from
the mouth of Lake Creek to the
head of Pond Creek.

Area B: Austin 1827-1835, Harris
1835-Jan. 1837, Washington Jan.
1837-Dec. 1837, Harris Dec. 1837-
Jan. 1840. Includes the area
west of the West Fork of the San
Jacinto River, south of the line southwest the mouth of
Lake Creek, and north of a due east line from the head of
Spring Creek.

Area C: Austin 1827-1835, Harris 1835-1840. Includes the
area west of the West Fork of the San Jacinto and south of
the due east line described in Area B.

Area D: Liberty 1831-1835, Harris 1835-1840. Includes the
area east of the West Fork of the San Jacinto and south of
the due east line described in Area B.

Area E: Liberty 1831-1838. Includes the area east of the
West Fork of the San Jacinto River and north of a northeast line from the mouth of Lake Creek.

Area F: Liberty 1831-1835, Harris 1835-1837, Liberty 1837-
1838. Includes the area east of the West Fork of the
San Jacinto River except Areas D and E.

Records available:
Deeds since 1838, marriages since 1838, probates since
1838, District Court minutes 1839 to 1841 and since 1845.

Liberty County records destroyed by fire in 1875 and damaged
by storm in 1900.

```
MOORE             Dumas         79029    Created     8-21-1876
                  Doo'mus       -0396    Organized   7-06-1892
```

Parent county or territory: Jack.

Records in:
Bexar 1831-1854, Cooke 1854-1860, Montague 1860-1873, Clay
(continued)

1873-1874, Jack 1874-1879, Wheeler 1879-1881, Oldham 1881-
1889, Potter 1889-1892.

Records available:
  Deeds since 1882, marriages since 1892, probates since
  1892, District Court minutes since 1892.

All records in Montague County 1860-1873 destroyed by fire.

MORRIS   Daingerfield 75638   Created   3-08-1875
                  Danger'field -1397   Organized   5-12-1875

Parent county or territory: Titus.

Records in:
  Area A: Nacogdoches 1831-1835, Red River 1835-1846, Titus
  1846-1875. Includes the area west of a southerly
  extension of the present Bowie-Red River line.
  Area B: Nacogdoches 1831-1835,
  Red River 1835-1840, Bowie 1840-
  1846, Titus 1846-1875. Includes
  the area east of said southerly
  extension.

Records available:
  Deeds since 1875, marriages since
  1875, probates since 1875,
  District Court minutes since 1875.

All Bowie records prior to 1889 destroyed
destroyed by several fires.

Titus records destroyed by fire in 1895.

MOTLEY   Matador   79244   Created   8-21-1876
Maht'lee   Mat'ah door   -9998   Organized   2-25-1891

Parent county or territory: Young.

Records in:
  Bexar 1831-1854, Cooke 1854-1858, Young 1858-1876, Jack
  1876-1881, Baylor 1881-1884, Donley 1884-1885, Hardeman
  1885-1887, Crosby 1887-1891.

Records available:
  Deeds since 1891, marriages since 1891, probates since
  1891, District Court minutes since 1891.

===

NACOGDOCHES   Nacogdoches   75961   Created   1-31-1831
Nack'o dough chess   -9998   Organized   -1831
(Created and organized as a Municipality
in 1831. The county was organized in 1837)

Parent county or territory: old Mexican Municipality.

Records in:
    Nacogdoches since 1831. Some records in Municipality of
    Nacogdoches 1831-1837 may be found in Nacogdoches County
    Archives.

Records available:
    Deeds since 1835, marriages since 1837, probates since
    1837, District Court minutes since 1837.

NAVARRO   Corsicana   75110   Created   4-25-1846
Nuh var'ro   Kawr see kan'a -0423   Organized 7-13-1846

Parent county or territory: Robertson.

Records in:
    Nacogdoches 1829-1838, Robertson 1838-1846.

Records available:
    Deeds since 1846, marriages since 1846, probates since
    1847, District Court minutes since 1855.

NEWTON   Newton   75966   Created   4-22-1846
                             -9998   Organized 7-13-1846

Parent county or territory: Jasper.

Records in:
    Area A: Liberty 1831-1835,
    Jasper 1835-1846. Includes
    the area south of Little Cow
    Creek and south of a line from
    said Creek to the mouth of
    Ayish Bayou on the present
    Jasper-San Augustine County
    line.
    Area B: Nacogdoches 1831-1834,
    San Augustine 1834-1835, Sabine
    1835-1837, Jasper 1837-1846.
    Includes the remainder of the county north of Area A.

(continued)

```
COUNTY              COUNTY SEAT    ZIP       DATE CREATED
PRONUNCIATION                                DATE ORGANIZED
============================================================
```

Records available:
    Deeds since 1846, marriages since 1846, probates since
    1846, physicians and naturalizations 1869-1909, District
    Court minutes since 1847.

Liberty County records destroyed by fire in 1875.

All Sabine records prior to 1876 destroyed by fire.

Jasper records destroyed by fire about 1850.

```
NOLAN             Sweetwater    79556    Created    8-21-1876
                                -9998    Organized  6-10-1881
```

Parent county or territory: Palo Pinto.

Records in:
    Bexar 1831-1858, Young 1858-1876, Shackelford 1876-1881.

Records available:
    Deeds since 1881, marriages since 1881, probates since
    1881, District Court minutes since 1881.

```
NUECES            Corpus Christi  78401  Created    4-18-1846
New a'sis         Kawr'pus Kris'te -3606 Organized  7-12-1846
```

Parent county or territory: San Patricio.

Records in:
    San Patricio 1834-1846.

Records available:
    Deeds since 1847, marriages since 1846, probates since
    1849, declaration records 1889, District Court minutes
    since 1850, declaration of intentions 1855-1906,
    naturalization and declarations 1855-1906.

    Prior to 1846, Nueces County was included in San Patricio
    County but actually was a part of Mexico.

```
OCHILTREE         Perryton      79070    Created    8-21-1876
Ah'kil tree                     -3154    Organized  2-21-1889
```

Parent county or territory: Clay.

(continued)

Records in:
   Bexar 1831-1854, Cooke 1854-1860, Montague 1860-1873, Clay
   1873-1879, Wheeler 1879-1889, Lipscomb 1889.

Records available:
   Deeds since 1889, marriages since 1889, probates since
   1889, District Court minutes since 1889.

Records in Montague County 1860-1873 destroyed by fire.

| OLDHAM | Vega | 79092 | Created | 8-21-1876 |
| | Vay'guh | -0009 | Organized | 6-12-1881 |

Parent county or territory: Jack.

Records in:
   Bexar 1831-1854, Cooke 1854-1860, Montague 1860-1873, Clay
   1873-1874, Jack 1874-1879, Wheeler 1879-1881.

Records available:
   Deeds since 1878, marriages since 1881, probates since
   1881, District Court minutes since 1881.

   Records in Montague County 1860-1873 destroyed by   fire.

| ORANGE | Orange | 77630 | Created | 2-05-1852 |
| | | -6353 | Organized | 3-20-1852 |

Parent county or territory: Jefferson.

Records in:
   Liberty and Jasper 1831-1835, Jefferson 1835-1852.

Records available:
   Deeds since 1852, marriages since 1852, probates since
   1852, District Court minutes since 1852.

Liberty County records destroyed by fire in 1875 and
damaged by storm in 1900.

Jasper County records destroyed by fire in 1850.

| PALO PINTO | Palo Pinto | 76072 | Created | 8-27-1856 |
| Paw'low Pen'toe | | -9998 | Organized | 4-27-1857 |

Parent county or territory: Tarrant, Bosque.

(continued)

===

Records in:
  Area A: Bexar 1831-1834, Milam
  1834-1837, Robertson 1837-1846,
  Navarro 1846-1850, Tarrant 1850-
  1856, Parker 1856-1857.
  Includes the area northeast of
  the Brazos River.
  Area B: Bexar 1831-1834, Milam
  1834-1850, McLennan 1850-1854,
  Bosque 1854-1857. Includes the
  area southwest of the Brazos
  River except Area C.
  Area C: Bexar 1831-1834, Milam 1834-1850, McLennan
  1850-1854, Bosque 1854-1860, Comanche 1860-1866. Includes
  a strip 2-1/4 miles wide taken from Eastland County on
  November 2, 1866.

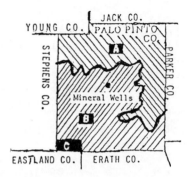

Records available:
  Deeds since 1858, marriages since 1858, probates since
  1858, District Court minutes since 1858.

Milam County records destroyed by fire April, 1874.

Tarrant County records destroyed by fires in 1864 and
1869.

Parker County records destroyed by fire in 1874.

| PANOLA | Carthage | 75633 | Created | 5-04-1846 |
| Pan o'la | | -2687 | Organized | 9- -1846 |

Parent county or territory: Rusk, Harrison.

Records in:
  Area A: Nacogdoches 1831-1834,
  San Augustine 1834-1835, Shelby
  1835-1840, Harrison 1840-1844,
  Rusk 1844-1846. Includes the
  area west of a due north line
  from the present northeast
  corner of Nacogdoches County.
  Area B: Nacogdoches 1831-1834,
  San Augustine 1834-1835, Shelby
  1835-1840, Harrison 1840-1846.
  Includes the area east of said
  due north line, west of the Sabine River, and northwest of

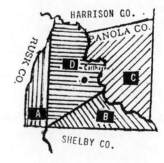

(continued)

a line drawn from the mouth of Murvaul Bayou on the Sabine
River southwest of the present northwest corner of
Nacogdoches County.
<u>Area C</u>: Nacogdoches 1831-1837, Shelby 1837-1840, Harrison
1840-1846. Includes the area east of the Sabine River.
<u>Area D</u>: Nacogdoches 1831-1834, San Augustine 1834-1835,
Shelby 1835-1841, Harrison 1841-1846. Includes the area
west of the Sabine River, excluding Areas A and B.

Records available:
    Deeds since 1846, marriages since 1846, probates since
    1846, District Court minutes since 1845.

    Panola County created in 1841 but declared illegal in 1845
    and re-created in 1846. Records from entire county from
    1841-1846 may have reverted to Harrison County.

Shelby County records destroyed by fires, the last in 1881.

PARKER   Weatherford   76086   Created   12-12-1855
                                 -4304   Organized   3-11-1856

Parent county or territory: Tarrant, Bosque.

Records in:
    <u>Area A</u>: Nacogdoches 1831-1834,
    Milam 1834-1837, Robertson
    1837-1846, Navarro 1846-1850,
    Tarrant 1850-1856. Includes the
    area northeast of the Brazos-
    Trinity divide.
    <u>Area B</u>: Bexar 1831-1834, Milam
    1834-1850, McLennan 1850-1854,
    Bosque 1854-1856. Includes the
    area southwest of the Brazos
    River.
    <u>Area C</u>: Bexar 1831-1834, Milam 1834-1837, Robertson 1837-
    1846, Navarro 1846-1850, Tarrant 1850-1856. Includes the
    area between the Brazos River and the Brazos-Trinity
    divide.

Records available:
    Deeds since 1874, marriages since 1874, probates since
    1874, District Court minutes since 1874.

Milam County records destroyed by fire April, 1874.

Tarrant County records destroyed by fires in 1864 and 1876.

- 145 -

PARMER   Farwell   79325   Created   8-21-1876
Pah'mer   -0356   Organized   -1907

Parent county or territory: Jack.

Records in:
   Bexar 1831-1854, Cooke 1854-1858, Young 1858-1874, Jack
   1874-1879, Wheeler 1879-1881, Oldham 1881-1891, Deaf Smith
   1891-1907.

Records available:
   Deeds since 1902, marriages since 1907, probates since
   1907, District Court minutes since 1907.

PECOS   Fort Stockton 79735   Created   5-03-1871
Pay'cuss   -1647   Organized   -1875

Parent county or territory: El Paso.

Records in:
   Bexar 1846-1866, El Paso 1866-1875.

Records available:
   Deeds since 1875, marriages since 1875, probates since
   1875, District Court minutes since 1875.

POLK   Livingston   77351   Created   3-30-1846
                                -3290   Organized   7-10-1846

Parent county or territory: Liberty, Houston.

Records in:
   Area A: Liberty 1831-1846.
   Includes the area south of the
   old Liberty-Houston line, which
   ran northeast from the present
   corner of Trinity and Polk
   Counties on the Trinity River to
   the mouth of Piney Creek on the
   Neches River.
   Area B: Nacogdoches 1831-1837,
   Houston 1837-1850, Trinity 1850-
   1875. Includes the area north of Area A.

Records available:
   Deeds since 1845, marriages since 1846, probates since
   1847, District Court minutes since 1848.

(continued)

==

Liberty County records destroyed by fire in 1875.

Houston County records badly damaged by two
fires.

POTTER   Amarillo   79101   Created   8-21-1876
            Am uh ril'o   -5250   Organized   9-10-1887

Parent county or territory: Jack.

Records in:
    Bexar 1831-1854, Cooke 1854-1860, Montague 1860-1873, Clay
    1873-1874, Jack 1874-1879, Wheeler 1879-1881, Oldham 1881-
    1887.

Records available:
    Deeds since 1876, marriages since 1887, probates since
    1887, District Court minutes since 1889.

Records in Montaque County 1860-1873 destroyed by fire.

PRESIDIO   Marfa   79843   Created   1-03-1850
Pruh sid' eo   Mahr'fuh   -9998   Organized   -1875

Parent county or territory: Bexar.

Records in:
    Bexar 1846-1866, El Paso 1866-1875.

Records available:
    Deeds since 1876, marriages since 1875, probates since
    1875, District Court minutes since 1876.

    All records from 1887-1897 from the strip 5 miles wide
    along the east line of Presidio County may be found in
    Brewster County.

RAINS   Emory   75440   Created   6-09-1870
                      -9998   Organized   12-01-1870

Parent county or territory: Wood, Hopkins, Hunt, Van Zandt.

Records in:
    <u>Area A</u>: Nacogdoches 1831-1846, Henderson 1846-1848, Van
    Zandt 1848-1850, Wood 1850-1870.

                                           (continued)

Includes the area east of a southward extension of the
present Hunt-Hopkins County line to the Sabine River
(hereafter called Line 1) and south of a westward
extension of the present Wood-Hopkins County line
(hereafter called Line 2).
Area B: Nacogdoches 1831-1840,
Lamar 1840-1846, Hopkins 1846-
1870. Includes the area east
of Line 1 and north of Line 2.
Area C: Nacogdoches 1831-1839,
Fannin 1839-1846, Hunt 1846-
1870. Includes the area west
of Line 1 and north of Line 2.
Area D: Nacogdoches 1831-1846,
Hunt 1846-1870. Includes the
area west of Line 1, south of
Line 2, and north of an eastward
extension of the present south line of Hunt County.
Area E: Nacogdoches 1831-1846, Henderson 1846-1848, Van
Zandt, 1848-1870. Includes the area west of Line 1 and
south of Area D.

The west half of Area E lying west of a north line 36 1/2
miles due east from the east line of present Dallas County
was included in Kaufman County from 1848-1850.

Records available:
  Deeds since 1879, marriages since 1880, probates since
  1880, District Court minutes since 1880.

Rains County records were destroyed by fire in late 1879.

RANDALL   Canyon   79015   Created   8-21-1876
                               -3890   Organized   7-27-1889

Parent county or territory: Jack.

Records in:
  Bexar 1831-1854, Cooke 1854-1860, Montague 1860-1873, Clay
  1873-1874, Jack 1874-1879, Wheeler 1879-1881, Oldham 1881-
  1883, Donley 1883-1887, Oldham 1887-1889, Potter 1889.

Records available:
  Deeds since 1878, marriages since 1889, probates since
  1889, District Court minutes since 1889.

Records in Montague County 1860-1873 were destroyed by fire.

==

| REAGAN | Big Lake | 76932 | Created | 3-07-1903 |
| Ray'gun | | -4515 | Organized | -1903 |

Parent county or territory: Tom Green.

Records in:
    Bexar 1831-1875, Tom Green 1875-1903.

Records available:
    Deeds since 1902, marriages since 1902, probates since
    1902, District Court minutes since 1902.

| REAL | Leakey | 78873 | Created | 4-03-1913 |
| Ree all' | Lake'e | -0656 | Organized | -1913 |

Parent county or territory: Edwards, Kerr, Bandera.

Records in:
    Area A: Bexar 1831-1860, Bandera
    1860-1861, Uvalde 1861-1866,
    Bandera 1866-1870, Kerr 1870-
    1883, Edwards 1883-1913.
    Includes the area west of a
    southern extension of the
    western most line of Kerr
    County.
    Area B: Bexar 1831-1856, Kerr
    1856-1913. Includes the area
    northeast of an extension of the south and western most
    lines of Kerr County to a corner.
    Area C: Bexar 1831-1854, Bandera 1854-1913. Includes the
    area east of a southern extension of the western most line
    of Kerr County excluding Area B.

Records available:
    Deeds since 1913, marriages since 1913, probates since
    1913, District Court minutes since 1913.

| RED RIVER | Clarksville | 75426 | Created | 11-11-1835 |
| | | -0749 | Organized | -1835 |

(Created and organized as a Municipality.
The county was created 3-17-1836 and organized in 1837)

Parent county or territory: Nacogdoches.

Records in:
    Nacogdoches 1831-1835.

(continued)

Records available:
    Deeds since 1830, marriages since 1845, probates since
    1838, mustering out records 1861-1867, District Court
    minutes since 1844, naturalization records 1908-1927.

```
REEVES            Pecos          79772      Created      4-14-1883
                  Pay'cuss       -0749      Organized    11-04-1884
```

Parent county or territory: Pecos County.

Records in:
    Bexar 1846-1866, El Paso 1866-1875, Pecos 1875-1884.

Records available:
    Deeds since 1884, marriages since 1884, probates since
    1884, District Court minutes since 1885.

```
REFUGIO           Refugio        78377      Created        -1825
Re fyou'rio                      -3151      Organized      -1826
```
(Created and organized as a Municipality.
The County was created in 3-17-1836 and organized in 1837)

Parent county or territory: old Mexican Municipality.

Records in:
    Refugio since 1826.

Records available:
    Deeds since 1835, marriages since 1851, probates since
    1840, District Court minutes since 1879, land grants to
    emmigrants 1840-1850, declaration of intentions and
    naturalization records 1854-1896.

Refugio records have suffered fire and hurricane damage.

```
ROBERTS           Miami          79059      Created      8-21-1876
                                 -9998      Organized    1-10-1889
```

Parent county or territory: Clay.

Records in:
    Bexar 1831-1854, Cooke 1854-1860, Montague 1860-1873, Clay
    1873-1879, Wheeler 1879-1889.

                                              (continued)

```
COUNTY          COUNTY SEAT   ZIP      DATE CREATED
PRONUNCIATION                          DATE ORGANIZED
================================================================
```

Records available:
    Deeds since 1889, marriages since 1889, probates since
    1889, District Court minutes since 1889.

Records in Montague County 1860-1873 destroyed by fire.

```
ROBERTSON       Franklin      77856    Created     12-12-1837
                              -0300    Organized        -1838
```

Parent county or territory: Milam.

Records in:
    Austin and Bexar 1827-1834, Milam 1834-1838.

Records available:
    Deeds since 1838, marriages since 1838, probates since
    1853, District Court minutes since 1838, records of
    declaration 1877-1903, minutes of final naturalization
    1901-1906, naturalization minutes 1892-1897.

    Some records relating to present Robertson County prior to
    1838 may be found in Austin and Bexar Counties.

All Milam County records destroyed by fire April 1874.

```
ROCKWALL        Rockwall      75087    Created      3-01-1873
                              -3796    Organized    4-23-1873
```

Parent county or territory: Kaufman.

Records in:
    Nacogdoches 1831-1846, Henderson 1846-1848, Kaufman 1848-
    1873.

Records available:
    Deeds since 1848, marriages since 1875, probates since
    1875, District Court minutes since 1888.

```
RUNNELS         Ballinger     76821    Created      2-01-1858
Ruhn'lz         Bal'in ger    -5726    Organized    2-16-1880
```

Parent county or territory: Bexar, Travis.

(continued)

Records in:
   Area A: Bexar 1831-1860, Brown
   1860-1876, Coleman 1876-1880.
   Includes the area west of a line
   running northwest from the
   junction of the Concho and
   Colorado Rivers.
   Area B: Bexar 1831-1848, Travis
   Brown 1860-1876, Coleman 1876-
   1880. Includes the area east of
   the above described line.

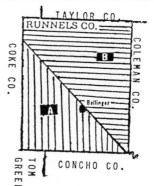

Records available:
   Deeds since 1876, marriages since 1880, probates since
   1880, District Court minutes since 1881.

All Brown County records destroyed by fire in 1880.

RUSK   Henderson   75652   Created   1-03-1844
                                -3147   Organized   -1844

Parent county or territory: Nacogdoches, Shelby.

Records in:
   Area A: Nacogdoches 1831-1844.
   Includes all the county except
   the small area in Area B.
   Area B: Nacogdoches 1831-1834,
   San Augustine 1834-1835, Shelby
   1835-1840, Harrison 1840-1841,
   Shelby 1841-1844. Includes the
   area north and east of Attoyac
   Creek.

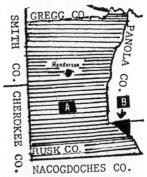

Records available:
   Deeds since 1843, marriages since 1843, probates since
   1847, District Court minutes since 1847.

Shelby County records destroyed by several fires, the last
in 1881.

SABINE   Hemphill   75948   Created   12-15-1835
Suh bean'   Hemp'hill   -0716   Organized   -1835
(Created and organized as a Municipality.
The county was organized in 1837 and was created in 1846)
(continued)

Parent county or territory: San Augustine, Nacogdoches.

Records in:
    Area A: Nacogdoches 1831-1834,
San Augustine 1834-1835.
Includes all the county south of
Patroon Bayou.
    Area B: Nacogdoches 1831-1835,
Shelby 1835. Includes the area
north of Patroon Bayou.

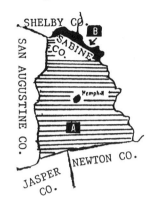

Records available:
    Deeds since 1876, marriages since
1875, probates since 1879, District
Court minutes since 1876.

All records prior to 1876 destroyed by fire.

SAN AUGUSTINE   San Augustine 75972   Created   3-06-1834
                              -1335   Organized   -1834
(Created and organized as a Municipality.
The county was organized in 1837)

Parent county or territory: Nacogdoches.

Records in:
    Area A: Nacogdoches 1831-1834.
Includes all the county except
Area B.
    Area B: Nacogdoches 1831-1834,
San Augustine 1834-1836, Sabine
1836-1837. Includes the area
lying east of Ayish Bayou and
south of a line from Big Prairie
on said Bayou northeast to the
south end of the north-south
portion of the present San
Augustine-Sabine County line running south from Shelby
County.

Records available:
    Deeds since 1833, marriages since 1837, probates since
1837, District Court minutes since 1837.

All Sabine County records prior to 1876 destroyed by fire.

| COUNTY | COUNTY SEAT | ZIP | DATE CREATED |
| PRONUNCIATION | | | DATE ORGANIZED |
==

| SAN JACINTO | Coldspring | 77331 | Created | 1-05-1869 |
| San Juh sin' toe | | -9998 | Organized | 12-01-1870 |

Parent county or territory: Polk, Liberty, Montgomery, Walker.

Records in:
Area A: Liberty 1831-1846, Polk 1846-1870. Includes the area bounded on the north by a line drawn from the present Polk-Tyler corner on the Neches River through the present Polk-Trinity corner on the Trinity River and extended southwest (hereafter called Line 1) and bounded on the west by a northwest extension of the present Montgomery-Liberty line (hereafter called Line 2) and bounded on the south by a west extension of the present Polk-Liberty County line.
Area B: Liberty 1831-1870. Includes the area east of Line 2 above and south of a west extension of the present Polk-Liberty County line.
Area C: Liberty 1831-1838, Montgomery 1838-1870. Includes the area west of Line 2 above and south of an east extension of the present Montgomery-Walker County line.
Area D: Liberty 1831-1838, Montgomery 1838-1846, Walker 1846-1870. Includes the L-shaped area north of Line 1 and north of an east extension of the present Montgomery-Walker line, and west of Line 2, except Area E.
Area E: Liberty 1831-1838, Montgomery 1838-1846, Walker 1846-1874. Includes a strip along the Walker County line lying west of a line drawn from the present Walker-San Jacinto corner on the Trinity River to a point on Peach Creek where the present Walker-Montgomery County line reaches said creek.

Records available:
Deeds since 1870, marriages since 1870, probates since 1871, District Court minutes since 1871.

Liberty County records destroyed by fire in 1875 and damaged by storm in 1900.

```
COUNTY           COUNTY SEAT    ZIP       DATE CREATED
PRONUNCIATION                             DATE ORGANIZED
=======================================================

SAN PATRICIO    Sinton         78387     Created    4-24-1834
San Puh trish'e o              -0578     Organized      -1834
(Created and organized as a Municipality)

Parent county or territory: Refugio.
```

Records in:
    Area A: Refugio 1825-1846.
Includes all the county except
Area B.
Area B: Refugio 1825-1834, San
Patricio 1834-1856, Live Oak
1856-1857. Includes the area
in the northwest part of the
county around Mathis.

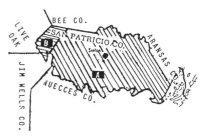

Records available:
    Deeds since 1846, marriages since
    1858, probates since 1847, District Court minutes since
    1848.

    Some records for the period 1827-1836 may be found in
    Bexar County.

San Patricio County records destroyed by fires in 1846 and
1867.

Refugio County records have been damaged by fire, hurricane.

```
SAN SABA        San Saba       76877     Created    2-01-1856
San Sah'buh                    -3608     Organized  5-03-1856
```

Parent county or territory: Bexar.

Records in:
    Bexar 1831-1856.

Records available:
    Deeds since 1857, marriages since 1857, probates since
    1857, District Court minutes since 11-02-1868.

District Court records destroyed by fire prior to 1868.

```
SCHLEICHER      Eldorado       76936     Created    4-01-1887
Shlye'ker       El duh ray'duh -0536     Organized      -1901
```

Parent county or territory: Kinney.

(continued)

```
COUNTY             COUNTY SEAT    ZIP      DATE CREATED
PRONUNCIATION                              DATE ORGANIZED
======================================================================
```

Records in:
    Bexar 1831-1875, Kinney 1875-1887, Menard 1887-1901.

Records available:
    Deeds since 1901, marriages since 1901, probates since
    1901, District Court minutes since 1892.

```
SCURRY          Snyder         79549    Created      8-21-1876
Skuh're                        -2581    Organized    6-28-1884
```

Parent county or territory: Young.

Records in:
    Bexar 1831-1858, Young 1858-1876, Shackelford 1876-1881,
    Mitchell 1881-1884.

Records available:
    Deeds since 1882, marriages since 1884, probates since
    1884, District Court minutes since 1885.

```
SHACKELFORD     Albany         76430    Created      2-01-1858
Shack'ul ferd                  -9998    Organized    9-12-1874
```

Parent county or territory: Bexar, Bosque.

Records in:
    <u>Area A</u>: Bexar 1831-1837, Milam
    1837-1850, McLennan 1850-1854,
    Bosque 1854-1858, Palo Pinto
    1858-1874. Includes the area
    south of the Clear Fork of the
    Brazos River.
    <u>Area B</u>: Bexar 1831-1858, Palo
    Pinto 1858-1874. Includes the
    two areas north of said stream.

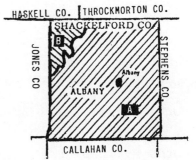

Records available:
    Deeds since 1872, marriages
    since 1874, probates since 1874,
    District Court minutes since 6-07-1875.

All Milam County records destroyed by fire April, 1874.

```
COUNTY              COUNTY SEAT    ZIP      DATE CREATED
PRONUNCIATION                               DATE ORGANIZED
===============================================================

SHELBY             Center         75935    Created    11-11-1835
                                  -0926    Organized      -1835
(Created and organized as the Municipality
of Tenehaw.  Shelby county was created in 1836 and organized
in 1837)
```

Parent county or territory: Old Municipality of Tenehaw.

Records in:

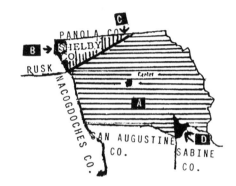

    Area A: Nacogdoches 1831-1834,
San Augustine 1834-1835.
Includes all the county except
Areas B, C, and D described
below.
    Area B: Nacogdoches 1831-1834,
San Augustine 1834-1835, Shelby
1835-1840, Harrison 1840-1841,
Shelby 1841-1844, Rusk 1844-
1845. Includes the area in the
northwest corner of the county
lying north of Attoyac Bayou
and west of a line drawn north
from the present northeast
corner of Nacogdoches County.
    Area C: Nacogdoches 1831-1834, San Augustine 1834-1835,
Shelby 1835-1840, Harrison 1840-1841. Includes the area
east of Area B and northwest of a line drawn from the
present northeast corner of Nacogdoches County to the
mouth of Murval's Bayou on the Sabine River.
    Area D: Nacogdoches 1831-1834, San Augustine 1834-1835,
Sabine 1835-1837. Includes the triangular area southwest
of Patroon Bayou and east of a north extension of the
north portion of the present Sabine-San Augustine County
line to intersect said Bayou.

Records available:
    Deeds since 1881, marriages since 1881, probates since
    1881, District Court minutes since 1882.

Shelby County records destroyed by several fires, the last
in 1881. All Sabine County records prior to 1876 destroyed
by fire.

```
SHERMAN            Stratford      79084    Created    8-21-1876
                                  -0145    Organized  6-13-1889
```

Parent county or territory: Jack.

(continued)

Records in:
    Bexar 1831-1854, Cooke 1854-1860, Montague 1860-1873, Clay
    1873-1874, Jack 1874-1879, Wheeler 1879-1881, Oldham 1881-
    1889, Potter 1889.

Records available:
    Deeds since 1875, marriages since 1889, probates since
    1889, District Court minutes since 1889.

Records in Montague County 1860-1873 destroyed by fire.

SMITH   Tyler   75701   Created   4-11-1846
                                   -7297   Organized   7-10-1846

Parent county or territory: Nacogdoches.

Records in:
    Nacogdoches 1831-1846.

Records available:
    Deeds since 1846, marriages since 1846, probates since
    1846, District Court minutes since 1846.

SOMERVELL   Glen Rose   76043   Created   3-13-1875
Suh'mer vel   -9998   Organized   4-12-1875

Parent county or territory: Hood.

Records in:
    Area A: Milam 1834-1850,
    McLennan 1850-1854, Johnson 1854-
    1866, Hood 1866-1875. Includes
    the area west of the Brazos
    River and east of the old
    Johnson County line, which ran
    northwest from a point on the
    present north line of Bosque
    County 8 miles from the Brazos
    River.
    Area B: Milam 1834-1838,
    Robertson 1838-1846, Navarro 1846-1853, Hill 1853-1854,
    Johnson 1854-1866, Hood 1866-1875. Includes the area east
    of the Brazos River.

(continued)

Area C: Milam 1834-1850, McLennan 1850-1854, Bosque 1854-
1866, Erath 1866, Hood 1866-1875. Includes the area west
of the old Johnson County line described above.

Records available:
Deeds since 1875, marriages since 1885, probates since
1875, District Court minutes since 1888.

All Milam County records destroyed by fire April 1874.

All Hood County records destroyed by fire in 1875.

STARR   Rio Grande City 78582 Created   2-10-1848
Star   Ree o Grahn'dee -2693 Organized   8-07-1848

Parent county or territory: Nueces.

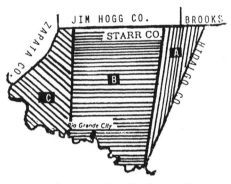

Records in:
Area A: Reynosa 1785-1846,
Nueces 1846-1848, Cameron 1848-
1852, Hidalgo 1852-1870.
Includes the triangular area
lying east of the old Cameron
County line which ran northeast
from the present southeast
corner of Starr County, and
which also was the approximate
line between the municipalities
of Reynosa and Camargo.
Area B: Camargo 1785-1846, Nueces 1846-1848. Includes the
central area lying west of the old Cameron County line
described above, and east of the old line between Camargo
and Mier, which ran northeast from the Rio Grande River.
Area C: Mier 1785-1846, Nueces 1846-1848. Includes the
area west of Area B being the area formerly in Mier.

Records available:
Deeds since 1848, marriages since 1858, probates since
1848, declaration records 1883-1902, District Court
minutes since 1848.

STEPHENS   Breckenridge 76024   Created   1-22-1858
                                 -3539   Organized   -1876
(Created as Buchanan County and name
changed 1861. Stephens County was temporarily organized but
soon lapsed)

(continued)

Parent county or territory: Bosque.

Records in:
   Bexar 1831-1834, Milam 1834-1850, McLennan 1850-1854,
   Bosque 1854-1860, Palo Pinto 1860-1876.

Records available:
   Deeds since 1854, marriages since 1876, probates since
   1876, District Court minutes since 1879.

No records of the temporarily organized county are in
existence.

STERLING   Sterling City 76951   Created   3-04-1891
                            -9998   Organized   6-03-1891

Parent county or territory: Tom Green.

Records in:
   Bexar 1831-1875, Tom Green 1875-1891.

Records available:
   Deeds since 1891, marriages since 1891, probates since
   1891, District Court minutes since 1891.

STONEWALL   Aspermont   79502   Created   8-21-1876
                  As'per mahnt -0614   Organized   12-20-1888

Parent county or territory: Young.

Records in:
   Fannin 1838-1846, Collin 1846-1849, Cooke 1849-1858, Young
   1858-1881, Throckmorton 1881-1883, Jones 1883-1886.

Records available:
   Deeds since 1887, marriages since 1888, probates since
   1888, District Court minutes since 1889.

SUTTON   Sonora   76950   Created   4-1-1887
Sut'tn   Suh no' rah   -0998   Organized   11-04-1890

Parent county or territory: Kinney.

Records in:
   Bexar 1831-1875, Kinney 1875-1887, Kimble 1887-1890.

(continued)

===

Records available:
    Deeds since 1890, marriages since 1890, probates since
    1890, District Court minutes since 1891.

SWISHER   Tulia   79088   Created   8-21-1876
                 Tool yuh   -2297   Organized   11-11-1890

Parent county or territory: Jack.

Records in:
    Bexar 1831-1854, Cooke 1854-1858, Young 1858-1874, Jack
    1874-1879, Wheeler 1879-1881, Oldham 1881-1883, Donley
    1883-1889, Hale 1889-1890.

Records available:
    Deeds since 1887, marriages since 1890, probates since
    1890, District Court minutes since 1890.

TARRANT   Fort Worth   76102   Created   12-20-1849
Tare'unt   -2101   Organized   8-05-1850

Parent county or territory: Navarro.

Records in:
    Area A: Nacogdoches 1831-1837,
    Robertson 1837-1846, Navarro
    1846-1850. Includes the area
    northeast of the Trinity River.
    Area B: Nacogdoches 1831-1834,
    Milam 1834-1837, Robertson 1837-
    1846, Navarro 1846-1850.
    Includes the area southwest of
    the Trinity River.

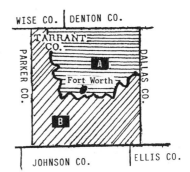

Records available:
    Deeds since 1876, marriages since 1876, probates since
    1876, District Court minutes since 1876.

Tarrant County records destroyed by fires in 1864 and in
1876.

```
COUNTY            COUNTY SEAT    ZIP       DATE CREATED
PRONUNCIATION                              DATE ORGANIZED
================================================================

TAYLOR            Abilene        79602     Created    2-01-1858
                  Ab'uh leen     -1582     Organized  7-03-1878
```

Parent county or territory: Bexar, Travis.

Records in:
  Area A: Bexar 1831-1858,
  Young 1858-1860, Comanche
  1860-1870, Palo Pinto 1870-
  1875, Shackelford 1875-1878.
  Includes all the county
  except Area B.
  Area B: Bexar 1831-1848,
  Travis 1858-1858, Young 1858-
  1860, Comanche 1860-1870,
  Palo Pinto 1870-1875,
  Shackelford 1875-1878. Includes the area south of the
  Brazos-Colorado divide and east of the old Travis County
  line which ran northwest from a point about 16 miles west
  of the present southeast corner of Taylor County.

Records available:
  Deeds since 1871, marriages since 1878, probates since
  1878, District Court minutes since 1879.

```
TERRELL           Sanderson      79848     Created    4-08-1905
                                 -4101     Organized     -1905
```

Parent county or territory: Pecos.

Records in:
  Bexar 1846-1866, El Paso 1866-1875, Pecos 1875-1905.

Records available:
  Deeds since 1906, marriages since 1905, probates since
  1905, District Court minutes since 1905.

```
TERRY             Brownfield     79316     Created    8-21-1876
                                 -4328     Organized     -1904
```

Parent County or territory: Young.

Records in:
  Bexar 1831-1854, Cooke 1854-1858, Young 1858-1881, Throckmorton 1881-1883, Howard 1883-1889, Martin 1889- 1904.
                                              (continued)

===

Records available:
    Deeds since 1880, marriages since 1904, probates since
    1904, District Court minutes since 1905.

| THROCKMORTON | Throckmorton | 76083 | Created | 1-13-1858 |
| | | -0698 | Organized | 3-18-1879 |

Parent county or territory: Bosque, Cooke.

Records in:
    Area A: Fannin 1838-1846, Collin
    1846-1849, Cooke 1849-1858,
    Young 1858-1866, Jack 1866-1870,
    Young 1870-1876, Shackelford
    1876-1879. Includes that part
    of the county northeast of the
    Salt Fork of the Brazos River.
    Area B: Fannin 1838-1846, Collin
    1846-1849, Cooke 1849-1858,
    Young 1858-1866, Jack 1866-1870,
    Young 1870-1876, Shackelford
    1876-1879. Includes that part of the county between Salt
    Fork and the Clear Fork of the Brazos River.
    Area C: Fannin 1838-1846, Collin 1846-1849, Cooke
    1849-1854, Bosque 1854-1858, Young 1858-1866, Jack 1866-
    1870, Young 1870-1876, Shackelford 1876-1879. Includes
    that part of the county south of the Clear Fork of the
    Brazos River.

Records available:
    Deeds since 1873, marriages since 1879, probates since
    1879, District Court minutes since 1879.

| TITUS | Mt. Pleasant | 75455 | Created | 5-11-1846 |
| | | -4447 | Organized | 7-13-1846 |

Parent county or territory: Red River.

Records in:
    Nacogdoches 1831-1835, Red River 1835-1846.

Records available:
    Deeds since 1895, marriages since 1895, probates since
    1895, District Court minutes since 1895.

Titus County records destroyed by fire prior to 1895.

```
COUNTY              COUNTY SEAT    ZIP        DATE CREATED
PRONUNCIATION                                 DATE ORGANIZED
================================================================

TOM GREEN           San Angelo     76901      Created      3-13-1874
                    San An'guh lo  -5850      Organized    1-05-1875

Parent county or territory: Bexar.

Records in:
  Bexar 1831-1875.

Records available:
  Deeds since 1869, marriages since 1875, probates since
  1875, District Court minutes since 1875.
-----------------------------------------------------------------

TRAVIS              Austin         78767      Created      1-25-1840
                                   -1748      Organized      -1840
```

Parent county or territory: Bastrop.

Records in:
  Area A: Bexar 1787-1832, Austin
  1832-1834, Bastrop 1834-1840.
  Includes the area north of the
  Colorado River and south of the
  north line of the Municipality
  of Mina (Bastrop), which line
  ran northwest from Elgin.
  Area B: Bexar 1787-1832, Austin
  1832-1836, Milam 1836-1838,
  Bastrop 1838-1840. Includes the
  two separate areas in the north-
  east and the northwest corners of the county lying north
  of the Bastrop line described above.
  Area C: Bexar 1787-1834, Bastrop 1834-1840. Includes the
  area south of the Colorado River.

Records available:
  Deeds since 1840, marriages since 1840, probates since
  1840, District Court minutes since 1840. Declaration
  minutes 1884-1906, Declaration intentions 1906,
  Naturalization records 1892-1903.

All Milam County records destroyed by fire April 1874.

```
COUNTY              COUNTY SEAT   ZIP      DATE CREATED
PRONUNCIATION                              DATE ORGANIZED
==========================================================

TRINITY             Groveton      75845    Created     2-11-1850
                                  -9998    Organized   4-01-1850

Parent county or territory: Houston.

Records in:
    Nacogdoches 1831-1837, Houston 1837-1850.

Records available:
    Deeds since 1873, marriages since 1876, probates since
    1876, District Court minutes since 1847, Index to
    naturalization 1886-1921, Record of declaration 1907-1925.

Trinity County records destroyed by fire in 1876.

Houston County records 1837-1850 destroyed by fire.
```

```
TYLER               Woodville     75979    Created     4-03-1846
                                  -5245    Organized   7-13-1846
(Created as the judicial county of Menard
on 1-22-1841.  Menard County was organized in 1843 and
functioned intermittently until the re-creation of Tyler
County in 1846)

Parent county or territory: Liberty.

Records in:
    Liberty 1831-1846.

Records available:
    Deeds since 1845, marriages since 1849, probates since
    1847, District Court minutes since 1847.

Liberty County records destroyed by fire in 1875 and
damaged by storm in 1900.
```

```
UPSHUR              Gilmer        75644    Created     4-27-1846
Up'sure             Gill'mer      -0730    Organized   7-13-1846

Parent county or territory: Harrison, Nacogdoches.

Records in:
    Area A: Nacogdoches 1831-1837, Shelby 1837-1840, Harrison
    1840-1846.  Includes all that area east of the Cherokee
    Trace except Area C.
```
                                                     (continued)

COUNTY   COUNTY SEAT   ZIP   DATE CREATED
PRONUNCIATION   DATE ORGANIZED
==

Area B: Nacogdoches 1831-1846.
Includes all that area west of
the Cherokee Trace except Area D.
Area C: Nacogdoches 1831-1837,
Shelby 1837-1840, Harrison 1840-
1846, Upshur 1846-1873, Gregg
1873-1882. Includes that area
east of the Cherokee Trace
and south of a line running
from the Marshall-Gilmer road
crossing of Glade Creek to the
northeast corner of Smith County.
Area D: Nacogdoches 1831-1846, Upshur 1846-1873, Gregg
1873-1882. Includes that area west of the Cherokee Trace
and south of the line described in Area C.

Records available:
Deeds since 1846, marriages since 1846, probates since
1846, District Court minutes since 1846.

Shelby County records destroyed by several fires, the last
in 1881.

UPTON   Rankin   79778   Created   2-26-1887
                            -0465   Organized   -1910

Parent county or territory: Tom Green.

Records in:
Bexar 1831-1875, Tom Green 1875-1887, Midland 1887-1910.

Records available:
Deeds since 1910, marriages since 1910, probates since
1910, District Court minutes since 1910.

UVALDE   Uvalde   78801   Created   2-08-1850
You'val de   -0284   Organized   4-21-1856

Parent county or territory: Bexar.

Records in:
Bexar 1831-1856.

Records available:
Deeds since 1856, marriages since 1856, probates since
1857, District Court minutes since 1857, records of
declaration 1884-1906.

(continued)

===

The creation of 2-8-1850 was of no practical effect since the county remained attached to the parent county of Bexar. Uvalde was re-created in 2-02-1856.

| VAL VERDE | Del Rio | 78840 | Created | 3-24-1885 |
| Val' ver'de | Dell Re'o | -9998 | Organized | 5-02-1885 |

Parent county or territory: Kinney, Pecos.

Records in:

    Area A: Bexar 1846-1875, Kinney 1875-1885. Includes all the county east of the Pecos River except Area C.
    Area B: Bexar 1846-1866, El Paso 1866-1875, Pecos 1875-1885. Includes the area west of the Pecos River.
    Area C: Bexar 1846-1860, Uvalde 1860-1871, Maverick 1871-1873, Kinney 1873-1885. Includes the area east of the Devils River and south of a west extension of the present north line of Kinney County.

Records available:
    Deeds since 1885, marriages since 1885, probates since 1885, District Court minutes since 1885.

| VAN ZANDT | Canton | 75103 | Created | 3-20-1848 |
| Van zant' | Can'tn | -9998 | Organized | 8-07-1848 |

Parent county or territory: Henderson.

Records in:
    Area A: Nacogdoches 1831-1846, Henderson 1846-1848. Includes the east part of the county bounded on the west by the following line: beginning in the Sabine River, thence due south to a point 36-1/2 miles due east from the present corner of Dallas County, thence due east 6-1/2 miles, thence due south to the south of the county.

(continued)

COUNTY   COUNTY SEAT   ZIP   DATE CREATED
PRONUNCIATION   DATE ORGANIZED
===

Area B: Nacogdoches 1831-1846, Henderson 1846-1848,
Kaufman 1848-1850. Includes the northwest part of the
county lying west of Area A and north of a line running
due east from the present southeast corner of Dallas
County.
Area C: Nacogdoches 1831-1846, Henderson 1846-1850.
Includes the area lying south of a due west line and west
of a due south line, both lines originating at a point 43
miles due east from the present southeast corner of Dallas
County.

Records available:
Deeds since 1848, marriages since 1848, probates since
1848, District Court minutes since 1848.

VICTORIA   Victoria   77903   Created   -1832
                               -6545   Organized   -1832
(Created and organized as a Municipality;
the county was organized in 1837)

Parent county or territory: old Mexican Municipality.

Records in:
Area A: Victoria since 1832.
Includes the area northeast of
Coleto Creek and northeast of
the Guadalupe River below the
mouth of said Creek, except Area D.
Area B: Refugio 1825-1846,
Includes the area between the
Guadalupe and San Antonio Rivers
lying southeast of the old
Goliad County line, which ran
southwest from the Guadalupe River
near the mouth of Coleto Creek so as
to coincide with the present Goliad-Refugio County line.
Area C: Goliad 1829-1861. Includes the area southwest of
Coleto Creek and northwest of the old Goliad County line
described in above in Area B.
Area D: Victoria 1832-1837, Jackson 1837-1846. Includes
a strip about 6 miles wide lying northeast of Garcitas
Creek.

(continued)

Records available:
  Deeds since 1838, marriages since 1838, probates since
  1838, naturalization book 1868-1870, records of
  declaration 1888-1894, declaration of intention 1896-1906,
  final naturalization record 1904-1906, District Court
  minutes since 1838, declaration of intention 1904, final
  naturalization 1879 and 1905, citizenship papers
  1849-1887.

Some records for Victoria County prior to 1838 may be
found in Bexar County records.

WALKER   Huntsville   77340   Created   4-06-1846
                                   -4601   Organized   7-16-1846

Parent county or territory: Montgomery, Houston.

Records in:
  Area A: Liberty 1831-1838,
  Montgomery 1838-1846. Includes
  the area southwest of the
  Trinity River, northeast of the
  San Jacinto River, and east of a
  line due north from the head of
  the San Jacinto River, which
  passes through a point about 9
  miles west of Huntsville.
  Area B: Austin 1829-1835,
  Washington 1835-1837, Montgomery
  1837-1846. Includes the area west of the above described
  line and southwest of the San Jacinto River, except Area D
  Area C: Nacogdoches 1831-1837, Houston 1837-1850, Trinity
  1850-1858. Includes the area northeast of the Trinity
  River.
  Area D: Austin 1829-1835, Washington 1835-1837, Montgomery
  1837-1846, Grimes 1846-1848. Includes a narrow strip just
  east of the present Grimes-Walker County line and lying
  west of the original Walker County line of 1846.

Records available:
  Deeds since 1846, marriages since 1846, probates since
  1846, District Court minutes since 1847, index to
  naturalization 1857-1920, records of intentions and
  naturalization 1888-1944.

Liberty County records destroyed by fire in 1875 and
damaged by storm in 1900.

| COUNTY | COUNTY SEAT | ZIP | DATE CREATED |
| PRONUNCIATION | | | DATE ORGANIZED |

===

| WALLER | Hempstead | 77445 | Created | 4-28-1873 |
| | Hem'sted | -9998 | Organized | 8-16-1873 |

Parent county or territory: Austin, Grimes.

Records in: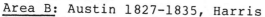

Area A: Austin 1827-1873.
Includes the area bounded on the
east by a line from the head of
Fish Pond Creek to the northeast
corner of the S. Isaacs league on
the Brazos River just north of
Richmond, and bounded on the
north by a line from the head of
Fish Pond Creek to the mouth of
Beasons Creek.
Area B: Austin 1827-1835, Harris
1835-1837, Austin 1837-1873. Includes the area east of
Area A and lying south of a line from the head of Fish
Pond Creek to the present northwest corner of Harris
County.
Area C: Austin 1827-1835, Washington 1835-1837, Montgomery
1837-1846, Grimes 1846-1873. Includes the area bounded on
the southeast by a line running from the head of Pond
Creek to the mouth of Lake Creek and bounded on the south
and west by a line from the head of Pond Creek to the
mouth of Beasons Creek.
Area D: Austin 1827-1835, Harris 1835-1836, Washington
1836-1837, Harris 1837-1840, Montgomery 1840-1846, Grimes
1846-1873. Includes the area bounded on the northwest by
a line from the head of Pond Creek to the mouth of Lake
Creek, and bounded on the south by a line from the head of
Pond Creek to the head of Spring Creek and thence due
east.
Area E: Austin 1827-1835, Harris 1835-1840, Montgomery
1840-1846, Grimes 1846-1873. Includes the area south of a
line running due east from the head of Spring Creek
(present northwest corner of Harris County).

Records available:
Deeds since 1837, marriages since 1873, probates since
1873, District Court minutes since 1873, declaration of
intentions 1874-1885, record of declaration 1884-1906,
naturalization records 1894-1906, record of successions
1873-1880.

```
COUNTY             COUNTY SEAT    ZIP      DATE CREATED
PRONUNCIATION                              DATE ORGANIZED
===========================================================

WARD               Monahans       79756    Created     2-26-1887
                   Mah'nuh hanz   -9998    Organized   3-29-1892

Parent county or territory: Tom Green.

Records in:
    Bexar 1831-1875, Tom Green 1875-1887, Reeves 1887-1892.

Records available:
    Deeds since 1893, marriages since 1893, probates since
    1893, District Court minutes since 1893.
----------------------------------------------------------

WASHINGTON         Brenham        77833    Created    10-16-1835
                   Bren'm         -0950    Organized     -1835

Parent county or territory: Austin, Bastrop.
```

Records in:
    Area A: Austin 1827-1835.
    Includes most of the county
    except Areas B and C.
    Area B: Austin 1827-1834,
    Bastrop 1834-1837. Includes
    the area in the extreme western
    portion of the county north-
    west of the La Bahia Road (the
    present road from Round Top to
    Burton) and southwest of the old
    line of Bastrop (Mina) which ran
    northwest from the point where Palmito Creek (West Fork
    of Mill Creek) crosses said road.
    Area C: Austin 1827-1842. Includes the area along the
    present Austin County line lying south of a line running
    due west from the head of Caney Creek.

Records available:
    Deeds since 1834, marriages since 1837, probates since
    1837, District Court minutes since 1837, naturalizatin
    records 1857-1913, final naturalization records 1887-1906.

```
WEBB               Laredo         78040    Created     1-28-1848
                   Luh ray'do     -9998    Organized   3-16-1848

Parent county or territory: Bexar, Nueces.
```
                                                    (continued)

Records in:

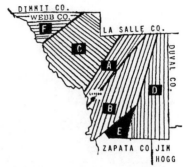

Area A: Municipality of Laredo
1784-1848, also Bexar 1838-
1848. Includes the area northwest of the Bexar-San Patricio
line of 1838, which ran from
Tilden to Laredo, and southeast
of the original northwest line of
Webb which ran northeast from the
upper corner of the Municipality
of Laredo on the Rio Grande
River near Delores.

Area B: Municipality of Laredo 1874-1848, also San
Patricio 1838-1846, Nueces 1846-1848. Includes the area
southeast of the 1838 Bexar-San Patricio line and northwest of the original east line of Webb County which ran
northeast from the Rio Grande River at the mouth of the
Salado River to the Nueces River, except a portion of Area
E described below.

Area C: Bexar 1831-1850. Includes the area northwest of
the original northwest line of Webb County (see Area A)
and southeast of the Webb County line of 1850 which ran
northeast from a point on the Rio Grande River 10 miles
above Palafox.

Area D: Municipality of Guerrero 1785-1848, also San
Patricio 1838-1846, Nueces 1846-1858. Includes the area
east of the original east line of Webb (see Area B) except
Area E.

Area E: Municipality of Guerrero 1785-1848, also San
Patricio 1838-1846, Nueces 1846-1848, Starr 1848-1858,
Zapata 1858-1870. Includes the area included in Zapata in
1858 lying south and east of a line beginning on the Rio
Grande River at the present Webb-Zapata corner, thence
northeast approximately 28 miles to intersection with the
orginal east line of Webb, thence southeast to the present
east line of Webb County.

Area F: Bexar 1831-1866. Includes the northwest
triangular area lying northwest of the 1850 Webb County
line described in Area C.

Records available:

Deeds since 1848, marriages since 1849, probates since
1871, District Court minutes from 1851-1853 and 1856-1862,
and since 1867.

The municipality of Laredo was created and organized in
1784 and functioned until 1848. Its jurisdictional limits
extended from the present Webb-Zapata corner of the Rio

(continued)

Grande River, up said river to the vicinity of Delores,
comprising Area A and most of Area B.

The "ghost" County of Encinal was created on 2-10-1858 but
was never organized and for all practical purposes was a
part of Webb County from the time of its creation.
Encinal County was bounded on the south, east, and north
by the present lines of Webb County and was bounded on the
west by a southward extension of the west line of La Salle
County.

WEGEFARTH   Never organized   Created   6-02-1873
                                       Repealed   8-21-1876
              Included portions of Wheeler, Gray, Donley, Hall,
              Collingsworth, and Childress Counties.

WHARTON   Wharton   77488   Created   4-03-1846
                             -5093   Organized   7-13-1846

Parent county or territory: Colorado, Jackson, Matagorda,
                            Brazoria.

Records available:
  Area A: Austin 1829-1836,
  Colorado 1836-1846. Includes
  the north part of the county on
  both sides of the Colorado
  River, bounded on the south by
  the following lines: beginning
  at a point where the 1844 line
  of Jackson County from the mouth
  of Smithers (Rocky) Creek on the
  Lavaca River to the common
  corner of the Alexander Jackson
  and Wm. Kincheloe leagues on
  the Colorado River at Wharton
  (hereafter called Line 1)
  intersects the present northwest
line of Wharton County, thence southeast along said Line 1
to the 1844 northeast corner of Jackson County (hereafter
called Point A and located about 5 miles west of Wharton),
thence southeast to an intersection with a line running
southwest from the mouth of Turkey Creek on the east bank
of the San Bernard River, thence northeast to said river.
  Area B: Austin 1829-1834, Matagorda 1834-1835, Jackson
  1835-1846. Includes the southwest part of the county
lying south of Line 1 and west of the original (1835) east
line of Jackson (hereafter called Line 2) which ran from a
                                              (continued)

- 173 -

COUNTY   COUNTY SEAT   ZIP   DATE CREATED
PRONUNCIATION   DATE ORGANIZED
==

point on Line 1 due south to the head of Tres Palacious Creek, at El Campo, and thence southwest to a point on the present southeast line of Wharton County about 2 miles from the south corner.

Area C: Austin 1829-1836, Colorado 1836-1844, Jackson 1844-1846. Includes the area south of Line 1, east of Line 2, northwest of a line running southwest from the mouth of Turkey Creek (see Area A), and west of a line running southeast from Point A (see Area A).

Area D: Austin 1829-1832, Brazoria 1832-1835, Matagorda 1835-1844, Jackson 1844-1846. Includes the area southeast of the line running southwest from the mouth of Turkey Creek, west of the line running southeast from Point A, and northeast of Tres Palacios Creek.

Area E: Austin 1829-1835, Matagorda 1835-1844, Jackson 1844-1846. Includes the area southwest of Tres Palacios Creek, and east of Line 2.

Area F: Austin 1829-1832, Brazoria 1832-1835, Matagorda 1835-1846. Includes the area on both sides of the Colorado River lying southeast of a line running southwest from the mouth of Turkey Creek and east of a line running southeast from Point A, except Areas G and H.

Area G: Austin 1829-1832, Brazoria 1832-1834, Matagorda 1834-1846. Includes the area east of Tres Palacios Creek and south of a line running due west from the point where the present Wharton-Matagorda County line crosses the Colorado River.

Area H: Austin 1829-1832, Brazoria 1832-1846. Includes the area along the San Bernard River south of the line running southwest from the mouth of Turkey Creek and east of a line running northwest from the head of Linnville Bayou.

Area I: Austin 1829-1832, Brazoria or Austin 1832-1835, Matagorda or Jackson 1835-1846. Includes the area along and near the present Jackson-Matagorda line and a northward extension of the same line which was not included in Areas B, C, D, and E. This particular area was shifted from county to county so often that the residents had no idea which county that they were in at any given time.

Records available:

Deeds since 1847, marriages since 1847, probates since 1848, District Court minutes since 1848, Index to naturalization records 1880-1936, Final naturalization records 1904-1906, naturalization petitions and records 1907-1919.

```
COUNTY              COUNTY SEAT    ZIP      DATE CREATED
PRONUNCIATION                               DATE ORGANIZED
=========================================================

WHEELER             Wheeler        79096    Created      8-21-1876
                                   -9998    Organized    4-12-1879
```

Parent county or territory: Clay.

Records in:
    Bexar 1831-1854, Cooke 1854-1860, Montague 1860-1873, Clay
    1873-1879.

Records available:
    Deeds since 1881, marriages since 1879, probates since
    1879, District Court minutes since 1879.

Records in Montague County 1860-1873 destroyed by fire.

```
WICHITA             Wichita Falls 76301    Created       2-01-1858
Witch'ah taw                      -2441    Organized     6-21-1882
```

Parent county or territory: Cooke.

Records in:
    Fannin 1838-1846, Grayson 1846-1849, Cooke 1849-1858,
    Young 1858-1860, Montague 1860-1873, Clay 1873-1882.

Records available:
    Deeds since 1873, marriages since 1882, probates since
    1882, District Court minutes since 1882.

Records in Montague County 1860-1873 destroyed by fire.

```
WILBARGER           Vernon         76384    Created      2-01-1858
Wil'bahr ger                       -4792    Organized    10-10-1881
```

Parent county or territory: Cooke.

Records in:
    Fannin 1838-1846, Grayson 1846-1849, Cooke 1849-1858,
    Young 1858-1860, Montague 1860-1873, Clay 1873-1883.

Records available:
    Deeds since 1883, marriages since 1881, probates since
    1882, District Court minutes since 1882.

Records in Montague County 1860-1873 destroyed by fire.

```
COUNTY            COUNTY SEAT    ZIP      DATE CREATED
PRONUNCIATION                             DATE ORGANIZED
==========================================================

WILLACY          Raymondville   78580    Created      4-02-1921
Will'ah c                       -3597    Organized        -1921
```

Parent county or territory: Hidalgo, Cameron.

Records in:
    <u>Area A</u>: Matamoros 1790-1846,
Nueces 1846-1848, Cameron 1848-
1921. Includes the area lying
east of a northern extension of
the present Hidalgo-Cameron
County line.
    <u>Area B</u>: Reynosa 1780-1846,
Nueces 1846-1848, Cameron 1848-
1852, Hidalgo 1852-1921.
Includes the area lying west of
a northern extension of the
present Hidalgo-Cameron County line.

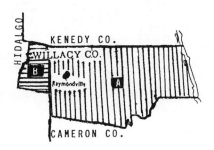

Records available:
    Deeds since 1921, marriages since 1921, probates since
1921, District Court minutes since 1921.

Matamoros Municipality records destroyed by fire.

```
WILLIAMSON       Georgetown     78626    Created      3-13-1848
                                -5846    Organized    8-07-1848
```

Parent county or territory: Milam.

Records in:
    <u>Area A</u>: Milam 1834-1850, Bell
1850-1853. Includes the area
northwest of a line drawn
southwest from the point where
the present Bell-Williamson
County line crosses Salado
Creek.
    <u>Area B</u>: Bastrop 1834-1838, Milam
1838-1848. Includes the small
area adjacent to Travis County
and south of the 1834 line of
Bastrop (Mina), which crosses Williamson County on a
course northwest through a point about 1 mile north of
McNeil.
    <u>Area C</u>: Milam 1834-1848.
Includes all the county except Areas A and B.

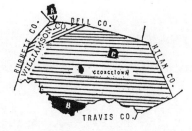

(continued)

Records available:
    Deeds since 1848, marriages since 1850, probates since
    1848, naturalization index 1875-1933, records of
    declaration 1891-1906, minutes of final naturalization
    1892-1906, District Court minutes since 1848, minutes
    of final naturalization 1891-1902, records of declaration
    1887-1906.

All Milam County records destroyed by fire in 1874.

WILSON   Floresville   78114   Created   2-13-1860
                    Floorz'ville -0027   Organized   8-06-1860
Wilson County was called Cibolo County
from 1869 to about 1874.

Parent county or territory: Bexar, Karnes, Guadalupe.

Records in: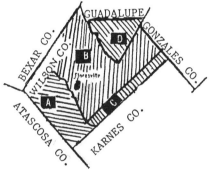
    Area A: Bexar 1787-1834, San
    Patricio 1834-1838, Bexar 1838-
    1860. Includes the area west of
    the San Antonio River.
    Area B: Bexar 1787-1860.
    Includes all the county except
    Areas A, C, and D.
    Area C: Goliad 1829-1854, Karnes
    1854-1860, (small southwest
    part of Area C was in San
    Patricio 1834-1838). Includes a
    strip 4-3/4 miles wide adjacent
    and parallel to the present
    Karnes County line.
    Area D: Bexar 1787-1846, Guadalupe 1846-1860. Includes
    the area northeast of Cibolo Creek and northwest of the
    present Guadalupe-Gonzales County line extended southwest
    of Cibolo Creek.

Records available:
    Deeds since 1877, marriages since 1860, probates since
    1862, naturalization records applications 1891-1906,
    naturalization and final papers 1891-1896, District Court
    minutes since 1884, naturalization records 1903,
    naturalization petition 1904-1924.

San Patricio County records destroyed by fire in 1846 and
1867.

Goliad County records destroyed in 1870 and since damaged by
storm.

```
COUNTY              COUNTY SEAT    ZIP        DATE CREATED
PRONUNCIATION                                 DATE ORGANIZED
===========================================================

WINKLER             Kermit         79745      Created      2-26-1887
                                   -9998      Organized    4-05-1910
```

Parent county or territory: Tom Green.

Records in:
  Bexar 1831-1875, Tom Green 1875-1887, Reeves 1887-1910.

Records available:
  Deeds since 1911, marriages since 1910, probates since
  1910, District Court minutes since 1910.

```
WISE                Decatur        76234      Created      1-23-1856
                    De Kay'tur     -0423      Organized    5-05-1856
```

Parent county or territory: Cooke.

Records in:
  Nacogdoches 1831-1838, Fannin 1838-1846, Collin 1846-1849,
  Cooke 1849-1856.

Records available:
  Deeds since 1855, marriages since 1886, probates since
  1852, District Court minutes since 1894.

Wise County records 1856-1881 destroyed by fire. Some
transcribed and re-recorded records exist for this
period.

```
WOOD                Quitman        75783      Created      2-05-1850
                                   -9998      Organized    8-05-1850
```

Parent county or territory: Van Zandt.

Records in:
  Nacogdoches 1831-1846, Henderson 1846-1848, Van Zandt
  1848-1850.

Records available:
  Deeds since 1879, marriages since 1879, probates since
  1879, District Court minutes since 1879.

Wood County records destroyed by fire in winter of 1878.

```
COUNTY              COUNTY SEAT   ZIP      DATE CREATED
PRONUNCIATION                              DATE ORGANIZED
=========================================================

YOAKUM              Plains        79355    Created      8-21-1876
Yo'kum                            -0309    Organized        -1907
```

Parent county or territory: Young.

Records in:
    Bexar 1831-1854, Cooke 1854-1858, Young 1858-1881,
    Throckmorton 1881-1883, Howard 1883-1889, Martin 1889-
    1905, Terry 1905-1907.

Records available:
    Deeds since 1900, marriages since 1907, probates since
    1907, District Court minutes since 1907.

```
YOUNG               Graham        76046    Created      2-02-1856
                                  -9998    Organized        -1858
```

Parent county or territory: Cooke.

Records in:
    Fannin 1838-1846, Collin 1846-1854, Cooke 1854-1858.

Records available:
    Deeds since 1858, marriages since 1858, probates since
    1858, District Court minutes since 1858.

    Between 1866-1870, Young County was attached to Jack
    County; some records for this period may be found there.

```
ZAPATA              Zapata        78076    Created      1-22-1858
Zuh pah'tah                       -9998    Organized    4-26-1858
```

Parent county or territory: Starr, Webb.

Records in:
    Area A: Guerrero 1785-1846,
    Nueces 1846-1848, Starr 1848-
    1858. Includes the area east
    of the original Webb-Starr
    County line which ran north-
    east from the mouth of the
    Salado River on the Rio Grande
    River near the present town of
    Zapata.
    Area B: Guerrero 1785-1846,
    Nueces 1846-1848, Webb 1848-

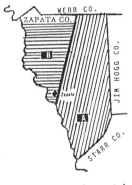

(continued)

==

1858. Includes the area west of the Webb-Starr County
line described above.
Entire county: Zapata 1858-1863, Webb 1863-1868, Zapata
1868-1870, Webb 1870-1887.

Records available:
Deeds since 1868, marriages since 1873, probates since
1895, District Court minutes since 1874.

Organization of Zapata functioned intermittently from 1858
until finally organized in 1887.

ZAVALLA   Crystal City 78839   Created   1-01-1858
Zuh vahl'a   -3590   Organized   2-25-1884

Parent county or territory: Uvalde, Bexar.

Records in:
Area A: Bexar 1831-1834, San
Patricio 1834-1838, Bexar 1838-
1856, Uvalde 1856-1860.
Includes the area east of the
Nueces River.
Area B: Bexar 1831-1860.
Includes the area west of the
Nueces River.
Entire county: Uvalde 1860-1870,
Maverick 1870-1871, Uvalde 1871-
1873, Frio 1873-1884.

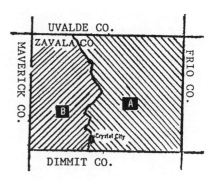

Records available:
Deeds since 1884, marriages since 1884, probates since
1884, District Court minutes since 1884.

San Patricio County records destroyed by fire in 1846 and
in 1867.

ADDITIONAL DEFUNCT COUNTIES

The counties listed below were created but never organized to the extent that records were created. Because they might be referred to from time to time in Texas history and be of interest to the researcher, these defunct counties are listed here. There are a number of other counties that once existed in Texas but are now defunct. They are listed elsewhere in this chapter because they remained in existance long enough to create records and the researcher needs to know where these records may be found.

BUCHEL   Created   03-15-1887
                                    Abolished   04-   1897

   Created out of Presidio County and attached to Brewster
   County for surveying purposes.

FOLEY   Created   03-15-1887
                                    Abolished   04-   1897

   Created out of Presidio County and attached to Brewster
   County for surveying purposes.

LATIMER

   Created by declaration of Constitutional Convention
   of 1868-1869. It was never organized or legalized
   by the Texas Legislature.

PASCHAL   Created   01-28-1841

   Created for judicial purposes, it included all of the
   present counties of Hopkins, Franklin, Titus, Morris, and
   Cass. It was abolished by Texas Supreme Court decision in
   1842.

NAVASOTA

   Created in 1841, it was renamed Brazos County in 1842.

SANTA FE   Created   03-15-1848

   Included practically all of the area of New Mexico claimed
   by the Republic of Texas and later by the state of Texas.
   In January 1850, Santa Fe was subdivided into Worth, El
   Paso, Presidio, and Santa Fe counties. On November 25,
   1850 Texas ceded to the United States (Compromise of
   1850) for 1 million dollars, her claims to the upper Rio
   Grande area. Worth and Santa Fe Counties became defunct.

SPRING CREEK   Created   01-25-1841

   Created for judicial purposes, it included parts of
   present counties of Grimes, Montgomery and Harris. It was
   abolished by Texas Supreme Court decision in 1842.

WACO   Created   01-29-1842

   Created for judicial purposes, it included all of Falls
   County. It was abolished by Texas Supreme Court
   decision in 1842.

WORTH   Created   01-03-1850

   Created out of Santa Fe County. On November 25,
   1850 Texas ceded to the United States (Compromise of
   1850) for 1 million dollars, her claims to the upper Rio
   Grande area. Worth and Santa Fe Counties became defunct.

CHAPTER 7

RECORDS AVAILABLE IN THE COUNTY COURTHOUSE

The county courthouse in Texas has a wealth of information for the researcher. Our desire is to guide you in your quest for this information by providing you with data on which department holds each kind of record. The Constitution of the State of Texas specifies the duties of each department of county government and which records they must maintain. Although the Constitution that sets forth these requirements was not enacted until 1876, most counties had already maintained vital records for many years and these records are available as indicated in Chapter 6, Formation and Organization of Counties.

COMMISSIONERS COURT

The Commissioners Court serves as the administrative body of the county. The court consists of four commissioners, two of whom are elected every two years, each for a four year term. The County Judge, elected from the county as a whole for a four year term, presides over Commissioners Court.

Two of the most important duties of the court are the setting of the tax rate and the approval of the county budget. Other functions of this court include the disposition of school lands; provide necessary government buildings and for their repair and maintenance; establishing and repairing roads and bridges; auditing and settling accounts for and against the county; providing for the support and care of paupers and mentally incompetent citizens of the county who are unable to support themselves; and to serve as a board of equalization of state and county tax assessments. The court has powers usually considered as separate since they include limited legislative power, and also judicial and executive powers.

While many duties of the Commissioners Court are assigned to various departments within the government, they are responsible to see that duties are carried out and records are maintained of these transactions.

COUNTY CLERK

The present constitution provides that the County Clerk shall

> be clerk of the County and Commissioners Courts and recorder of the county, whose duties, prerequisites and fees of office shall be prescribed by the legislature, and a vacancy in whose office shall be filled by the Commissioners Court, until the next general election. In counties with a population of less than 8,000 persons, there may be an election of a single clerk for both county and district courts.

Clerk as a Recorder:

During the time when Texas was a Republic, the statutory
duties of the County Clerk had, to a large extent, been
defined. The Clerk was to record all deeds, conveyances,
mortgages, and other liens on land; to record all estrays; to
issue and record all marriage licenses; to issue and record
various types of business licenses; and to post a list of
taxpayers. State laws enacted after 1846 also required the
Clerk to record deeds of trust, bonds, covenants, defeasances
and other instruments relating to property including marriage
contracts, powers of attorney, abstracts of judgement, and
land titles. He is also to record all livestock marks and
brands in the county and to provide an alphabetical list of
all names that appear in records maintained by this office.

Important: Any marriage record, if one exists, prior to 1836
is held by the Catholic Church. County clerks maintain
marriage records after this time.

Since 1903, the Clerk has been required to record all births
and deaths in the county, and since 1919, to record official
military service discharges.

As a result of laws enacted over the years, the duties of the
County Clerk have been increased to include the recording of
business and professional records, such as assumed name certificates; licenses for dentists, nurses, optometrists, and
mortitians; plats; reports of animals killed on railroad
rights of way; and condominium records.

Clerk of the County Court:

As Clerk of the County Court, the County Clerk has the duties
of recording all proceedings and preserving all books, papers
and effects of the Court. The County Court has original
jurisdiction over all misdemeanors (except those cases where
Justice Court has exclusive original jurisdiction), civil
cases of value between $200 and $500, general jurisdiction
for probate cases, and appointments of guardians for minors,
lunatics, idiots, and drunkards.

The jurisdiction of the County Clerk underwent a number of
changes between 1836 and 1876. Under the Republic of Texas
Constitution of 1836, was charged with hearing probate and
civil cases, including those affecting land titles, when the
amount in contoversy did not exceed $100. In 1839, this lim-
ited civil jurisdiction granted to County Court was repealed
by the State Legislature. The first constitution adopted
after Texas became a state in 1845, established inferior
courts in the various counties and divided the probate
jurisdiction between the inferior and district courts. The
inferior court at the county level made appointments in

probate matters, while the District Court was responsible for probate administration. In 1846, the State Legislature created probate courts in the established counties and granted sole probate jurisdiction to these courts. In 1848, the Legislature created county courts, with administrative as well as probate jurisdiction, to replace the probate courts.

The Constitution of 1866 created county courts exercising jurisdiction in misdemeanor, probate, and civil cases where the amount in controversy did not exceed $500. While this "Reconstruction Constitution" was held invalid by the Federal Courts, several Texas counties organized such courts and heard cases for several years. The Constitution of 1869, as approved by the federal courts, abolished county courts and transferred their jurisdiction to the district courts until changes were effected under the Constitution of 1876 under which, as amended, we currently operate.

Clerk of the Commissioners Court:

The final broad area of responsibility of the County Clerk includes attendance at all Commissioners Court meetings, posting notices of such meetings, preparing the agenda for each meeting, taking minutes of each meeting, and indexing and maintaining records of all meetings.

DISTRICT COURT

The Texas Constitution provides for division of the State into as many judicial districts as may be provided by law. The District Court has jurisdiction in

> all criminal cases of the grade of a felony; in all suits in behalf of the State to recover penalties, forfeitures, and escheats; of all cases of divorce; of all misdemeanors involving official misconduct; of all suits to recover damages of slander or defamation of character; of all suits for trial of title to land and for the enforcement of liens thereon; of all suits for the trial of the right of property levied upon the virtue of any writ of execution, sequestration or attachment when the property levied on shall equal to or exeed in value five hundred dollars; of all suits, complaints, or pleas whatever, without regard to any distinction between law and equity, when the matter in controversy shall be valued at or amount to five hundred dollars exclusive of interest; of contested elections, and said court and the judges thereof, shall have power to issue writs of habeaus corpus, mandamus, injunction and certiorari, and all writs necessary to enforce their jurisdiction.

The District Court also has appellate jurisdiction over the County Court in probate cases and County Commissioners Court as well as general supervisory control over the later. Since 1931 the District Court presides over adoption proceedings. The Constitution provides that

> there shall be a Clerk for the District Court of each county, who shall be elected by the qualified voters for state and county officers, and who shall hold this office for four years, subject to removal by information, or by indictment of a grand jury, and conviction of a petit jury. In case of vacancy, the Judge of the District Court shall have the power to appoint a Clerk, who shall hold until the office can be filled by election.

The District Clerk is responsible for recording and preserving all records created by the District Court as well as recording licenses of physicians, chiropodists, and chiropractors. The District Clerk must make reports to various agencies as required by law including the Texas Industrial Accident Board, the Texas Judicial Council, and the Department of Public Safety. The District Clerk is also responsible for the preparation of the ballot boxes for all elections.

JUSTICE OF THE PEACE

The office of the Justice of the Peace was first included in the Constitution of the Republic of Texas and has been a part of each constitution since that time. The Justice of the Peace, under the present constitution, has

> jurisdiction in criminal matters of all cases where the penalty or fine to be imposed by law may not be more than two hundred dollars, and in civil matters of all cases where the amount in controversy is two hundred dollars or less.

This court is often called the "poor man's court" because of its limited jurisdiction.

The Justice of the Peace has authority to issue warrants and writs, arraign prisoners, and hold preliminary hearings, as well as to conduct inquests in cases where doubt exists as to the cause of death. In towns of less than 2,500 people, the Justice of the Peace may act as registrar of vital statistics in his precinct.

SHERIFF

This is probably the oldest office in American local government, tracing its roots back to our Anglo-Saxon heritage of English speaking people. It has been provided for in every Texas Constitution. The present constitution provides that

> there shall be elected by the qualified voters of each county, a Sheriff, who shall hold his office for the term of four years, whose duties and prerequisites, and fees of office, shall be prescribed by the Legislature, and vacancies in whose office shall be filled by the Commissioners Court until the next general election.

Chief duty of the Sheriff is that of peace officer of the county, but he is also an officer of both county and district courts in which he is responsible for the services of writs and processes. The Sheriff is also charged with the maintenance of the county jail and the supervision of its prisoners.

TAX ASSESSOR-COLLECTOR

The Assessor and Collector of Taxes is elected to a four year term in each county. As assessor, he must make a list of taxable property in the county, and assessing the value of it. As collector, he receives and collects all taxes assessed in the county. In most counties, the duties of the Tax Assessor have been transferred to an appointed official since 1980.

During the Republic of Texas, a Tax Assessor was appointed for each county and the Sheriff served as collector. In 1846, the offices of tax assessor and collector were combined into an elective position whose duties were expanded to include the preparation of a list of delinquent taxpayers.

The Constitution of 1876 provided for the election of a Tax Assessor for each county and for a Tax Collector in counties of 10,000 population or more. The Sheriff served as Tax Collector in smaller counties. In 1932, the offices of Tax Assessor and Collector were combined in counties of 10,000 population or more, and the Sheriff held both positions in smaller counties. Since 1954, smaller counties have been authorized to create a separate office of Tax Assessor-Collector upon the approval of the voters of the county.

From the time of its creation, the County Tax Assessor-Collector has been authorized to collect both county and state taxes on real and personal property. In addition this official is the " Registrar of Voters " for the county and is responsible for the registration of voters, keeping of records, preparation of voting lists, and such other duties involving voter registration as are placed upon him by law.

The Tax Assessor-Collector is also charged by statutory law with the registration of all motor vehicles in the county.

After 1980, with the enactment of the Peveto Bill, the duties of the Tax Assessor were transferred to an appointed Appraisal District while the elected official remains the Tax Collector for the County.

COUNTY TREASURER

This office was first created as an appointive position in 1840. The Constitution now provides for the election of a County Treasurer, who serves a four year term.

The primary responsibility of the County Treasurer is to receive and disburse county funds as authorized by Commissioners Court.

COUNTY AUDITOR

The office of County Auditor is not required by the Texas Constitution but is a requirement of statuary law which states that any county with a population of 35,000 or more, or taxable valuation in excess of $15 million, is required to have an auditor. Smaller counties may create this office by action of Commissioners Court.

The County Auditor is appointed by the District Judge, or Judges of the county who may also remove that official for incompetence or misconduct.

The Auditor's main duties are the general oversight of all books and records of all officers of the county, district or state, who may be authorized or required by law, to receive or collect any money, funds, fees, or other property, for theuse of, or belonging to the county; and shall see to the strict enforcement of the law governing county finances.

In counties of less than 225,000 population, the Auditor estimates revenues and expenditures so that a county budget can be formulated by Commissioners Court. In counties of over 225,000 population, the Auditor is the budget officer and prepares the budget to be approved by Commissioners Court.

COUNTY SUPERINTENDENT OF SCHOOLS

The office of County Superintendent of Schools was created by amendment to the School Law of 1876, and the establishment of the office was left to the discretion of Commissioners Court.

A County Superintendent is elected for a term of four years in counties having a scholastic population of 3,000 or more. This official advises the Board of Education on the establishment and maintenance of common schools and their educational policies, including rules and regulations and prescribed courses of study. He prepares annual school budgets for approval by the board; submits annual reports to the State School Superintendent; and transmits rules and regulations of the State Board of Education to local Boards of Education and to school employees.

With the increase in number of consolidated school districts, each with its own superintendent, the need for this office has decreased to the extent that it is either filled by the County Judge or has been eliminated by Commissioner Court.

COUNTY SURVEYOR

This position dates back to the days of the Republic of Texas when each County Surveyor was elected by Congress and required to make a map with plats of all deeded land in the county and to record field notes of all surveys. The duties of the office have remained essentially unchanged since then although the office was made elective in 1840.

The current constitution states that the County Surveyor shall be elected for a four year term but the importance of the office has decreased in recent years to the extent that the position is no longer filled in many counties.

NOTICE

It is important to note that there is a fee charged for copies of any records available to the public under the so called " Freedom of Information Act " and that this fee is set by the State Legislature and is subject to change from year to year. This fee is to cover the cost of reproduction as well as any time spent on research by an employee of the County, District, or State. It is not intended to cover the cost of the " goodwill effort of those wonderful public employees who are so interested in giving the public the information from public records that is so valuable to research into the history of our State and our ancestors.

CHAPTER 8

RECORDS AVAILABLE IN THE TEXAS STATE LIBRARY

The Lorenzo de Zavala State Archives and Library building is located on Brazos Street, directly to the east of the Texas State Capitol. The Library and its offices occupy most of the building with the exception of the Archives which is located in the south wing of the first floor.

The Genealogy Department is located in the north wing of first floor. The genealogist will find many materials for research in this library, much of which can be found in no other place. It is open Monday through Saturday from 8 AM to 5 PM, with the exception of State and Federal holidays.

The genealogy collection covers the whole field of American genealogy with some publications in the European field. The emphasis, of course, is on the works of the southern states, since this was the homeland of most families who moved to Texas in earlier years. Types of material included in this collection are guides to genealogical research, general books on heraldry, family histories, and state and county records and information. The index to Texas births and deaths from 1903 to 1973 is available in book form. These books list the place of death and death certificate number of every recorded death as well as every birth certificate issued during this period, including delayed certificates.

While most books are not available on interlibrary loan, the State Library has supplied most local libraries with a list of duplicates that they have accumulated that are available through them. Consult your librarian for this list.

Most books are shelved in open stacks and may be read at the convenience of the researcher. The library staff will help readers identify and locate publications that relate to the subject of their research and will explain how to use the indexes and other material in the room. Detailed research can not, of course, be done by the staff.

The staff can not answer questions by mail or phone that involve lengthy research, but will check indexes for needed information as time permits. There is a minimum charge for photocopies ordered by mail that is currently $1.00. The library has a list of qualified persons who will, for a fee, search records for family information.

In addition to books and periodicals, the collection contains microfilm of census records, some military records, Texas tax rolls, and the Nacogdoches Archives. All the Federal Census for every state, 1790 through 1910, are on file as well as special censuses such as the State of Texas, 1850-1880, including the mortality schedules, the 1880 soundex for Texas, Mississippi, and South Carolina, and the 1900 soundex for Texas and Oklahoma.

Most of the collection of Confederate Service records on film are those of Texas State Troops and Militia. There is also an index to records held by the National Archives.

The Texas tax rolls for all counties, from the formation of the county through 1921, are a part of the genealogy collection and are circulated on interlibrary loan.

The Mexican Archives gives information on births, marriages, deaths, and some judicial proceedings, a few as early as 1726. This film includes records from different parts of the state of Nuevo Leon. No other Mexican states are represented.

Among the books to be found in the Texas State Library Genealogy collection are valuable volumes of county marriage records; county cemetery records; county histories, most of them compiled by local genealogists; some county courthouse records as abstracted by local citizens in various counties; Daughters of the American Revolution and Daughters of the Confederacy lineage books; and, indexed census records for most states through 1850, and for some Texas and other southern counties.

This library has a collection of periodicals published by major genealogy societies throughout America and Quarterly publications for many Texas county and area genealogy societies. A great deal of local history can be obtained from the material published in these periodicals.

The genealogist who wishes to continue research elsewhere, will want to consult the indexes maintained by the Texas State Library. These indexes will assist the researcher in locating information through genealogy periodicals; Bibliography of Local Histories in the Library of Congress; American Libraries; American Genealogical Index; American State Papers; Southwestern Historical Quarterly; and Confederate Veteran Magazine, among others.

The mailing address is

> Texas State Library
> Box 12927
> Capitol Station
> Austin, Texas   78711

CHAPTER   9

RECORDS AVAILABLE IN TEXAS STATE ARCHIVES

A wealth of information about early residents, soldiers, and settlers of Texas can be found in our State Capitol. Much of this information is in the Texas State Archives which is located in the Texas State Library Building.

Many records that are available in the State Archives have been copied and can be examined at Genealogy Departments of City and County Libraries throughout Texas. It is wise, therefore, to begin your research at your local or nearest library in order to be able to get the most possible good from your contact with the State Library and Archives.

Your local library will probably have a copy of a very handy book, "A Guide to Genealogical Resources in the Texas State Archives," which gives valuable tips on research and what is available for your examination.

In the next few pages we will attempt to give you a summary of historical information and documents that could be beneficial to you in your genealogical research in Texas. Please remember that the Archives contains many documents that are very old and great care must be exercised in their use; careful attention must be paid to rules for working with them so that they can be preserved for future generations.

Military records of Texans who served in the state troops from 1836 until around 1898 are kept in the Texas State Archives. Beginning with the Mexican War, records for the United States troops serving in Texas are held in the National Archives. This includes records of Confederate States Army activities.

TEXAS STATE ARCHIVES

Genealogical Information for Certain Categories

Bonds and Oaths	1836-1920. Records of bonds and/or oaths administered to County, District, or State officeholders.
Colonial Records	1760-1836. Available records of persons living or immigrating to Texas during this period.
Colonization Papers	1836-1846. Records of persons immigrating to the Republic of Texas as part of an organized effort to settle this area.
Commissioner of Deeds	1846-1912. Records of notorial agents in foreign countries or in states other than Texas.
Confederate Claims	1861-1865. Records on claims filed by military and civilian personnel engaged in the Texas war effort during this period.
Confederate Home Records	1886-1954. Records of indigent or disabled veterans, their wives or widows.
Confederate Indigent Families List	1863-1865. Records of service men of the Confederacy or their indigent "heads of household."
Confederate Pensions	1900-1975. Records of Indigent Veterans or their widows.
Customs House Records	1836-1846. Records of ship masters, merchants, and some passengers arriving in, or doing business with the Republic of Texas.
Election Registers and Returns	1836-1960s. Record of persons running for state or county office and persons appointed or elected to state or county office during this period.

General Land Office
Muster Roll
        1835-1846. Records of men who fought in the Texas Revolution and in some Republic-era military engagements.

General Service Records
        1836-1902. Records of men who served in Texas military organizations.

Memorials and Petitions
        1836-1937. Record of persons who signed petitions for or against legislation in Texas.

Muster Rolls
        1836-1917. Rolls of men who served in Texas military units.

Payments for Services
to the Republic
        1836-1846. Record of payments to military and civilians who rendered service to the Republic of Texas.

Scholastic Census Records
        1854-1855. Records of free white children, six to sixteen years old, or their families.

Supreme Court Records
        1838-1940. Record of litigants in appellate civil and criminal cases.

Voters Registration
        1867. List of franchised voters in Texas.

Workers on Texas
State Capitol Building
        1882-1888. List and records of laborers, craftsmen, and supervisors engaged in the building of the present State Capitol Building.

Under the above rather broad catagories can be found records, or lists of names, of many men who came to Texas during the early days of its existence. As is the case with most records of this period, the recorded names were of the male head of household except in the case of claims by widows or surviving family members.

The only records maintained in the Texas Archives are of people who lived in Texas, acted for Texas in an official capacity in another state or territory, or served in Texas but did not receive compensation for their services until after they moved from Texas.

Adjutant General Record Group

Muster Rolls, 1836-1911

REPUBLIC:

Texas Army of the Republic:	Rolls for 1837-1841. Commanding officer files. Filed by company designation.
Texas Militia:	Rolls for 1838-1842. Commanding officer files. Filed by company designation.
Texas Rangers:	Rolls for 1838-1845. Commanding officer files. Filed by captain.
Texas Volunteers:	Rolls for 1836-1840. Commanding officer files. Filed by captain.
U.S. Volunteer Companies:	Rolls for 1836, 1837, 1842. Commanding officer files.
Minute Men:	Rolls for 1840-1841. Commanding officer files. Filed by county.
Texas Navy:	Rolls for 1839-1843. Filed by ship. Officers lists.

ALL OTHER:

Texas Rangers:	Rolls for 1855-1874, 1900-1901. Commanding officer files. Filed by captain.
Mounted Volunteers:	Rolls for 1847-1876. Commanding officer files. Filed by captain.
Minute Men:	Rolls for 1858-1874 Commanding officer files. Filed by county.
Confederate Muster Rolls:	Rolls for 1861-1865. Transcribed in Muster Roll Card Index. Originals too worn for routine research.

Union Muster Rolls:	Rolls for 1861-1865 Filed by company designation.
"Official Roster" of Union Soldiers of Texas.	A "full and correct" roster of men enrolled in the 1st and 2nd Regiment of the Texas Cavalry Volunteers, Companies A-M and A-E, along with the roll of Captain A.J. Vidal's Company of Independent Partisan Rangers. Also contains some service records.
Reserve Militia:	Rolls for 1870-1871. Commanding officer files. Filed by company designation.
State Police:	Rolls for 1870-1871. Commanding officer files. Filed by commanding officer under each district, 1st-4th.
State Guard:	Rolls for 1870-1871. Commanding officer files. Filed by company designation, 1st-10th Regiments, Infantry. Cross indexed by captain and county.
Frontier Forces:	Rolls for 1870-1871. Commanding officer files. Filed by company designation.
Frontier Battalion:	Rolls for 1874-1901. Commanding officer files. Filed by Company, A-E.

Texas Volunteer Guard:	Rolls for 1881-1902.
	commanding officer files.
	1st Regiment Infantry 1881-1900
	2nd Regiment Infantry 1883-1900
	3rd Regiment Infantry 1886-1900
	4th Regiment Infantry 1891-1900
	   all above Companies A-M.
	5th Regiment Infantry 1889-1895
	   Companies A-I.
	6th Regiment Infantry 1889-1895
	   Companies A-H.
	1st Cavalry Regiment 1881-1901
	   Companies A-H.
	1st and 2nd Brigades 1891-1899
	Artillery Battalion 1891-1900.

U.S. Volunteers: Spanish American War, 1898.
                                    Commanding officer files.
                                    Muster-in rolls only, 1st-4th
                                    Volunteer Infantry and 1st
                                    Volunteer Calvary. Co. A-M.
                                    Filed by company designation.

Texas National Guard: Rolls for 1903-1911.
                                    Commanding officer files.
                                    1st-4th Infantry Regiments, 1st
                                    Calvary Regiment, 1st Artillery
                                    Battalion, Colored Battalion
                                    Infantry, Companies A-M.
                                    Filed by Company.

MUSTER ROLL CARDS:

Muster roll data for individual soldiers in each of the
following listed six military organizations has been
transcribed on index cards which are available for inspec-
tion in the Texas State Archives. Copies of the information
on these cards is accepted as proof of service by the Sons
and Daughters of the Republic of Texas, the Sons of
Confederate Veterans, the United Daughters of the
Confederacy, and similar organizations.

Minute Men   Rolls for 1837,1839,1841-1842,
                                    1860.
                                    1,780 cards.
                                    Militia companies formed prior
                                    to the civil war. Gives dates
                                    of service, name and rank, and
                                    organization.

Texas Navy   Rolls for 1836-1844.
                                    4,000 cards
                                    Gives name and rank, date of
                                    enlistment and some discharge
                                    dates as well as ship and
                                    commanding officer assignment.

Republic Rangers   Rolls for 1836-1845.
                                    2,900 cards.
                                    Most effective militia for
                                    policing Texas borders and vast
                                    unclaimed land.
                                    Gives name and rank, commanding
                                    officer, organization, enlist-
                                    ment and discharge dates, and
                                    sometimes, place of enlistment.
                                    Salmon colored cards are for

soldiers serving under
Zachary Taylor in July 1845.
White cards are for Texas
Volunteer Army in July, 1836.
Yellow cards are for J. D.
Lilly's "Texas Forces" who
served June, 1841.
Turquoise cards used for all
other Republic Rangers.

Texas Rangers:

Rolls for 1839-1880s.
8,300 cards.
Index for several policing
organizations formed after
the Civil War.
Roll card gives name, birth-
place, or place of enlistment,
discharge date, description,
occupation and age.

Confederate:

Rolls of 1861-1865.
77,000 cards.
These cards were for militia
who protected the borders and
frontiers of Texas during the
Civil War. Many of these men
later served in the Confederate
Army.
Roll card gives name and rank,
commanding officer, enlistment
and discharge dates, organization, description and remarks.

Texas Volunteer Guard:

Rolls of 1876-1902.
4,600 cards.
This was the forerunner of our
present National Guard. These
men were brought under federal
law in 1903.

Roll cards give name and rank,
commanding officer, organization, description (includes age
color of hair, eyes, and
complexion as well as
occupation and native state)
and enlistment and discharge
dates.

A microfilm copy of these cards is also available in the
Genealogy Section of Texas State Library and in the Ranger
Museum at Fort Fisher in Waco, Texas.

The staff will check muster roll cards for information on an individual. Whenever possible the researcher should furnish a date span and branch of military service when inquiring by mail or phone.

MILITARY SERVICE RECORDS:

The service record series for the period between 1836 and 1902 is a combination of official service record files and alphabetical files created by a state agency in reference to an individual's service in a military unit. This information may consist of a single strip of paper containing a sentence up to a complete file on the individual during some phase of his military service.

These files during this period cover service in the following areas:

Army of the Republic: 1363 files
    1. Enlistment
    2. Discharge
    3. Affidavit of service.

Navy of the Republic: 897 files
    1. Copies of vouchers for payment for services.

Mounted Volunteers: 373 files
    1. Paymasters Certificate
    2. Assignment of Power of Attorney
    3. Affidavits of service.

Minute Men: 68 files
    1. Power of Attorney
    2. Adjutant General Service Record verification.

Texas State Troops: 480 files
    1. Voucher: Name
    2. Copies of orders and special orders.
    3. Carbons of Adjutant General replies regarding service.

State Police: 811 files
    1. Pay voucher
    2. Sub voucher

Regular Rangers: 1,374 files

    1. Adjutant General's Warrant of authority and descriptive list.
    2. Enlistment, oath of service and description.

Special Rangers: 4,158 files

    1. Application

Railroad Rangers: 1,081 files

    1. Application

Loyalty Rangers: 486 files

    1. Application

Frontier Forces: 792 files

    1. Pay vouchers

Frontier Battalion: 2,848 files

    1. Certificate of pay or debt.
    2. Discharge
    3. Descriptive List.

Texas Volunteer Guard- 1890s-1902: 4,294 files

    1. Enlistment oath (This is all most files contain.)
    2. Discharge
    3. Officer Record Questionnaire
    4. Application and descriptive list.

United States Volunteers- 1898-1899: 4,394 files

    1. Receipt for pay owed for service in Texas prior to Spanish-American War.
    2. Voucher Affidavit
    3. Oath of Enlistment
    4. Receipt for Texas service for volunteers killed in action
    5. Description and Assignment Card for Volunteers

The condition of the records will determine whether or not an individuals records may be copied.

Brigade Correspondence
Texas State Troops   1861-1865

    The State Militia Law of 1861 divided Texas into 33 Brigade Districts by Counties. These men were to protect Texas and be at the call of the State in case of an emergency.

Special Pardons   1866-ca 1870   322 applications
                                     The information found in these
                                     files usually has character
                                     affidavit and description of
                                     War record. Many records do
                                     contain valuable genealogical
                                     information.

Capitol Building Commission Records   1881-1888
                                     Records of the construction of
                                     the State Capitol Building and
                                     contractors and workmen who
                                     built it.

Colonization Records: 1836-1846

                                     The only records in the State
                                     Archives to contain very much
                                     information about immigration
                                     are those produced by organized
                                     European emigration companies
                                     such as Castro, Fisher-Miller,
                                     and Peters Colonies.

Commissioners of Deeds: 1846-1912

                                     Information in these records is
                                     limited to correspondence of
                                     applicants for this position as
                                     well as the oath of office and
                                     bond for successful candidates.

Confederate Claims: 1861-1865

                                     Claims for state legislative
                                     expenses during Civil War era.
                                     This has nothing to do with
                                     claims by service personnel or
                                     their families.

Confederate Home Records: 1886-1954

                                     The Texas Confederate Home
                                     opened in 1886 to provide for
                                     indigent and disabled veterans
                                     of the Civil War. Privately
                                     funded until 1891 when it was
                                     made the responsibility of the
                                     State. Records contain much
                                     valuable information about
                                     residents of home.

Confederate Indigent Families Lists: 1863-1865

> This lists only payments made to County Courts who kept all records of families receiving assistance. Some County records are in State Archives but most are in County Clerks files.

Confederate Pensions: 1899-1975

> The first Confederate Pension law was passed in 1899 and was amended several times before the final 1917 legislation. The State Archives has records on Confederate veterans and their families who received benefits for their service.

Custom House Records   1846-1846

> Records from custom houses in Galveston, Aransas, Matagorda, Brazos, Sabine & San Augustine Revenue Districts until ended in 1846 by Annexation agreement

Election Registers   1836-1970
> Official records of all people elected to Republic and State offices.

Election Returns   1835-1973
> Early returns records listed only names of winners in Republic and early state races for county, district, state, and national races.

> Early statehood and Republic records include poll lists in some precincts.

Memorials and Petitions   1836-1937
> Petitions presented to the State with requests for redress of wrong or grant of favor by the state to a person or group are filed in the Archives if not with the bill in the legislature acknowledging the petition.

REQUEST FOR
TEXAS VETERAN SEARCH

Mail form to:
   Texas State Archives
   Texas State Library
   Box 12927
   Austin, Texas 78711

Print your name and address in
the space below:

* Submit a separate form for each veteran.

* There is a $1.00 minimum charge for mail requests. An additional 10¢ per page will be charged for any copies over the initial ten included in the minimum charge.

* DO NOT SEND MONEY WITH THIS FORM. THE ARCHIVES WILL BILL.

****

1. Name of Veteran *(Last, first, middle)*   2. Birth Date   3. Death Date   4. Place of Death

5. Name of Widow *(Last, first, middle)*   6. Birth Date   7. Death Date   8. Place of Death

9. Dates of Military Service   10. Name or Number of Military Unit   11. County of Residence

12. Pension Number   13. Do you need additional blank Texas Veteran Search forms (how many)? _____

14. Check appropriate category. (Records searched in each category are listed on reverse in Part I.)

☐ REPUBLIC OF TEXAS (1836-1845)   ☐ RANGER UNITS (1836-1935)
☐ CIVIL WAR (1861-1865)   ☐ STATE POLICE (1870-1871)
☐ SPANISH-AMERICAN WAR (1898-1899)   ☐ TEXAS VOLUNTEER GUARD (1873-1902)

****

REPLY (Archives Use Only)

☐ RECORDS FOUND:
   ☐ Audited Military Claim, Republic
   ☐ Pension, Republic
   ☐ Public Debt Paper, Republic
   ☐ GLO Muster Roll Book
   ☐ Muster Roll Abstract
   ☐ Audited Military Claim, Texas State Troops

   ☐ Confederate Home Records
   ☐ Indigent Family Lists
   ☐ Pension, Confederate
   ☐ Pension, Confederate Widow's
   ☐ Service Record
   ☐ Biographical Index
   ☐ Other_____

☐ Please remit _____ for the enclosed copies. Make check payable to the TEXAS STATE LIBRARY

☐ We located no records for the above individual. This does not necessarily mean that he did not serve in a Texas military organization or that there are no pertinent records either in the Texas State Archives or elsewhere. See Part II on reverse.

Nacogdoches Archives

1753-1836
National, regional, and local
officials records and reports
of the Mexican government
during this period plus
municipal records of the
Nacogdoches vicinity.
These records include records
and oaths of citizenship for
those who filed for
certificates of citizenship
during this period.

Miscellaneous Records

Elections (1825-1835)

Military Reviews (1773-1830)

Payments for service to the
  Republic

Audited Civil & Military
  claims.

Republic Pensions (1870-1900)

Public Debt Papers (1848-1860)

Graves of Civil War Veterans.

Scholastic Census (1854-1855)

Supreme Court Records
  (1838-1893)

Voters Registration (1867-1870)

CHAPTER 10

RECORDS AVAILABLE IN THE REGIONAL HISTORICAL RESOURCES DEPOSITORIES

The Regional Historical Resources Depositories function under the auspices of the Local Records Department of the Texas State Library. This program was created by legislation passed in 1972 and amended in 1973 and 1979 to provide a uniform statewide system for the retention and preservation of historical resources.

The Local Records Department of the Texas State Archives is responsible for collecting, preserving, and making available historical records of cities, counties, and other local governments.

Each of the depositories contain microfilm of primary source material from the counties designated in their respective area. These records consist of deeds, wills, administration records, marriage records, naturalization records, district court minutes, etc. The records date primarly through 1885; although some of the probate and marriage records date through 1915.

Of great value to the genealogical researcher, this microfilm may be ordered on interlibrary loan through your local library. One should first obtain a list of the microfilm roll numbers assigned to each roll of film from the depository involved in order to enable your local librarian to make the loan using standard ILL forms. At the present time, this service is available without charge.

Each of the depositories has some original material about that area of the state. Some of this material is in the form of manuscripts and records which have been donated by residents of the area or was taken from courthouses or city halls within the region.

A list of the depositories and their addresses, and the counties that are assigned to each depository is provided on the following pages of this chapter so that the depository for your county can quickly be determined.

REGIONAL HISTORICAL RESOURCE DEPOSITORIES

Persons whose names are starred (*) are Texas State Library staff members stationed at Depositories. Others are staff of host institutions where no TSL staff member is stationed.

ANGELO STATE UNIVERSITY

Joe B. Lee, Head Librarian
Angelo State University
San Angelo, TX 76909
(915) 942-2222

AUSTIN PUBLIC LIBRARY

Audray Bateman, Curator
Austin History Center
Austin Public Library
P.O. Box 2287
Austin, TX 7876-2287
(512) 473-4283

BAYLOR UNIVERSITY

Richard Veit
Texas Collection
Baylor University
P.O. Box 6396
Waco, TX 76706-6396
(817) 755-1268

DALLAS PUBLIC LIBRARY

Cindy Smolovic, Archivist
Texas-Dallas History and
Archives Division
Dallas Public Library
1515 Young Street, 7th Floor
Dallas, TX 75201
(214) 749-4158

EAST TEXAS STATE UNIVERSITY

James H. Conrad,
University Archivist
James G. Gee Library
East Texas State University
Commerce, TX 75428
(214) 886-5737

HOUSTON PUBLIC LIBRARY

Louis Marchiafava, Dir.
HMRC - Houston Public
  Library
500 McKinney Avenue
Houston, TX 77002
(713) 224-5441
NOTE: Reference and
interlibrary loan requests
should be sent to Sally
Rogers, Sam Houston Regional
Library, (see listing)

MIDWESTERN STATE UNIVERSITY

Melba Harvill
  Director of Libraries
Midwestern State University
Wichita Falls, TX 76308
(817) 692-6611, ext. 4165

NORTH TEXAS STATE UNIVERSITY

Texas Dallas History &
Richard Himmel,
University Archives
North Texas State University
Box 5188, NTSU Station
Denton, TX 76203
(817) 565-2766

PAN AMERICAN UNIVERSITY

George Gause
Special Collections Librarian
Pan American University
Edinburg, TX   78539-2999
(512) 381-2799

PARIS JUNIOR COLLEGE

Daisy Harvill, Archivist
Learning Resource Center
Paris Junior College
Paris, TX   75460-6298
(214) 785-7661

SAM HOUSTON REGIONAL LIBRARY
& RESEARCH CENTER

*Robert Schaadt, Director
Sam Houston Regional Library
  & Research Center
P.O. Box 989
Liberty, TX   77575-0989
(713) 336-7097

SAM HOUSTON STATE UNIVERSITY

Paul Culp
Special Collections Librarian
Sam Houston State University
Huntsville, TX   77341
(409) 294-1619

SAN ANTONIO   REGIONAL OFFICE

*Carmela Leal, Field Archivist
G. J. Sutton Building
321 Center Street
Room B-031
San Antonio, TX   78202
(512) 226-5926

SHERMAN PUBLIC LIBRARY

Jacqueline Banfield
Assistant Libarary Director
Sherman Public Library
P.O. Box 1106
Sherman, TX   75090
(214) 892-4545, Ext. 240

STEPHEN F. AUSTIN STATE
  UNIVERSITY

Linda Nicklas
Special Collections Librarian
Stephen F. Austin State
  University
Box 13055 SFA Station
Nacogdoches, TX   75962
(409) 568-4100

TARLETON STATE UNIVERSITY

Gertrude Carlson
Special Collections Librarian
Tarleton Station
Stephenville, TX   76402
(817) 968-9246

TEXAS A & I UNIVERSITY

Mrs. Patricia Scott
South Texas Archives
Campus Box 134
Texas A & I University
Kingsville, TX   78363
(512) 595-2819

TEXAS A & M UNIVERSITY

*Paul R. Scott, Field
  Archivist
University Archives
Texas A & M University
College Station, TX   77843
(409) 845-1815

TEXAS TECH UNIVERSTIY

Gloria Lyerla
Reference/Interlibrary Loans
Special Collections
Texas Tech Univesity
Lubbock, TX   79409
(806) 742-2242

TEXAS STATE LIBRARY

*Wendie Hill
Local Records Division
Texas State Libraray
P.O. Box 12927
Austin, TX   78711
(512) 463-5478

UNIVERSITY OF TEXAS AT
   ARLINGTON

Marcelle Hull
Special Collections
University of Texas at
   Arlington
University Library
P.O. Box 19497
Arlington, TX   76019
(817) 273-3392

UNIVERSITY OF TEXAS AT DALLAS

Larry Sall, Assistant Director
for Special Collections
University of Texas at Dallas
P.O. Box 830643   MC 3.3
Richardson, TX   75083-0643
(214) 690-2570

UNIVERSITY OF TEXAS AT EL PASO

Cesar Caballero, Head
Special Collections Department
University of Texas at El Paso
El Paso, TX   79968-0582
(915) 747-5697

UNIVERSITY OF TEXAS AT
   PERMIAN BASIN

Bobbie Klepper
Special Collections Librarian
University of Texas of the
   Permian Basin
4901 East University Blvd.
Odessa, TX   79762
(915) 367-2128

VICTORIA COLLEGE

Virginia Allen
Archives Librarian
VC-UHVC Library
2602 North Ben Jordan
Victoria, TX   77901
(512) 576-3151, ext. 201

WEST TEXAS STATE UNIVERSITY

Claire R. Kuehn, Librarian
Panhandle-Plains Historical
   Museum
Box 967, WT Station
Canyon, TX   79016
(806) 655-7191, Ext. 8

ALPHABETICAL LIST OF TEXAS COUNTIES AND THEIR RHRD DEPOSITORIES

Starred (*) counties do not have their county records
microfilmed at the time of the printing of this book.

ANDERSON
  Sam Houston State Univ.

ANDREWS
  Univ. of Texas-Permian Bas.

ANGELINA
  Stephen F. Austin Univ.

ARANSAS
  Texas A & I Univ.

ARCHER*
  Midwestern Univ.

ARMSTRONG
  West Texas Univ.

ATASCOSA
  no regional depository

AUSTIN
  Texas A & M Univ.

BAILEY*
  Texas Tech Univ.

BANDERA
  no regional depository

BASTROP
  Texas State Archives

BAYLOR*
  Midwestern Univ.

BEE
  Texas A & I Univ.

BELL*
  Baylor Univ.

BEXAR
  no regional depository

BLANCO
  Texas State Archives

BORDEN*
  Univ. of Texas-Permian Bas.

BOSQUE
  Baylor Univ.

BOWIE*
  East Texas Univ.

BRAZORIA
  Houston Public Library

BRAZOS
  Texas A & M Univ.

BREWSTER*
  Univ. of Texas-El Paso

BRISCOE*
  West Texas State Univ.

BROOKS*
  Texas A & I Univ.

BROWN*
  Tarleton State Univ.

BURLESON
  Texas A & M Univ.

BURNET
  Baylor Univ.

CALDWELL
  Texas State Archives

CALHOUN
  Univ. of Houston-Victoria

CALLAHAN*
  Tarleton State Univ.

CAMERON
  Pan American Univ.

CAMP
  East Texas State Univ.

CARSON
West Texas State Univ.

CASS
East Texas State Univ.

CASTRO*
West Texas State Univ.

CHAMBERS
Sam Houston Regional
Library & Research Center

CHEROKEE
Stephen F. Austin State Univ.

CHILDRESS*
West Texas State Univ.

CLAY*
Midwestern Univ.

COCHRAN*
Texas Tech Univ.

COKE*
Angelo State Univ.

COLEMAN*
Tarleton State Univ.

COLLIN
Univ. of Texas-Dallas

COLLINGSWORTH*
West Texas State Univ.

COLORADO
Texas A & M Univ.

COMAL
no regional depository

COMANCHE*
Tarleton State Univ.

CONCHO*
Angelo State Univ.

COOKE
North Texas State Univ.

CORYELL
Baylor Univ.

COTTLE*
Texas Tech Univ.

CRANE*
Univ. of Texas-Permian Bas.

CROCKETT*
Angelo State Univ.

CROSBY*
Texas Tech Univ.

CULBERSON*
Univ. of Texas-El Paso

DALLAM*
West Texas State Univ.

DALLAS*
Dallas Public Library

DAWSON*
Univ. of Texas-Permian Bas.

DE WITT
Univ. of Houston-Victoria

DEAF SMITH*
West Texas State Univ.

DELTA
Paris Junior College

DENTON
North Texas State Univ.

DICKENS*
Texas Tech Univ.

DIMMIT
no regional depository

DONLEY*
West Texas State Univ.

DUVAL
Texas A & I Univ.

EASTLAND*
Tarleton State Univ.

ECTOR*
Univ. of Texas-Permian Bas.

EDWARDS*
Angelo State Univ.

EL PASO*
Univ. of Texas-El Paso

ELLIS
Univ. of Texas-Dallas

ERATH
Tarleton State Univ.

FALLS
Baylor Univ.

FANNIN
Paris Junior College

FAYETTE
Texas A & M Univ.

FISHER*
Angelo State Univ.

FLOYD*
Texas Tech Univ.

FOARD*
Midwestern Univ.

FORT BEND
Houston Public Library

FRANKLIN
East Texas State Univ.

FREESTONE
Sam Houston State Univ.

FRIO
no regional depository

GAINES*
Univ. of Texas-Permian Bas.

GALVESTON
Houston Public Library

GARZA*
Texas Tech Univ.

GILLESPIE
Texas State Archives

GLASSCOCK*
Univ. of Texas-Permian Bas.

GOLIAD
Univ. of Houston-Victoria

GONZALES
Univ. of Houston-Victoria

GRAY*
West Texas State Univ.

GRAYSON
Sherman Public Library

GREGG*
East Texas State Univ.

GRIMES
Sam Houston State Univ.

GUADALUPE
no regional depository

HALE*
Texas Tech Univ.

HALL*
West Texas State Univ.

HAMILTON
Baylor Univ.

HANSFORD*
West Texas State Univ.

HARDEMAN*
Midwestern Univ.

HARDIN
Sam Houston Regional
Library & Research Center

HARRIS
  Houston Public Library

HARRISON*
  East Texas State Univ.

HARTLEY*
  West Texas State Univ.

HASKELL*
  Midwestern Univ.

HAYS
  Texas State Archives

HEMPHILL*
  West Texas State Univ.

HENDERSON*
  Univ. of Texas-Dallas

HIDALGO
  Pan American Univ.

HILL
  Baylor Univ.

HOCKLEY*
  Texas Tech Univ.

HOOD
  Univ. of Texas-Arlington

HOPKINS
  East Texas State Univ.

HOUSTON
  Sam Houston State Univ.

HOWARD*
  Univ. of Texas-Permian Bas.

HUDSPETH*
  Univ. of Texas-El Paso

HUNT
  East Texas State Univ.

HUTCHINSON*
  West Texas State Univ.

IRION*
  Angelo State Univ.

JACK*
  Midwestern Univ.

JACKSON
  Univ. of Houston-Victoria

JASPER
  Sam Houston Regional
    Library and Archives

JEFF DAVIS*
  Univ. of Texas-El Paso

JEFFERSON
  Sam Houston Regional
    Library & Research Center

JIM HOGG*
  Pan American Univ.

JIM WELLS*
  Texas A & I Univ.

JOHNSON*
  Univ. of Texas-Arlington

JONES*
  Angelo State Univ.

KARNES
  no regional depository

KAUFMAN
  Univ. of Texas-Dallas

KENDALL
  no regional depository

KENEDY*
  Texas A & I Univ.

KENT*
  Texas Tech Univ.

KERR
  no regional depository

KIMBLE*
  Angelo State Univ.

KING*
  Texas Tech Univ.

KINNEY
  no regional depository

KLEBURG*
  Texas A & I Univ.

KNOX*
  Midwestern Univ.

LA SALLE
  no regional depository

LAMAR
  Paris Junior College

LAMB*
  Texas Tech Univ.

LAMPASAS*
  Baylor Univ.

LAVACA
  Univ. of Houston-Victoria

LEE
  Texas A & M Univ.

LEON
  Sam Houston State Univ.

LIBERTY
  Sam Houston Regional
    Library & Research Center

LIMESTONE
  Baylor Univ.

LIPSCOMB*
  West Texas State Univ.

LIVE OAK
  Texas A & I Univ.

LLANO
  Texas State Archives

LOVING*
  Univ. of Texas-Permian Bas.

LUBBOCK*
  Texas Tech Univ.

LYNN*
  Texas Tech Univ.

MADISON*
  Sam Houston State Univ.

MARION*
  East Texas State Univ.

MARTIN*
  Univ. of Texas-Permian Bas.

MASON*
  Angelo State Univ.

MATAGORDA
  Houston Public Library

MAVERICK
  no regional depository

McCULLOCH*
  Angelo State Univ.

McLENNAN
  Baylor Univ.

McMULLEN
  no regional depository

MEDINA
  no regional depository

MENARD*
  Angelo State Univ.

MIDLAND*
  Univ. of Texas-Permian Bas.

MILAM
  Texas A & M Univ.

MILLS*
  Tarleton State Univ.

MITCHELL*
  Univ. of Texas-Permian Bas.

MONTAGUE
North Texas State Univ.

MONTGOMERY
Sam Houston State Univ.

MOORE*
West Texas State Univ.

MORRIS*
East Texas State Univ.

MOTLEY*
Texas Tech Univ.

NACOGDCHES
Stephen F. Austin Univ.

NAVARRO
Univ. of Texas-Dallas

NEWTON
Sam Houston Regional
   Library & Research Center

NOLAN*
Angelo State Univ.

NUECES
Texas A & I Univ.

OCHILTREE*
West Texas State Univ.

OLDHAM*
West Texas State Univ.

ORANGE
Sam Houston Regional
   Library & Research Center

PALO PINTO*
Tarleton State Univ.

PANOLA
Stephen F. Austin Univ.

PARKER
Univ. of Texas-Arlington

PARMER*
West Texas State Univ.

PECOS*
Univ. of Tex-Permian Bas.

POLK
Sam Houston Regional
   Library & Research Center

POTTER*
West Texas State Univ.

PRESIDIO*
Univ. of Texas-El Paso

RAINS*
East Texas State Univ.

RANDALL*
West Texas State Univ.

REAGAN*
Univ. of Texas-Permian Bas.

REAL*
no regional depository

RED RIVER
Paris Junior College

REEVES*
Univ. of Texas-Permian Bas.

REFUGIO
Texas A & I Univ.

ROBERTS*
West Texas State Univ.

ROBERTSON
Texas A & M Univ.

ROCKWALL
Univ. of Texas-Dallas

RUNNELS*
Angelo State Univ.

RUSK
Stephen F. Austin Univ.

SABINE
Stephen F. Austin Univ.

SAN AUGUSTINE
   Stephen F. Austin Univ.

SAN JACINTO
   Sam Houston Regional
      Library & Research Center

SAN PATRICIO
   Texas A & I Univ.

SAN SABA*
   Angelo State Univ.

SCHLEICHER*
   Angelo State Univ.

SCURRY*
   Univ. of Texas-Permian Bas.

SHACKELFORD*
   Tarleton State Univ.

SHELBY*
   Stephen F. Austin Univ.

SHERMAN*
   West Texas State Univ.

SMITH*
   East Texas State Univ.

SOMERVELL
   Univ. of Texas-Arlington

STARR
   Pan American Univ.

STEPHENS*
   Tarleton State Univ.

STERLING*
   Angelo State Univ.

STONEWALL*
   Texas Tech Univ.

SUTTON*
   Angelo State Univ.

SWISHER*
   West Texas State Univ.

TARRANT*
Univ. of Texas-Arlington

TAYLOR*
   Angelo State Univ.

TERRELL*
   Univ. of Texas-Permian Bas.

TERRY*
   Texas Tech Univ.

THROCKMORTON*
   Midwestern Univ.

TITUS*
   East Texas State Univ.

TOM GREEN*
   Angelo State Univ.

TRAVIS
   Austin Public Library

TRINITY
   Sam Houston State Univ.

TYLER
   Sam Houston Regional
      Library & Research Center

UPSHUR*
   East Texas State Univ.

UPTON*
   Univ. of Texas-Permian Bas.

UVALDE
   no regional depository

VAL VERDE*
   Angelo State Univ.

VAN ZANDT*
   East Texas State Univ.

VICTORIA
   Univ. of Houston-Victoria

WALKER
   Sam Houston State Univ.

WALLER
  Texas A & M Univ.

WARD*
  Univ. of Texas-Permian Bas.

WASHINGTON
  Texas A & M Univ.

WEBB
  Pan American Univ.

WHARTON
  Houston Public Library

WHEELER*
  West Texas State Univ.

WICHITA*
  Midwestern Univ.

WILBARGER*
  Midwestern Univ.

WILLACY*
  Pan American Univ.

WILLIAMSON
  Baylor Univ.

WILSON
  no regional depository

WINKLER*
  Univ. of Texas-Permian Bas.

WISE
  North Texas State Univ.

WOOD*
  East Texas State Univ.

YOAKUM*
  Texas Tech Univ.

YOUNG*
  Midwestern Univ.

ZAPATA
  Pan American Univ.

ZAVALA
  no regional depository

CHAPTER 11

RECORDS AVAILABLE IN THE TEXAS GENERAL LAND OFFICE

The General Land Office was created by the Constitution of 1836 making it one of the oldest agencies in state government. The primary purpose of this agency was to determine how much and what land was granted to colonists and to collect and maintain the records, in the capitol of the Republic, and later the state capital, that recorded such land grants.

The Archives and Records Division of the General Land Office is the repository for those early land grants dating back to the 1700's and for the land grants by the Republic and State of Texas. These grants are the nucleus of title to every inch of land in Texas and must be considered the most important collection of records on the history of our development.

When Texas joined the Union in 1845, the young Republic offered 175 million acres of public land to the federal government in exchange for the assumption of Texas $10 million debt. Congress refused the offer and Texas became the only state to retain title to its public land.

If the researcher is fortunate enough to find their ancestor in the Republic of Texas or shortly after statehood, the resources of the General Land Office can provide a "Gold Mine" of information about the issuance of land grants giving the original title to land in what is now the state of Texas.

It is important to remember that the General Land Office maintains records, maps, etc., only of the original land grants. The information on the disposal of the property can be found through the deed records as maintained in each county. The original records and survey maps that are found in this office, however, can offer valuable information to the genealogist who finds a record of their ancestor here.

Some of the records and materials that would be of interest to the genealogist are listed on the following page. All of this material is available for examination and abstracting. Much of it can be reproduced by photostat although it can not be photocopied because of the size and condition of the original material. No charge is made for the examination of the records found here and you will find a most courteous staff available to assist you in understanding the material that they will show you. A nominal charge is made for the reproduction of any records you wish to have.

The General Land Office was created in 1836 by the Republic of Texas to oversee the administration of its public lands.

The government was then and still is, the largest landowner in Texas and these lands and their resources are managed by this agency. The Land Commissioner was directed by the First Congress to "take charge of all records, books, and papers in any way pertaining to the lands of the republic..and the said records, books, and papers should become and be deemed the books and papers of said office." These are the materials we find so valuable to our research today.

ORIGINAL LAND RECORDS:

Grant and land records issued by the Crown of Spain.
Grant and land records issued by the Republic of Mexico.
Grant and land records of the Republic of Texas.
Grant and land records issued by the State Of Texas.

These grants were issued to people who settled in Texas and to men who fought in the Texas Revolution.

SPANISH COLLECTION:

Spanish and Mexican Land Grants in Texas

Character Certificates

Austin's Census of 1826

Family Registers: Stephen F. Austin, Benjamin R. Milam, Arthur Wavell, and Charles S. Taylor

Spanish and Mexican Land Grants in Tamaulipas and Nuevo Santander, including porciones on north bank of Rio Grande

Empresario Contracts and Appendix to Empresario Contracts

Mission records

Minutes of Ayuntamiento of San Felipe de Austin: 1829, 1830, 1831

Colony atlases

Titles to town lots in Liberty

English field notes

Government communications, correspondence, and legal records

A Spanish Translator and research specialists are available
to provide assistance in the use of this collection.

REPUBLIC AND STATE OF TEXAS:

Bounty Grants — 320 acres for each 3 months service in the Army of the Republic of Texas.

Donation Grants — 640 acres for special service during Texas Revolution. Men who fought at any battle were eligible, and other donations were later given to widows and surviving veterans.

Headrights — given to heads of families and to single men who settled in the Republic of Texas as follows:

FIRST CLASS: Those who arrived before 1836 received one league (4,428.4 acres) and one labor (177.1 acres) per family or one-third league (1,476.1 acres) per single man.

SECOND CLASS: Those who arrived between March 2, 1836 and October 1, 1837, received 1280 acres per family or 640 acres per single man.

THIRD CLASS: Those who arrived between October 1, 1837 and 1840 received 640 acres per family or 320 acres per single man.

FOURTH CLASS: Those who arrived between January 1, 1840 and 1842 received 640 acres per family or 320 acres per single man.

Pre-emption Grants — (Homestead or Settler's Claims) Individuals who lived on a tract of no more than 320 acres for at least 3 consecutive years between January 22, 1845 and 1854, could receive title to that land. After 1854, the limit was 160 acres and in 1870 single men were limited to 80 acres. The last grants were approved in 1898.

School Lands — Sold to individuals under an act of 1874.

Patents   The final title issued by the
                                     Republic or State of Texas on a
                                     survey of any land grant.

MISCELLANEOUS SOURCES:

   Colonies under the Republic and State of Texas, such as
   Peters', Mercer's, Castro's, Fisher-Miller's (also
   German Emigration Company with miscellaneous transfers
   showing ship lists). See third class index for colonies.

   German Contracts (circa 1846)

   Confederate Scrip is a special donation of 1280 acres
   given to men who served from Texas and were permanently
   disabled or killed.

   Special Acts Certificates were given under special acts of
   the legislature such as relief acts for individuals.

   Court of Claims are records of individuals who appealed to
   the court for land claims.

   Muster Roll Book contains the muster rolls from the Army
   of the Republic of Texas.

   County Maps show the original surveys in each county in
   Texas.

   "Abstracts of All Original Texas Land Titles Comprising
   Grants and locations to August 31, 1941." This is a set
   of eight volumes listed by counties.

   Austin City Lots and Outlots, original deeds to lots and
   outlots, patents and maps of city lots and outlots.

Genealogical information may be requested by writing:

                 Archives and Records Division
                 General Land Office
                 Austin, Texas 78701
                 Telephone: 1-(512) 463-5277

When requesting information please give the name of the
person who received the grant and the county in which the
grant is located, if known.

The original papers may be examined in person at the General
Land Office in the Stephen F. Austin State Office Building,
Room 811, 1700 North Congress Avenue, Austin, Texas.

A most courteous and efficient staff will be happy to assist
you in your research in the Archives and Records Division of
the General Land Office of Texas.

CHAPTER 12

TEXAS LIBRARIES WITH RESOURCES FOR GENEALOGICAL RESEARCH

Most libraries in Texas have some material that is valuable to the genealogist. It may be local history, old telephone books, manuscripts, diaries, old photographs, old newspapers, or oral history. The library in the area where your ancestor lived should be contacted to find out if they have holdings that could help you in your search. This chapter, however, is written about those libraries that have specific resources to help the genealogy researcher.

Most of the larger cities have libraries with excellent genealogy research facilities. Dallas, and Fort Worth have large genealogy departments in their libraries where they have set aside a great amount of space for those who wish to research their collections. Houston's major research center is Clayton Library for Genealogical Research; it has a reputation for having one of the best genealogy collections in the south. In 1968 when the genealogy department had outgrown its facilities, it was moved to its present location on Caroline Street where it has continued to grow and to expand into new buildings as they are required. Montgomery County Library, in Conroe has an excellent collection serving that area of the state.

The Texas State Library has an excellent genealogy department and a complete chapter in this book has been devoted to information on this library.

Academic libraries often are an unexplored source for many researchers. Many have good collections of materials not available elsewhere.

Genealogist in the Southwest are fortunate to have the Region 7 of the National Archives and Records Center in Ft. Worth, Texas, where all of the Federal Census are available for research. In addition to the Census, this records center has much of the material on microfilm that is in the National Archives in Washington D.C.. You will find the location of this facility listed under Tarrant County in this chapter.

Once again we urge the researcher to visit the local library in any county in which research is being done. Many times information will be discovered that is least expected but very valuable.
==
KEY:

GEN = Genealogy collection   LH = Local history collection
OH = Oral history collection

LIBRARIES WITH RESOURCES FOR GENEALOGICAL RESEARCH

ANGELINA COUNTY

Kurth Memorial Library   GEN, LH
101 Calder Square
Lufkin, TX 75901   Tel (409) 634-7923

T L L Temple Memorial Library   OH
300 Park St., PO Box 597
Diboll, TX 75941-0597   Tel (409) 829-5497

AUSTIN COUNTY

Bellville Public Library   GEN
106 N. Holland
Bellville, TX 77418   Tel (409) 865-3731

BASTROP

Bastrop Public Library,   GEN
1008 Water St., Box 738
Bastrop, TX 78602-0738   Tel (512) 321-5441

BEE COUNTY

Bee County Public Library   GEN
210 E. Corpus Christi
Beeville, TX 78102   Tel (512) 358-5541

BELL COUNTY

Teinert Memorial Public Library   LH, OH
Dalton and Allen Sts., PO Box 12
Bartlett, TX 76511   Tel (817) 527-3208

Belton City Library   GEN, LH
301 East 1st St.
Belton, TX 76513   Tel (817) 939-1161

Killeen Public Library   LH
711 N Gray
Killeen, TX 76541   Tel (817) 526-6527

Railroad and Pioneer Museum, Inc. Library   LH, OH
710 Jack Baskin St., PO Box 5126
Temple, TX 76501-5372   Tel (817) 778-6873

Temple Public Library   GEN
101 North Main St.
Temple, TX 76501   Tel. (817) 778-5555

BEXAR COUNTY

    Daughters of the Republic of Texas Library
    The Alamo
    PO Box 259
    San Antonio, TX 78299   Tel (512) 225-1391

    Saint Mary's University Academic Library
    One Camino Santa Maria
    San Antonio, TX 78284   Tel (512) 436-3441
    SPANISH ARCHIVES OF LARADO

    San Antonio College Library   GEN
    1001 Howard Dr.
    San Antonio, TX 78284   Tel (512) 733-2480

    San Antonio Genealogical and Historical Society GEN
    P. O. Box 17461
    San Antonio, TX 72217-0461
    Private Library

    San Antonio Public Library   GEN
    203 So. Saint Mary's St.,
    San Antonio, TX 78205   Tel (512) 299-7790

    University of Texas at San Antonio Library   LH
    San Antonio, TX 78285   Tel (512)B 691-4570

BOWIE COUNTY

    Texarkana Historical Museum Research Library   LH
    219 State Line Ave, PO Box 2343
    Texarkana, TX 75501   Tel (214) 793-4831

    Texarkana Public Library   GEN
    600 W Third St.
    Texarkana, TX   Tel (214) 794-2149

BRAZORIA COUNTY

    Brazoria County Library System   GEN
    Central Headquarters, 401 E. Cedar
    Angleton, TX 77515   Tel (409) 849-5711

BRAZOS COUNTY

    Bryan Public Library   GEN
    201 East 26th St.
    Bryan, TX 77803   Tel (409) 779-5622

    Texas A and M University   OH
    Sterling C. Evans Library
    College Station, TX 77843   Tel (409) 845-8111

BROWN COUNTY

Brownwood Public Library   GEN
600 Carnegie Blvd.
Brownwood, TX 76801   Tel (915) 646-0155

Howard Payne University   GEN
Walker Memorial Library, Center Ave.
Brownwood, TX 76801   Tel (915) 646-2502

BURNET

Herman Brown Free Library   GEN
100 East Washington
Burnet, TX 78611   Tel (512) 756-2328

CALDWELL COUNTY

Dr. Eugene Clark Library   OH
217 South Main, PO Box 209
Lockhart, TX 78644   Tel (512) 398-3223

Luling Public Library   GEN
215 South Pecan Ave.
Luling, TX 78648   Tel (512) 875-2813

CAMERON COUNTY

Arnulfo L. Oliveira Memorial Library   GEN, LH
1825 May St.
Brownsville, TX 78520   Tel (512) 544-8221

Lon C Hill Memorial Library   GEN
502 East Taylor Ave.
Harlingen, TX 78550   Tel (512) 423-3563

CHEROKEE COUNTY

Lon Morris College   OH
Simon and Louise Henderson Library
College Ave.
Jacksonville, TX 75766   Tel (214) 586-2471

Singletary Memorial Library   GEN, LH
E. Sixth St.
Rusk, TX 75785   Tel (214) 683-5916

COLLIN COUNTY

Richardson Public Library   LH, OH
900 Civic Center Dr.
Richardson, TX 75080   Tel (214) 238-8251

COMANCHE COUNTY

    Comanche Public Library   LH
    311 N. Austin, PO Box 411
    Comanche, TX 76442-0411   Tel (915) 356-2122

COOKE COUNTY

    Cooke County Library   GEN, LH
    200 Weaver St.
    Gainesville, TX 76240   Tel (817) 665-2401

CORYELL COUNTY

    Gatesville Public Library   LH
    805 Main St.
    Gatesville, TX 76528   Tel (817) 865-5367

DALLAS COUNTY

    Carrollton Public Library   LH
    2001 Jackson St.
    Carrollton, TX 75006   Tel (214) 323-5014

    Dallas Public Library   GEN
    Genealogy Section
    1515 Young St.
    Dallas, TX 75201-9987   Tel (214) 749-4100

    Genealogical Research Library   GEN
    4524 Edmondson Ave.
    Dallas, TX 75205

    Highland Park Library   GEN
    4700 Drexal Dr.
    Dallas, TX 75205   Tel (214) 521-4150

    Duncanville Public Library   GEN
    103 E. Wheatland Rd
    Duncanville, TX 75116   Tel (214) 298-5400

    Farmers Branch Library   LH
    13613 Webb Chapel
    Farmers Branch, TX 75234   Tel (214) 247-3131

    Nicholson Memorial Library   OH
    625 Austin St.
    Garland, TX 75040-6365   Tel (214) 494-7187

    Grand Prairie Memorial Library   LH, OH
    901 Conover Dr.
    Grand Prairie, TX 75051   Tel (214) 264-1571

Grapevine Public Library   GEN
307 W. Dallas Rd.
Grapevine, TX 76051   Tel (817) 488-0413

Mesquite Public Library   GEN
300 Grubb Drive
Mesquite, TX 75149   Tel (214) 285-6369

Richardson Public Library   LH, OH
900 Civic Center Dr.
Richardson, TX 75080   Tel (214) 238-8251

DAWSON COUNTY

Dawson County Public Library   GEN
511 N. Third, PO Box 1090
Lamesa, TX 79331   Tel (806) 872-7042

DENTON COUNTY

Denton Public Library   OH
502 Oakland St.
Denton, TX 76201   Tel (817) 566-8470

Pilot Point Community Library   GEN
105 Jefferson St.,
Pilot Point, TX 76258

ECTOR COUNTY

Ector County Library   GEN, LH
Genealogical and Historical Room, 321 W. Fifth St.,
Odessa TX 79761-5066   Tel (915) 333-9633

EL PASO COUNTY

El Paso Genealogical Library   GEN
3651 Douglas St.
El Paso, TX 79903

El Paso Public Library   GEN
Document Dept., 501 North Oregon St.
El Paso, TX 79901   Tel (915) 541-4864

ELLIS COUNTY

Nicholas P. Sims Library   GEN, LH
515 W. Main
Waxahachie, TX 75165   Tel (214) 937-2671

FAYETTE COUNTY

Fayette County Public Library GEN
855 So. Jefferson
LaGrange, Texas 78945 Tel (409) 968-3765

FISHER COUNTY

Rotan Public Library LH
404 E. Snyder Ave.
Rotan, TX 79546 Tel (915) 735-3362

FORT BEND COUNTY

Ft. Bend County Library GEN, LH
1001 Golfview
Richmond, TX 77519 Tel (713) 342-4455

FREESTONE COUNTY

Fairfield Library Association, Inc. GEN
350 W. Main
Fairfield, TX 75840 Tel (214) 389-3574

GALVESTON COUNTY

Rosenberg Library GEN
2310 Sealy Ave.
Galveston, TX 77550 Tel (409) 763-8854

League City Public Library LH
100 W. Walker
League City, TX 77573 Tel (713) 554-6612

Moore Memorial Library GEN
1701 Ninth Ave. N.
Texas City, TX 77590 Tel (713) 948-3111

GONZALES COUNTY

Gonzales Public Library GEN
415 Saint Matthew, PO Box 220
Gonzales, TX 78629-0220 Tel (512) 672-6315

GRAYSON COUNTY

Denison Public Library GEN, LH
300 W. Gandy
Denison, TX 75020 Tel (214) 465-1797

Sherman Public Library GEN, LH
Local History and Genealogy Dept.
421 North Travis
Sherman, TX 75090 Tel (214) 892-4545

Whitesboro Public Library   GEN
308 W. Main
PO Box B
Whitesboro, TX 76273   Tel (214) 564-5432

GREGG COUNTY

Nicholson Memorial Public Library   LH
400 S. Green St.
Longview, TX 75601   Tel (214) 758-4252

GUADALUPE COUNTY

Sequin-Guadalupe County Public Library   LH
707 E. College St.
Sequin, TX 78155   Tel (512) 379-1531

HALE COUNTY

Hale Center Public Library   LH
609 Main St.
PO Box 214
Hale Center, TX 79041-0214   Tel (806) 839-2055

HANSFORD COUNTY

Hansford County Library   OH
121 Main
Spearman, TX 79081   Tel (806) 659-2231

HARRIS COUNTY

Lee College   OH
Learning Resources Center
PO Box 818
Baytown, TX 77522-0818   Tel (713) 427-5611

Sterling Municipal Library   OH
Public Library Ave.
Baytown, TX 77520   Tel (713) 427-7331

Clayton Library for Genealogical Research   GEN
5300 Caroline
Houston, TX 77004   Tel (713) 524-0101

Houston Public Library   LH
Texas and Local History Dept.
500 McKinney St.
Houston, TX 77002   Tel (713) 224-5441

Rice University
Fondren Library
Houston, TX 77251-1892   Tel (713) 527-4022

```
Pasadena Public Library                              GEN, LH
1201 Minerva
Pasadena, TX 77506              Tel (713) 477-0276

Chaparral Genealogical Library and Society     GEN, LH
P.O. Box 606
Tomball, TX 77375               Tel (713) 255-9081
```

HARRISON COUNTY

```
Nicholson Memorial Public Library              LH
400 So. Green St.
Longview, TX 75601              Tel (214) 758-4252
```

HAYS COUNTY

```
San Marcos Public Library                      LH
PO Box 907
San Marcos, TX 78667-0907       Tel (512) 392-8124
```

HEMPHILL COUNTY

```
Hemphill County Library                        GEN
Fifth and Main
Canadian, TX 79014              Tel (806) 323-5282
```

HENDERSON COUNTY

```
Clint W Murchison Memorial Library             GEN
121 So. Prairieville
Athens, TX 75751                Tel (214) 675-1717

Malakoff Public Library                        OH
Mitcham St.
Malakoff, TX 75148              Tel (214) 489-1818
```

HIDALGO COUNTY

```
McAllen Memorial Library                       GEN
601 North Main St.
McAllen, TX 78501-4688          Tel (512) 682-4531

Porter Doss Memorial Library                   OH
515 S. Kansas St.
Weslaco, TX 78596               Tel (512) 968-4533
```

HILL COUNTY

```
Hill Junior College Library              CIVIL WAR,OH
PO Box 619
Hillsboro, TX 76645-0619        Tel (817) 582-2555 ext 40
```

HOOD COUNTY

    Hood County Library   GEN
    222 North Travis
    Grandbury, TX 76048   Tel (817) 573-3569

HOUSTON COUNTY

    Crockett Public Library   GEN
    708 E. Goliad, PO Box 1226
    Crockett, TX 75835-1226   Tel (409) 544-3089

HOWARD COUNTY

    Howard County Library   GEN
    Fourth and Surry,
    Big Spring, TX 79720   Tel (915) 267-5295

HUNT COUNTY

    Commerce Public Library   LH
    1210 Park St., PO Box 308
    Commerce, TX 75428-0308   Tel (214) 886-6858

    East Texas State University   OH
    James Gilliam Gee Library, ET Station
    Commerce, TX 75428-2951   Tel (214) 886-5717

    Walworth Harrison Public Library   GEN
    Genealogy Room, 3716 Lee St.
    Greenville, TX 75401   Tel (214) 455-2205

HUTCHINSON COUNTY

    Hutchinson County Library   GEN
    625 No. Weatherly St.
    Borger, TX 79007   Tel (806) 274-6221

JEFFERSON COUNTY

    Tyrell Public Library   GEN
    695 Pearl St.
    Beaumont, TX 77701   Tel (409) 838-0780

    Port Arthur Public Library   LH, OH,
    3601 Cultural Center Dr.
    Port Arthur, TX 77642-3136   Tel (409) 985-8838

JOHNSON COUNTY

    Cleburne Public Library   LH
    302 W. Henderson, PO Box 657
    Cleburne, TX 76031-0657   Tel (817) 641-3326

KARNES COUNTY

    Karnes County Library System   LH
    303 W. Main
    Kenedy, TX 78119   Tel (512) 583-9673

KERR COUNTY

    Butt-Holdsworth Memorial Library   OH
    505 Water St.
    Kerrville, TX 78028   Tel (512) 257-8422

KLEBERG COUNTY

    Robert J. Kleberg Public Library   GEN
    Fourth and Henrietta
    Kingsville, TX 78363-6309   Tel (512) 592-6381

    Texas A and I University   OH
    James C Jernigan Library,
    West Santa Gertrudis Ave., PO Box 197
    Kingsville, TX 78363-0197   Tel (512) 595-3416

LIBERTY COUNTY

    Austin Memorial Library   OH
    220 S. Bonham
    Cleveland, TX 77327   Tel (713) 592-3920

    Sam Houston Regional Library and Research Center   GEN,LH
    Robert Schaadt, Director, PO Box 989
    Liberty, TX 77575-0989   Tel (713) 294-1619

LIMESTONE COUNTY

    Maffett Memorial Library   LH
    601 W. Yeagua
    Groesbeck, TX 76642   Tel (817) 729-3667

LLANO COUNTY

    Llano County Public Library   GEN, LH
    107 W. Sandstone
    Llano, TX 78643   Tel (915) 247-5248

LUBBOCK COUNTY

    Lubbock City-County Library   GEN
    1306 9th St.
    Lubbock, TX 79401   Tel (806) 762-6411

    Texas Tech University Health Sciences Center   OH
    Lubbock, TX 79430   Tel (806) 743-2200

McCULLOCH COUNTY

F. M. Richards Memorial Library   GEN
1106 S. Blackburn
Brady, TX 76825   Tel (915) 597-2617

McLENNAN COUNTY

Baylor University Library   OH
CSB 356
Waco, TX 76798-0356   Tel (817) 755-3590

Masonic Grand Lodge Library and Museum of Texas
715 Columbus
PO Box 446
Waco, TX 76703-0446   Tel (817) 753-7395
TEXAS MASONIC RECORDS

Waco-McLennan County Library   GEN
1717 Austin Ave.
Waco, TX 76701   Tel (817) 754-4694

MADISON COUNTY

Madison County Library   GEN
605 S. May St.
Madisonville, TX 77864   Tel (409) 348-6118

MATAGORDA COUNTY

Bay City Public Library   GEN
1900 Fifth St.
Bay City, TX 77414   Tel (409) 245-6931

MEDINA COUNTY

Castroville Public Library   GEN, OH
1209 N. Florella
PO Box 532
Castroville, TX 78009-0532   Tel (512) 538-2656

MIDLAND COUNTY

Midland County Public Library   GEN
301 W. Missouri
Midland, TX 79702-1191   Tel 915-683-2708

Nita Stewart Haley Memorial Library   OH
1804 W. Indiana
Midland, TX 79701   Tel. (915) 682-5785

MILAM COUNTY

Cameron Public Library   GEN
304 E. Third St.
Cameron, TX 76520   Tel (817) 697-2401

MITCHELL COUNTY

Mitchell County Public Library   OH
340 Oak St.
Colorado City, TX 79512   Tel (915) 728-3968

MONTGOMERY COUNTY

Montgomery County Library   GEN, LH, OH
Genealogy Department
San Jacinto at Phillips, PO Box 579
Conroe, TX 77305-0579   Tel (409) 756-4484

Splendorah City Library   LH
300 FM 2090 E, PO Box 1097
Splendorah, TX 77372   Tel (713) 689-1818

MOORE COUNTY

Killgore Memorial Library   OH
124 Bliss,
Dumas, TX 79029   Tel (806) 935-4941

NACOGDOCHES

Stephen F Austin University   OH
Ralph W Steen Library
PO Box 13055, SFA Station
Nacogdoches, TX 75962   Tel (409) 569-4109

NAVARRO COUNTY

Corsicana Public Library   GEN
100 North 12th St.
Corsicana, TX 75110   Tel (214) 872-3071

NOLAN COUNTY

Sweetwater County-City Library   GEN
206 Elm St., PO Box 780
Sweetwater, TX 79556-0780   Tel (214) 885-4926

NUECES COUNTY

Corpus Christi State University
6300 Ocean Dr.
Corpus Christi, TX 78412   Tel (512) 991-6810
MAPS AND LAND TITLES

La Retama Public Library   GEN, LH
505 North Mesquite St.
Corpus Christi, TX 78401   Tel (512) 882-1937

Bell-Whittington Public Library   GEN
Memorial at Ganem Dr.
Portland, TX 78374   Tel (512) 643-6527

OCHILTREE COUNTY

Perry Memorial Library   LH
22 S.E. Fifth
Perryton, TX 79070   Tel (806) 435-5801

ORANGE COUNTY

Orange Public Library   GEN, LH, OH
220 N. Fifth
Orange, TX 77630-5796   Tel (409) 833-7323

Vidor Public Library   GEN
365 Claiborne
Vidor, TX 77662   Tel (409) 769-7148

PANOLA COUNTY

East Texas Genealogical Society Library   GEN
412 #A West College St.
Carthage, TX 75633-1406   Tel (214) 693-3444

PARKER COUNTY

Azle Public Library   LH
613 Southeast Parkway
Azle, TX 76020   Tel (817) 444-1331

Weatherford Public Library   GEN, LH
1214 Charles St.
Weatherford, TX 76086   Tel (817) 594-2767

POTTER COUNTY

Amarillo Public Library   GEN
413 E. Fourth St.
PO Box 2171
Amarillo, TX 79189-2171   Tel (806) 378-3050

RANDALL COUNTY

Amarillo Public Library   GEN
413 E. Fourth St.
PO Box 2171
Amarillo, TX 79189-2171   Tel (806) 378-3050

West Texas State University   OH
Cornette Library
2nd Ave. and 26th St.
PO Box 748, WTS Station
Canyon, TX 79016-0748   Tel (806) 656-2761

REFUGIO COUNTY

Refugio County Public Library   GEN
815 S. Commerce St.
Refugio, TX 78377   Tel (512) 526-2608

RUSK COUNTY

Rusk County Memorial Library   LH
514 N. High
Henderson, TX 75652   Tel (214) 657-8557

SAN AUGUSTINE COUNTY

San Augustine Public Library   GEN
413 E. Columbia
San Augustine, TX 75972   Tel (409) 275-5367

SAN PATRICIO COUNTY

Bell-Whittington Public Library   GEN
Memorial at Ganem Dr.
Portland, TX 78374   Tel (512) 643-6527

San Patricio County Library   GEN, OH
313 N. Rachal, PO Box 397
Sinton, TX 78387-0397   Tel (512) 364-4863

SCURRY COUNTY

Scurry County Library   GEN
1916 23rd St.
Snyder, TX 79549   Tel (915) 573-5572

SMITH COUNTY

Tyler Public Library   GEN
Genealogy Dept.
201 S. College Ave.
Tyler, TX 75702-7381   Tel (214) 595-4267

TARRANT COUNTY

Arlington Public Library   GEN
101 E. Abram
Arlington, TX 76010   Tel (817) 275-2763

University of Texas at Arlington
PO Box 19497, UTA   Station
Arlington, TX 76019   Tel (817) 273-3391
ROBERTSON'S COLONY PAPERS

Azle Public Library   LH
613 Southeast Parkway
Azle, TX 76020   Tel (817) 444-1331

Fort Worth Public Library   GEN, OH
300 Taylor St.
Fort Worth, TX 76102-7309   Tel (817) 870-7700

National Archives and Records Center, Region 7
4900 Hemphill Street, Building 1
PO Box 6216
Fort Worth, TX 76115   Tel (817) 334-5525

Southwestern Baptist Theological Seminary
Roberts Library
2001 W. Seminary Dr., Box 22,000-2 E
Fort Worth, TX 76122   Tel (817) 923-1921
BAPTIST HISTORY

Grapevine Public Library   GEN
307 W. Dallas Rd.
Grapevine, TX 76051   Tel (817) 488-0413

Hurst Public Library   OH
901 Precinct Line Rd.
Hurst, TX 76053   Tel (817) 485-5320

Keller Public Library   OH
137 Taylor St., PO Box 770
Keller, TX 76248-0770   Tel (817) 431-9011

Saginaw Public Library   LH
404 S. Saginaw Blvd.
Saginaw, TX 79070   Tel (817) 232-2100

TAYLOR COUNTY

Abilene Public Library   OH
202 Cedar St.
Abilene, TX 79601-5793   Tel (915) 677-2474

McMurry College   GEN
Jay-Rollins Library
Scarborough Library of Genealogy, History
and Biography of the South and Southwest
14 St. at Sayles Blvd.
PO Box 218, McMurry Station
Abilene, TX 79697-0218   Tel (915) 692-4130

TERRY COUNTY

    Kendrick Memorial Library   LH
    301 W. Tate
    Brownfield, TX 79316   Tel (806) 637-3848

TITUS COUNTY

    Mount Pleasant Municipal Library   GEN
    213 N. Madison, PO Box 1285
    Mount Pleasant, TX 75455   Tel (214) 572-2705

TOM GREEN COUNTY

    Fort Concho Museum Library   OH
    213 E. Ave. D
    San Angelo, TX 76903-7099   Tel (915) 655-9121

TRAVIS COUNTY

    Austin Public Library   OH
    800 Guadalupe St., PO Box 2287
    Austin, TX 78768-2287   Tel (512) 472-5433

    Daughters of the Confederacy Museum Library
    112 E. 11th
    Austin, TX 78701   Tel (512) 472-2596

    University of Texas Libraries
    Eugene C Barker History Center
    PO Box P
    Austin, TX 78712-7330   Tel (512) 471-5961
    MANUSCRIPT AND NEWSPAPER COLLECTION

    Texas Catholic Historical Society
    Catholic Archives of Texas
    PO Box 13327, Capitol Station
    Austin, TX 78711   Tel (512) 476-4888

    Texas Confederate Museum Library
    112 E. 11th
    Austin, TX 78701   Tel (512) 477-1822

    Texas State Library, Genealogy Department   GEN
    1200 Brazos St.
    Box 12927 Capital Station
    Austin, TX 78711   Tel (512) 475-2166

UPTON COUNTY

    Rankin Public Library   OH
    205 E. Tenth, PO Box 6
    Rankin, TX 79778-0006   Tel (915) 693-2881

UVALDE COUNTY

El Progreso Memorial Library   GEN, LH
129 W. Nopal St.
Uvalde, TX 78801   Tel (512) 278-2017

VICTORIA COUNTY

Victoria College - University of Houston   LH
2602 N. Ben Jordan
Victoria, TX 77901-5699   Tel (512) 576-3177

Victoria Public Library   GEN
302 N. Main
Victoria, TX 77901   Tel (512) 578-6241

WALKER COUNTY

Huntsville Public Library   GEN
1216 14th St.
Huntsville, TX 77340   Tel (409) 291-5472

WASHINGTON COUNTY

Nancy Carol Roberts Memorial Library   OH
100 W. Academy
Brenham, TX 77833   Tel (409) 836-2312

WEBB COUNTY

Laredo Junior College
Harold R Yeary Library
West End Washington St.
Laredo, TX 78040   Tel (512) 722-0521
LARADO ARCHIVES

Laredo Public Library   LH
Bruni Plaza
Laredo, TX 78040   Tel (512) 722-2435

WICHITA COUNTY

Burkburnett Library   GEN
215 E. Fourth St.
Burkburnett, TX 76354   Tel (817) 569-2991

Kemp Public Library   GEN
1300 Lamar St.
Wichita Falls, TX 76301   Tel (817) 322-5611, ext 377

```
Midwestern State University
George Moffett Library
3400 Taft Ave.
Wichita Falls, TX 76308-2099          Tel (817) 692-6611
                                              ext 4204

     MISSOURI-KANSAS-TEXAS RAILROAD MAP COLLECTION

WILLIAMSON COUNTY

     Teinert Memorial Public Library          LH, OH
     Dalton and Allen Streets
     P O Box 12
     Bartlett, TX. 76511-0012          Tel (817) 527-3208

     Round Rock Public Library                 OH
     216 E. Main St.
     Round Rock, TX 78664             Tel (512) 255-3939

WILSON COUNTY

     Wilson County Library                     OH
     One Library Lane
     Floresville, TX 78114           Tel (512) 393-2286

WOOD COUNTY

     Mineola Memorial Library                 GEN
     301 N. Pacific St.
     Mineola, TX 75773               Tel (214) 569-2767

YOUNG COUNTY

     Graham Public Library                  LH, OH
     1100 Cherry St.
     Graham, TX 76046-3898           Tel (817) 549-0600

     Olney Community Library and Arts Center    OH
     807 W. Hamilton
     PO Box 67
     Olney, TX 76374-0067            Tel (817) 564-5513
```

BIBLIOGRAPHY

CHAPTER 1.   EARLY MUNICIPALITIES IN TEXAS

Hubert Howe Bancroft, History of the North
Mexican States (San Francisco: The History Co,
1886.)

Herbert Eugene Bolton, Texas in the Middle
Eighteenth Century (Austin: University of Texas
Press, 1970.)

Carlos Eduardo Castaneda, Our Catholic Heritage
in Texas, 1519-1936 (Austin: Von Boeckmann-
Jones Co., 1936), vols I-V.

MAPS

General Land Office, Austin, Texas.

Texas State Archives, Austin, Texas.

CHAPTER 2.   MEXICAN LAWS CONCERNING COLONIZATION

Hans Peter Nielson Gammel, ed., Gammel's
Laws of Texas (Austin: Austin Printing Co.,
1905.)

CHAPTER 3.   SPANISH TERMS USED IN LAND GRANTS AND EARLY
DEEDS

Edwin B. Williams, ed., Webster's Spanish and
English Dictionary (Secausus: Castle Books,
1980.)

Old list printed by the General Land Office,
Austin, Texas. No publication date.

CHAPTER 4.   ORIGINAL COLONIES OF TEXAS

Hans Peter Nielson Gammel, ed., Gammel's
Laws of Texas (Austin: Austin Printing Co.,
1905.)

Malcolm D. McLean, Papers Concerning Robertson's
Colony in Texas (Fort Worth: Texas Christian
University, 1974-   ), vol. I - III.

MAPS

General Land Office, Austin, Texas.

Texas State Archives, Austin, Texas.

CHAPTER 5.   LAND DISTRICTS OF TEXAS

General Land Office, Austin, Texas.

Texas State Archives, Austin, Texas.

CHAPTER 6.   FORMATION AND ORGANIZATION OF COUNTIES

Zip Code information was obtained from:
Texas ZIP + 4 State Directory (Washington, DC:
United States Postal Service, 1985.)

The information on each county listed in this chapter was
obtained from Gammel's Laws of Texas, unless otherwise noted.
Because space is limited, however, only the citation for the
creation date of each county will be given.

ANDERSON -   Hans Peter Nielson Gammel, ed., Gammel's
                  Laws of Texas (Austin: Austin Printing Co.,
                  1905), vol. II, p. 1326.
ANDREWS -   Ibid, vol. VIII, p. 1075.
ANGELINA -   Ibid, vol. II, p. 1426.
ARANSAS -   Ibid, vol. VII, p. 3.
ARCHER -   Ibid, vol. IV, p. 230.
ARMSTRONG -   Ibid, vol. VIII, p. 1072.
ATASCOSA -   Ibid, vol. IX, p. 205.
AUSTIN -   Ibid, vol. I, p. 307.
BAILEY -   Ibid, vol. VIII, p. 1073.
BANDERA -   Ibid, vol. IV, p. 211.
BASTROP -   Walter Prescott Webb, ed., The Handbook of
                  Texas (Austin: The Texas State Historical
                  Association, 1952), vol. I, p. 120-121.
BAYLOR -   Hans Peter Nielson Gammel, ed., Gammel's Laws
                  of Texas (Austin: Austin Printing Co.,
                  1905), vol. IX, p. 959.
BEE -   Ibid, vol. IV, p. 883.
BELL-   Ibid, vol. III, p. 501.
BEXAR -   Walter Prescott Webb, ed., The Handbook of
                  Texas (Austin: The Texas State Historical
                  Association, 1952), vol. II, pp. 241-242.
BLANCO -   Hans Peter Nielson Gammel, ed., Gammel's Laws
                  of Texas (Austin: Austin Printing Co.,
                  1905), vol IV, p. 1070.
BORDEN -   Ibid, vol. VIII, p. 1074.
BOSQUE -   Ibid, vol. III, p. 1492.

- 241 -

BOWIE -   Hans Peter Nielson Gammel, ed., Gammel's Laws
                     of Texas (Austin: Austin Printing Co.,
                     1905), vol II, p. 561.
BRAZORIA -   Walter Prescott Webb, ed., The Handbook of
                     Texas (Austin: The Texas State Historical
                     Association, 1952), vol. I, pp. 207-208.
BRAZOS -   Hans Peter Nielson Gammel, ed., Gammel's Laws
                     of Texas (Austin: Austin Printing Co.,
                     1905), vol. II, p. 550. (changed from
                     Navasota Co.).
BREWSTER -   Ibid, vol. IX, p. 802.
BRISCOE -   Ibid, vol. VIII, p. 1073.
BROOKS -   Walter Prescott Webb, ed., The Handbook of
                     Texas (Austin: The Texas State Historical
                     Association, 1952), vol. I, p. 222.
BROWN -   Hans Peter Nielson Gammel, ed., Gammel's Laws
                     of Texas (Austin: Austin Printing Co.,
                     1905), vol. IV, p. 484.
BURLESON -   Ibid, vol. II, p. 708.
BURNET -   Ibid, vol. II, p. 558.
BUCHEL -   Ibid, vol. IX, p. 824. (see Brewster Co.)
BUCHANAN -   Ibid, vol. IV, p. 930. (see Stephens Co.)
CALDWELL -   Ibid, vol. III, p. 53.
CALHOUN -   Ibid, vol. II, p. 1354.
CALLAHAN -   Ibid, vol. IV, p. 959.
CAMERON -   Ibid, vol. III, p 27.
CAMP -   Ibid, vol. VIII, p. 67.
CARSON -   Ibid, vol. VIII, p. 1071.
CASS -   Ibid, vol. III, p. 1441.
CASTRO -   Ibid, vol. VIII, p. 1073.
CHAMBERS -   Ibid, vol. IV, p. 1064.
CHEROKEE -   Ibid, vol. II, p. 1369.
CHILDRESS -   Ibid, vol. VIII, p. 1072.
CLAY -   Ibid, vol. IV, p. 905.
COCHRAN -   Ibid, vol. VIII, p. 1073.
COKE -   Ibid, vol. IX, p. 1114.
COLEMAN -   Ibid, vol. IV, p. 959.
COLLIN -   Ibid, vol. II, p. 1350.
COLLINGSWORTH -   Ibid, vol. VII, p. 1072.
COLORADO -   Ibid, vol. I, p. 1034.
COMAL -   Ibid, vol. II, p. 1319.
COMANCHE -   Ibid, vol. IV, p. 207.
CONCHO -   Ibid, vol. IV, p. 959.
COOKE -   Ibid, vol. III, p. 186.
CORYELL -   Ibid, vol. III, p. 1490.
COTTLE -   Ibid, vol. VIII, p. 1073.
CRANE -   Ibid, vol. IX, p. 806.
CROCKETT -   Ibid, vol. VIII, p. 374.
CROSBY -   Ibid, vol. VIII, p. 1074.
CULBERSON -   Walter Prescott Webb, ed., The Handbook of
                     Texas (Austin: The Texas State Historical
                     Association, 1952), vol. I, pp. 443-444.

DALLAM –	Hans Peter Nielson Gammel, ed., <u>Gammel's Laws</u> <u>of Texas</u> (Austin: Austin Printing Co., 1905), vol. VIII, p. 1071.
DALLAS –	<u>Ibid</u>, vol. II, p. 1332.
DAWSON –	<u>Ibid</u>, vol. IV, p. 959.
DEAF SMITH –	<u>Ibid</u>, vol. VIII, p. 1072.
DELTA –	<u>Ibid</u>, vol. VI, p. 61.
DENTON –	<u>Ibid</u>, vol. II, p. 1363.
DEWITT –	<u>Ibid</u>, vol. II, p. 762.
DICKENS –	<u>Ibid</u>, vol. VIII, p. 1074.
DIMMIT –	<u>Ibid</u>, vol. IV, p. 959.
DONLEY –	<u>Ibid</u>, vol. VIII, p. 1072.
DUVAL –	<u>Ibid</u>, vol. IV, p. 959.
EASTLAND –	<u>Ibid</u>, vol. IV, p. 959.
ECTOR –	<u>Ibid</u>, vol. IX, p. 806.
EDWARDS –	<u>Ibid</u>, vol. IV, p. 959.
ELLIS –	<u>Ibid</u>, vol. III, p. 454.
EL PASO –	<u>Ibid</u>, vol. III, p. 462.
ENCINAL –	<u>Ibid</u>, vol. IV, p. 959.
ERATH –	<u>Ibid</u>, vol. IV, p. 208.
FALLS –	<u>Ibid</u>, vol. III, p. 525.
FANNIN –	<u>Ibid</u>, vol. I, p. 1395.
FAYETTE –	<u>Ibid</u>, vol. I, p. 1377
FISHER –	<u>Ibid</u>, vol. VIII, p. 1074.
FLOYD –	<u>Ibid</u>, vol. VIII, p. 1073.
FOARD –	<u>Ibid</u>, vol. X, p. 19.
FOLEY –	<u>Ibid</u>, vol. X, p. 824. (abolished)
FORT BEND –	<u>Ibid</u>, vol. I, p. 1460.
FRANKLIN –	<u>Ibid</u>, vol. VIII, p. 467.
FREESTONE –	<u>Ibid</u>, vol. III, p. 859.
FRIO –	<u>Ibid</u>, vol. IV, p. 959.
GAINES –	<u>Ibid</u>, vol. VIII, p. 1075.
GALVESTON –	<u>Ibid</u>, vol. I, p. 1482.
GARZA –	<u>Ibid</u>, vol. VIII, p. 1075.
GILLESPIE –	<u>Ibid</u>, vol. III, p. 35.
GLASSCOCK –	<u>Ibid</u>, vol. X, p. 934.
GOLIAD –	Walter Prescott Webb, ed., <u>The Handbook of</u> <u>Texas</u> (Austin: The Texas State Historical Association, 1952), vol. I, p. 699.
GONZALES –	<u>Ibid</u>, vol. I, pp. 707-708.
GRAY –	Hans Peter Nielson Gammel,ed., <u>Gammel's Laws</u> <u>of Texas</u> (Austin: Austin Printing Co., 1905), vol. VIII, p. 1075.
GRAYSON –	<u>Ibid</u>, vol. II, p. 1313.
GREER –	<u>Ibid</u>, vol. VI, p. 1500.
GREGG –	<u>Ibid</u>, vol. VII, p. 489.
GRIMES –	<u>Ibid</u>, vol. II, p. 1356.
GUADALUPE –	<u>Ibid</u>, vol. II, p. 750.
HALE –	<u>Ibid</u>, vol. VIII, p. 1072.
HALL –	<u>Ibid</u>, vol. VIII, p. 1072.
HAMILTON –	<u>Ibid</u>, vol. II, p. 763.
HANSFORD –	<u>Ibid</u>, vol. VIII, p. 1070.
HARDEMAN –	<u>Ibid</u>, vol. IV, p. 909.

HARDIN -   Hans Peter Nielson Gammel,ed., <u>Gammel's Laws</u>
                        <u>of Texas</u> (Austin: Austin Printing Co.,
                        1905), vol. IV, p. 930.
HARRIS-   <u>Ibid</u>, vol. I, p. 1022.
HARRISON -   <u>Ibid</u>, vol. II, p. 159.
HARTLEY-   <u>Ibid</u>, vol. III, p. 1071.
HASKELL -   <u>Ibid</u>, vol. IV, p. 909.
HAYES -   <u>Ibid</u>, vol. III, p. 48.
HEMPHILL -   <u>Ibid</u>, vol. VIII, p. 1071.
HENDERSON -   <u>Ibid</u>, vol. II, p. 1445.
HIDALGO -   <u>Ibid</u>, vol. III, p. 918.
HILL -   <u>Ibid</u>, vol. III, p. 1321.
HOCKLEY -   <u>Ibid</u>, vol. VIII, p. 1073.
HOOD -   <u>Ibid</u>, vol. V, p. 1001.
HOPKINS -   <u>Ibid</u>, vol. III, p. 1330.
HOWARD -   <u>Ibid</u>, vol. VIII, p. 1075.
HOUSTON -   <u>Ibid</u>, vol. I, p. 1330.
HUDSPETH -   Walter Prescott Webb, ed., <u>The Handbook of</u>
                        <u>Texas</u> (Austin: The Texas State Historical
                        Association, 1952), vol. I, p. 588.
HUNT -   Hans Peter Nielson Gammel,ed., <u>Gammel's Laws</u>
                        <u>of Texas</u> (Austin: Austin Printing Co.,
                        1905), vol. II, p. 1364.
HUTCHINSON -   <u>Ibid</u>, vol. VIII, p. 1071.
IRION -   <u>Ibid</u>, vol. IX, p. 1127.
JACK -   <u>Ibid</u>, vol. IV, p. 480.
JACKSON -   <u>Ibid</u>, vol. I, p. 949.
JASPER -   <u>Ibid</u>, vol. I, p. 946.
JEFF DAVIS -   <u>Ibid</u>, vol. IX, p. 828.
JEFFERSON -   <u>Ibid</u>, vol. I, p. 955.
JIM HOGG -   Walter Prescott Webb, ed., <u>The Handbook of</u>
                        <u>Texas</u> (Austin: The Texas State Historical
                        Association, 1952), vol. I, pp. 912-913.
JIM WELLS -   <u>Ibid</u>, vol. I, p. 913.
JOHNSON -   Hans Peter Nielson Gammel,ed., <u>Gammel's Laws</u>
                        <u>of Texas</u> (Austin: Austin Printing Co.,
                        1905), vol. III, p. 1548.
JONES -   <u>Ibid</u>, vol. VIII, p. 1076.
KARNES -   <u>Ibid</u>, vol. III, p. 1488.
KAUFMAN -   <u>Ibid</u>, vol. III, p. 40.
KENDALL -   <u>Ibid</u>, vol. V, p. 476.
KENEDY -   Walter Prescott Webb, ed., <u>The Handbook of</u>
                        <u>Texas</u> (Austin: The Texas State Historical
                        Association, 1952), vol. I, p. 947.
KENT -   Hans Peter Nielson Gammel,ed., <u>Gammel's Laws</u>
                        <u>of Texas</u> (Austin: Austin Printing Co.,
                        1905), vol. VIII, p. 1074.
KERR -   <u>Ibid</u>, vol. IV, p. 210.
KIMBALL -   <u>Ibid</u>, vol. IV, p. 930.
KING -   <u>Ibid</u>, vol. VIII, p. 1074.
KINNEY -   <u>Ibid</u>, vol. IV, p. 253.

KLEBERG -   Walter Prescott Webb, ed., <u>The Handbook of</u>
                 <u>Texas</u> (Austin: The Texas State Historical
                 Association, 1952), vol. I, p. 969.
KNOX -   Hans Peter Nielson Gammel,ed., <u>Gammel's Laws</u>
                 <u>of Texas</u> (Austin: Austin Printing Co.,
                 1905), vol. IV, p. 939.
LAMAR -   <u>Ibid</u>, vol. II, p. 561.
LAMB -   <u>Ibid</u>, vol. VIII, p. 1073.
LAMPASAS -   <u>Ibid</u>, vol. IV, p. 221.
LA SALLE -   <u>Ibid</u>, vol. IV, p. 939.
LATIMER -   <u>Ibid</u>, vol. VI, p. 122. (abolished)
LAVACA -   <u>Ibid</u>, vol. II, p. 747.
LEE -   <u>Ibid</u>, vol. VIII, p. 96.
LEON -   <u>Ibid</u>, vol. II, p. 1314.
LIBERTY -   Walter Prescott Webb, ed., <u>The Handbook of</u>
                 <u>Texas</u> (Austin: The Texas State Historical
                 Association, 1952), vol. II, p. 54.
LIMESTONE -   Hans Peter Nielson Gammel,ed., <u>Gammel's Laws</u>
                 <u>of Texas</u> (Austin: Austin Printing Co.,
                 1905), vol. II, p. 1378.
LIPSCOMB -   <u>Ibid</u>, vol. VIII, p. 1070.
LIVE OAK -   <u>Ibid</u>, vol. IX, p. 234.
LLANO -   <u>Ibid</u>, vol. VI, p. 225.
LOVING -   <u>Ibid</u>, vol. IX, p. 806.
LUBBOCK -   <u>Ibid</u>, vol. VIII, p. 1074.
LYNN -   <u>Ibid</u>, vol. VIII, p. 1074.
MADISON -   <u>Ibid</u>, vol. II, p. 763.
MARION -   <u>Ibid</u>, vol. IV, p. 1419.
MARTIN -   <u>Ibid</u>, vol. VIII, p. 1075.
MASON -   <u>Ibid</u>, vol. IV, p. 930.
MATAGORDA -   <u>Ibid</u>, vol. I, p. 352.
MAVERICK -   <u>Ibid</u>, vol. IV, p. 252.
McCULLUCH -   <u>Ibid</u>, vol. IV, p. 478.
McLENNAN -   <u>Ibid</u>, vol. III, p. 500.
McMULLEN -   <u>Ibid</u>, vol. IV, p. 959.
MEDINA -   <u>Ibid</u>, vol. III, p. 27.
MENARD -   <u>Ibid</u>, vol. IV, p. 930.
MIDLAND -   <u>Ibid</u>, vol. IX, p. 644.
MILAM -   Walter Prescott Webb, ed., <u>The Handbook of</u>
                 <u>Texas</u> (Austin: The Texas State Historical
                 Association, 1952), vol. II, p. 192.
MILLS -   Hans Peter Nielson Gammel,ed., <u>Gammel's Laws</u>
                 <u>of Texas</u> (Austin: Austin Printing Co.,
                 1905), vol. IX, p. 823.
MINA -   <u>Ibid</u>, vol. I, p. 384. (see Bastrop Co.)
MITCHELL -   <u>Ibid</u>, vol. VIII, p. 1075.
MONTAGUE -   <u>Ibid</u>, vol. IV, p. 903.
MONTGOMERY -   <u>Ibid</u>, vol. I, p. 1375.
MOORE -   <u>Ibid</u>, vol. VIII, p. 1071.
MORRIS -   <u>Ibid</u>, vol. VIII, p. 469.
MOTLEY -   <u>Ibid</u>, vol. VIII, p. 1073.

NACOGDOCHES -   Walter Prescott Webb, ed., <u>The Handbook of</u>
                 <u>Texas</u> (Austin: The Texas State Historical
                 Association, 1952), vol. II, p. 257.
NAVARRO -   Hans Peter Nielson Gammel,ed., <u>Gammel's Laws</u>
                 <u>of Texas</u> (Austin: Austin Printing Co.,
                 1905), vol. II, p. 1438.
NAVASOTA -   (see Brazos County.)
NEWTON -   <u>Ibid</u>, vol. II, p. 1428.
NOLAN -   <u>Ibid</u>, vol. VIII, p. 1075.
NUECES -   <u>Ibid</u>, vol. II, p. 1396.
OCHILTREE -   <u>Ibid</u>, vol. VIII, p. 1070.
OLDHAM -   <u>Ibid</u>, vol. VIII, p. 1072.
ORANGE -   <u>Ibid</u>, vol. III, p. 956.
PALO PINTO -   <u>Ibid</u>, vol. IV, p. 483.
PANOLA -   <u>Ibid</u>, vol. II, p. 618.
PARKER -   <u>Ibid</u>, vol. IV, p. 183.
PARMER -   <u>Ibid</u>, vol. VIII, p. 1073.
PASCHAL -   <u>Ibid</u>, vol. II, p. 521. (abolished)
PECOS -   <u>Ibid</u>, vol. VI, p. 985.
POLK -   <u>Ibid</u>, vol. II, p. 1333.
POTTER -   <u>Ibid</u>, vol. VIII, p. 1072.
PRESIDIO -   <u>Ibid</u>, vol. III, p. 462.
RAINES -   <u>Ibid</u>, vol. VI, p. 176.
RANDALL -   <u>Ibid</u>, vol. VIII, p. 1072.
REAGAN -   <u>Ibid</u>, vol. XII, p. 44.
RED RIVER -   <u>Ibid</u>, vol. I, p. 1431.
REEVES -   <u>Ibid</u>, vol. IX, p. 411.
REFUGIO -   <u>Ibid</u>, vol. II, p. 1067.
ROBERTS -   <u>Ibid</u>, vol. VIII, p. 1071.
ROBERTSON -   <u>Ibid</u>, vol. I, p. 1398.
ROCKWALL -   <u>Ibid</u>, vol. VII, p. 462.
RUNNELS -   <u>Ibid</u>, vol. IV, p. 359.
RUSK -   <u>Ibid</u>, vol. II, p. 959.
SABINE -   <u>Ibid</u>, vol. I, p. 983.
SAN AUGUSTINE - <u>Ibid</u>, vol. I, p. 352.
SAN JACINTO -   <u>Ibid</u>, vol. VII, p. 78.
SAN PATRICIO -   <u>Ibid</u>, vol. I, p. 384.
SAN SABA -   <u>Ibid</u>, vol. IV, p. 225.
SANTA FE -   <u>Ibid</u>, vol. III, p. 95. (abolished)
SCHLEICHER -   <u>Ibid</u>, vol. IX, p. 893.
SCURRY -   <u>Ibid</u>, vol. VIII, p. 1074.
SHACKELFORD -   <u>Ibid</u>, vol. IV, p. 959.
SHELBY -   <u>Ibid</u>, vol. I, p. 532.
SHERMAN -   <u>Ibid</u>, vol. VIII, p. 1071.
SMITH -   <u>Ibid</u>, vol. II, p. 759.
SOMERVELL -   <u>Ibid</u>, vol. VIII, p.471.
SPRING CREEK -   <u>Ibid</u>, vol. II, p. 513. (abolished)
STARR -   <u>Ibid</u>, vol. III, p. 24.
STEPHENS -   <u>Ibid</u>, vol. IX, p. 1.
STERLING -   <u>Ibid</u>, vol. X, p. 20.
STONEWALL -   <u>Ibid</u>, vol. VIII, p. 1074.
SUTTON -   <u>Ibid</u>, vol. IX, p. 893.
SWISHER -   <u>Ibid</u>, vol. VIII, p. 1073.

```
TARRANT -          Hans Peter Nielson Gammel,ed., Gammel's Laws
                   of Texas (Austin:  Austin Printing Co.,
                   1905), vol. III, p. 458.
TAYLOR -           Ibid, vol. IV, p. 959.
TENEHAW -          Ibid, vol. I, p. 532. (see Shelby Co.)
TERRY -            Ibid, vol. VIII, p. 1074.
TERRELL -          Ibid, vol. XII, p. 96.
THROCKMORTON -     Ibid, vol. IX, p. 908.
TITUS -            Ibid, vol. II, p. 1504.
TOM GREEN -        Ibid, vol. VIII, p. 23.
TRAVIS -           Ibid, vol. II, p. 428.
TRINITY -          Ibid, vol. II, p. 379.
TYLER -            Ibid, vol. II, p. 1348.
UPSHUR -           Ibid, vol. II, p. 1445.
UPTON -            Ibid, vol. IX, p. 806.
UVALDE -           Ibid, vol. III, p. 570.
VAL VERDE -        Ibid, vol. IX, p. 668.
VAN ZANDT -        Ibid, vol. III, p. 149.
VICTORIA -         Walter Prescott Webb, ed., The Handbook of
                   Texas (Austin:  The Texas State Historical
                   Association, 1952), vol. II, p. 840.
WACO -             Hans Peter Nielson Gammel,ed., Gammel's Laws
                   of Texas (Austin:  Austin Printing Co.,
                   1905), vol. II, p. 752. (abolished)
WALKER -           Ibid, vol. II, p. 357.
WALLER -           Ibid, vol. VII, p. 501.
WARD -             Ibid, vol. II, p. 529.
WASHINGTON -       Ibid, vol. I, p. 1391.
WEBB -             Ibid, vol. III, p. 18.
WHARTON -          Ibid, vol. II, p. 1344.
WHEELER -          Ibid, vol. VIII, p. 1074.
WICHITA -          Ibid, vol. IV, p. 959.
WILBARGER -        Ibid, vol. IV, p. 909.
WILLACY -          Walter Prescott Webb, ed., The Handbook of
                   Texas (Austin:  The Texas State Historical
                   Association, 1952), vol. II, pp. 910-911.
WILLIAMSON -       Hans Peter Nielson Gammel,ed., Gammel's Laws
                   of Texas (Austin:  Austin Printing Co.,
                   1905), vol. III, p. 76.
WILSON -           Ibid, vol. IV, p. 1468.
WINKLER -          Ibid, vol. IX, p. 806.
WISE -             Ibid, vol. IV, p. 203.
WOOD -             Ibid, vol. III, p. 541.
WORTH -            Ibid, vol. III, p. 462.
YOAKUM -           Ibid, vol. VIII, p. 1074.
YOUNG -            Ibid, vol. IV, p. 252.
ZAPATA -           Ibid, vol. IV, p. 930.
ZAVALA -           Ibid, vol. IV, p. 959.
```

CHAPTER 7   RECORDS AVAILABLE IN THE COUNTY COURTHOUSE

               Hans Peter Nielson Gammel, ed., Gammel's
               Laws of Texas (Austin: Austin Printing Co.,
               1905).

CHAPTER 8   RECORDS AVAILABLE IN THE TEXAS STATE LIBRARY

               Genealogical Research at the Texas State Library
               (Austin: Texas State Library, 1985).

CHAPTER 9   RECORDS AVAILABLE IN THE TEXAS STATE ARCHIVES

               Jean Carefoot, Guide to Genealogical Resources
               in the Texas State Archives (Austin: Archives
               Division, Texas State Library, 1984).

CHAPTER 10   RECORDS AVAILABLE IN THE REGIONAL HISTORICAL
               RESOURCE DEPOSITORIES

               Finding Guide for Microfilm Holdings of the
               Regional Historical Resource Depositories and
               Local Records Division (Austin: Texas State
               Library, 1984?).

CHAPTER 11   RECORDS AVAILABLE IN THE GENERAL LAND OFFICE
               OF TEXAS

               Archives and Records Division, General Land
               Office, Austin, Texas.

CHAPTER 12.   TEXAS LIBRARIES WITH RESOURCES FOR GENEALOGICAL
               RESEARCH

               Jaques Cattell Press, ed., American Library
               Directory (New York: R. R. Bowker Company
               Publisher, 1985), vol. II, pp. 1487-1563.

               Personal investigation.